secrets

of

meditation

ALSO BY DAVIDJI

destressifying: The Real World Guide
to Personal Empowerment, Lasting
Fulfillment, and Peace of Mind

VIDEO TRAINING COURSES

The Art of Meditation with davidji
Hay House University's 5-Week Meditation Program

Lightseeker: The Path to Spiritual Awakening

How Do I Know What I'm Supposed to Do?
Making the Big Decisions in Life

Audio CDs and Digital Downloads

davidji Guided Meditations: Fill What Is Empty; Empty What Is Full,
featuring Snatam Kaur and Damien Rose

40 Days of Transformation

Journey to Infinity:
Music, Mantras, and Meditations with SacredFire Music

The davidji Meditation Experience—Volume 1

The davidji Meditation Experience—Volume 2

The Goddess Meditations, featuring Fionnuala Gill

Guided Meditations for Awakening Your Divine Self

davidji: Come Fly With Me
The Passenger's Guide to Stress-Free Flying

The Five Secrets of the SweetSpot: Rituals for Daily Meditation

davidji Guided Affirmations: Fill What Is Empty; Empty What Is Full

davidji Guided Meditations: Fill Your Chakras
Inspired by the Tulku Jewels Sacred Chakra Collection

davidji Guided Affirmations: Conscious Choices in Life and Love

secrets
of
meditation

a
practical
guide
to inner peace
and personal
transformation

davidji

HAY HOUSE, INC.
Carlsbad, California • New York City
London • Sydney • New Delhi

Published the United States by: Hay House, Inc.: www.hayhouse.com®
Published in Australia by: Hay House Australia Pty. Ltd.: www.hayhouse.com.au
Published in the United Kingdom by: Hay House UK, Ltd.: www.hayhouse.co.uk
Published in India by: Hay House Publishers India: www.hayhouse.co.in

Cover design: Charles McStravick • *Interior design:* Riann Bender
Interior illustrations: Courtesy of the author

The author gratefully acknowledges and credits the following for the right to reprint material in this book:
"Sandayu the Separate," by Patti Smith, from *Babel*; used in gratitude with permission from Patti Smith.
"There Is a Wonderful Game," from *I Heard God Laughing: Renderings of Hafiz*; used with sweet permission from Daniel Ladinsky. Thank you for being so gracious about my interpretation of your interpretation of Hafiz's interpretation of God.
Bhagwan Shree Rajneesh on the Fool, written by Osho Dang Dang Doko Dang; used in gratitude with permission from the Osho International Foundation.

The author of this book does not dispense medical advice or prescribe the use of any technique as a form of treatment for physical, emotional, or medical problems without the advice of a physician, either directly or indirectly. The intent of the author is only to offer information of a general nature to help you in your quest for emotional and spiritual well-being. In the event you use any of the information in this book for yourself, which is your constitutional right, the author and the publisher assume no responsibility for your actions.

Library of Congress Cataloging-in-Publication Data for the original edition

davidji.
   Secrets of meditation : a practical guide to inner peace and personal transformation / davidji. -- 1st ed.
      p. cm.
   ISBN 978-1-4019-4030-0 (tradepaper : alk. paper) 1. Meditation. I. Title.
   BL627.D385 2012
   158.1'2--dc23

                              2012011857

Tradepaper ISBN: 978-1-4019-5308-9
Digital ISBN: 978-1-4019-5411-6

12 11 10 9 8 7 6 5 4
1st edition, September 2012
1st revised edition, March 2017

Printed in the United States of America

"It all has to come from inside, though, I guess."

— JIMI HENDRIX

DEDICATION

This book is dedicated to my dear friend, loving brother, and relentless teacher, David Simon, an amazing being who has touched my life and my heart in more ways than one could ever imagine. He flows through me in each breath I take. He is in my heart with each day's meditation, each sunset I drink in, each herb I pick, and each tender moment I witness. Among the countless number of lifelong lessons he has shared with me, he taught me that in each moment and in each interaction we have with people, animals, and our beloved Mother Earth, we have a choice to leave behind either toxic residue (known in Sanskrit as *ama*) or nourishing vital nectar (known as *ojas*). This is a lesson I am still learning each day, and it has helped me evolve my emotional intelligence and awaken my emotional digestive fire so that I could move beyond much of my constricted conditioning, make more nourishing choices, and share more selflessly with the world.

I have always trusted his heart, and that has taught me to trust mine.

When the sky is dark and the stars are out, it brings me back to the innocence and sweet atmospheric vibration of our morning hikes and late-night strolls. I think about how deeply we shared in hundreds of quiet conversations as we toured the world from Dublin to Vancouver, Miami to Alaska, London to Whistler, Oxford to Los Angeles, and everywhere in between—with the universe as our witness, we shared our hearts, our dreams, our truest essence. The stars tell the whole story every night . . . and they will forever.

David introduced me to Daniel Ladinsky's interpretations of the great Sufi poet Hafiz. The poem "There Is a Wonderful Game" speaks so sweetly of our undying connection. Please accept it in deepest reverence.

There is a game we should play,

And it goes like this:

We hold hands and look into each other's eyes

And scan each other's face.

Then I say,

"Now tell me the difference you see between us."

And you might respond,

"Hafiz, your nose is ten times bigger than mine!"

Then I would say,

"Yes, my dear, almost ten times!"

But let's keep playing.

Let's go deeper,

Go deeper.

For if we do,

Our spirits will embrace

And interweave.

Our union will be so glorious

That even God

Will not be able to tell us apart.

There is a wonderful game

We should play with everyone

And it goes like this . . .

To you, my timeless Sufi master, may you laugh and love with Hafiz every day.

CONTENTS

FOREWORD

No doubt you've heard the expression "Silence is golden." Yet in this modern era, treasuring the experience of a quiet mind has not been that resonant in our world consciousness. As a practitioner of meditation for many decades and as a physician dedicated to healing and transformation, I've learned the value of meditation as a tool for quieting the mind is inestimable.

The message that most of us received from an early age is that an active mind is a valuable mind. We clearly need the skills of an awake and creative mind to function, create, achieve, accomplish, and enjoy life. At the same time, the value of a quiet mind is tremendous, though less commonly recognized or appreciated. When the thoughts and noisy chatter of the mind settle, we have access to deeper levels of awareness. And when we can combine these two skill sets—the active mind that allows us to explore the world of form and phenomena and the quiet mind that brings clarity and balance into our awareness—we are in the best position to determine how to direct our energies and make the most evolutionary choices that will serve us, humanity, and the planet.

In this beautiful book, davidji—a sweet yogi and a dedicated teacher—explores various technologies to help bring the mind from chaos to quietude. Along the way, you will awaken to deeper levels of stillness in your bodymind and effortlessly develop a regular practice. Taking time on a daily basis to go within and access the field of pure awareness brings us from activity to silence, from individuality to universality, and from the personal to the universal. Meditation is like a bath for the mind; it allows our mind to be clear and refreshed and to see the same experience from a slightly different point of view. This shift expands our capacity for happiness, well-being, love, and creativity.

The information lovingly contained within these chapters will help you find your pathway to expansion. I encourage you to explore and try the practices that most resonate with you. Then you will fulfill the purpose of meditation, which is to transform your sense of Self from constricted to expanded. As you awaken your body, heart, mind, and soul, you and all those in your life will benefit.

— **David Simon, M.D.**
Co-founder of the Chopra Center for Wellbeing

PREFACE

It is my hope that you meditate. It is my belief that we will change the world through meditation. It is my understanding that connecting to the stillness and silence within allows each of us to live life with expanded awareness, deeper compassion, and greater fulfillment. It is my experience that time spent in stillness and silence can open your heart to the true depth of your universal essence. Accessing this depth of pure, unbounded consciousness on a regular basis has allowed me to *see* and *feel* the world with an ever-expanding openness, deeper empathy, greater clarity, and a heightened connection to Source. At this point in my life, I think this is a good thing.

Aham brahmasmi is a Sanskrit expression meaning "I am the universe." When we can genuinely feel we are not in or of this world but rather the whole world is within us, we slowly begin to integrate that mind-set into our words, our thoughts, and our deeds. Once this is truly how you feel (and daily meditation will awaken that understanding), you will effortlessly tap into the limitless supply of what the universe has to offer you—a wellspring of effortless abundance, an unfolding of deeper fulfillment, and a sweeter, more loving world that you can walk through with greater grace and ease.

No different from when you are in a dream state, every experience you have in your waking state is self-derived, self-created, self-influenced, and self-motivated. This is not to say things outside of you don't happen; rather, it's how you respond to the unexpected or the uncertain—what you do with new information and old rituals—that ends up becoming the fabric of your life. And we all respond to everything: a kiss on our lips, the wind on our cheek, a diagnosis, a text, a cough, a comment, a sigh, a desire, a memory, a caress, the ringing of a phone, the honking of a horn, the wink of an eye, a fleeting thought, footsteps in the distance, the sun on our neck, the tone of an e-mail, the color of someone's hair, and even the reading of this sentence. Yet there is no such thing as an external force that can *make* us feel a certain emotion or respond in a certain way. Our moods, feelings, and emotions are multidimensional interpretations based on our conditioning. Most of it is probably imprinted into our subconsciousness before we reached our teens. The remainder is embedded over the past few decades as we drank life in and reinforced those early interpretations, weaving them into the fabric of our being. Our response to each moment is a blend of that conditioning, our DNA, our current circumstances, our emotional intelligence, and our state of mind in that instant. In his book *Man's Search for Meaning*, the Austrian neurologist and holocaust survivor, Viktor Frankl, wrote "Between stimulus and response there is a space. In that space is our power to choose our response. In our response lies our growth and our freedom."

Meditating every day has taught me we are all the masters of each moment. And effortlessly weaving this practice into every fiber of my being has given me tools and techniques for better choosing my responses—living life with less stress and anxiety, greater clarity and focus, expanded compassion and empathy, deeper love and more frequent joy. Meditation has also gifted me a viewpoint that is more receptive to other perspectives, which offers me increased possibilities in each moment. I believe that anyone who is willing to embrace meditation can access these tools as well. Feel free to consider this book your meditation tool kit.

Since I wrote the first edition of this book, I have meditated more than 5,000 additional hours, trained hundreds of thousands of people to connect to the stillness and silence within themselves, and immersed myself into the newest scientific discoveries regarding the human brain, our thought process, and how we make decisions. With my soul bursting to share this new information with you, I rebirthed *Secrets of Meditation* with additional meditation techniques, the most recent scientific studies, and juicy explorations into higher states of consciousness.

I thank you for taking the time to read this book, which came from my heart. I encourage you to try meditating and begin a meditation practice using the guidance contained in these pages. I hope you'll let me help you find what you are looking for. I would consider it a privilege.

Peace.

davidji

PART I

AWAKENING
TO NEW
POSSIBILITIES

Although I practice a particular type of meditation, I honor all schools of meditation. The gentle drifting from outside ourselves to inside and then back out again is one of the most magnificent processes a human can experience. As your thoughts, your breath, and your physiology slow and progressively quiet to more subtle expressions, your awareness will expand—at first during meditation and then in your life—which will awaken a world of infinite possibilities in every moment.

I am not a monk or an evangelist of any particular religion. I live in the real world, and my meditation training occurred under real-world circumstances. I wrote this book to share my journey to wholeness, which I found through meditation. Wholeness is our natural state of balance—of flowing our essence with grace and ease, and of seeing the Divine in each sacred, precious present moment. When our physical body, our tender heart, our intellect, our emotions, and our ability to make the best choices are all in sync, we experience this powerful spiritual merging of all the parts of our existence—and the result is profound joy, deep connection, overwhelming gratitude, true happiness, lasting fulfillment, and a feeling of being one with everything around us. This magnificent ability to live in the present moment is available to anyone who desires to tap into the stillness and silence that rests within. I offer these teachings to beginners and masters alike. I am humbled by the thought that more than a million seekers throughout the world have joined me in this voyage of profound reconnection. I invite you to join the celebration with those who have found greater purpose, clarity, compassion, fulfillment, healing, flexibility, love, purpose, creativity, peace, abundance, one-ness, and evolutionary transformation, through the daily practice of sitting in stillness and silence . . . and those who are taking their first step right now.

How to Use This Book

This book is designed as a meditation owner's manual. I suggest you read it once through from beginning to end, participating in all the exercises and guided meditations. When you have finished, you will have a deeper understanding of meditation, you will have experienced many different types of meditations, you will have gone beyond any description that one could share, and you will have felt the rich benefits of a daily practice as your life unfolds with a joy and a calming ease that perhaps has eluded you. If you find yourself drawn to a particular form of meditation, I encourage you to explore it further; do online research, find a class, read more, and see where it goes. If you are interested in having a personal guide in your meditation practice, I invite you to explore all the free resources on **davidji.com**, including information about connecting with me or one of my many Certified Masters of Wisdom and Meditation Teachers to help you take your practice to the next level. Keep exploring and keep trusting your heart.

As you read *Secrets of Meditation* and come upon knowledge that resonates with you, feel free to make notes, highlight, and dog-ear the pages providing guidance or information with which you connect. And if you are stirred to share these teachings with others, consider becoming one of my certified teachers—our community is global and growing—and together we will transform the world as we transform ourselves.

A Word about Language

Many of these teachings were first articulated in Sanskrit, the ancient language of India, and in Pali, the ancient language of Buddhism. I have shared the original languages as well as the translations and transliterations into English. I encourage you to not torture yourself over pronunciation or grammar. There is an entire vocabulary of meditation, and the goal is for you to meditate rather than become a walking meditation encyclopedia. In time, these words will evolve into the fabric of your daily language, and in the meantime, these pages can be a helpful resource for learning to speak *consciousness as a second language*.

CHAPTER 1

SEARCHING FOR THE GURU

"To reach to the ultimate realization of truth, you will have to create the path by walking yourself; the path is not ready-made, lying there and waiting for you. It is just like the sky: the birds fly, but they don't leave any footprints. You cannot follow them; there are no footprints left behind."

— OSHO

How do you spell *guru*?

GEEE! . . . You . . . Are . . . You!

I began to meditate over 30 years ago, while attending college in upstate New York. I was young, impressionable, and a curious reader, who had stumbled onto five books that changed my life: (1) the *Bardo Thodol* (known in English as *The Tibetan Book of the Dead* or *The Tibetan Book of Living and Dying*); (2) the ancient Vedic text called the *Bhagavad Gita*; (3) *The Teachings of Don Juan* by the mystical storyteller Carlos Castaneda; (4) the consciousness classic *Be Here Now* by Ram Dass; and (5) *The Way of Zen* by the brilliant British philosopher Alan Watts. This group of books, dating back more than 3,500 years and as current as this century, opened my eyes to new answers to some of my fundamental life questions: Who am I? Why am I here? What is reality? Why are we all here? What does it all mean? What is my purpose? Is there more?

Reading these books also led me to my first meditation experience—an extra-credit weekly Zen meditation session offered to the students enrolled in an experimental Eastern philosophy course I was taking. The twelve of us sat in a circle, and our Zen master walked clockwise around us. We had been instructed that when we noticed a thought drifting into our mind, we were to raise our hand. In his hand, the Zen master carried an 18-inch bamboo stick known as a *keisaku*. On seeing one of our hands rise, our teacher would gently nod, silently walk over, and thwack the hand-raiser on the back with his keisaku. I don't know if it stopped the thought, but it certainly created a new one.

I found deep stillness and several cosmic moments in those sessions, but I also had lots of thoughts. Ouch! I only lasted in that school of meditation for two weeks. I found myself *not* raising my hand to avoid the thwack of the keisaku . . . and when you find yourself lying to your Zen master, that's when it's time to move on. As Alan Watts once said, "When you get the message, hang up the phone." I had gotten the message. But I wasn't really sure what to do with it. *What now?* I asked myself.

Over the next 30 years, I would explore many other forms of meditation, occasionally resonating with a particular modality enough to comfortably practice it for extended periods of time. But with the same ease that I would drift into a practice, I would drift away from it as work, home, relationships, the corporate world, and life's twists and turns spun me in varying directions, ultimately bringing me to my knees.

The Journey from Biofeedback to Mindfulness

After moving on from Zen, I embraced biofeedback for a few years. Biofeedback is a practice in which you focus on slowing your breath and controlling your heart rate. I got really good at it, and for the first time ever experienced a deep sense of relaxation in my life. But my pulse became so low that I kept passing out in elevators whenever I went above 10 stories.

I then moved on to a series of techniques that took me from listening to sound waves to Kundalini dancing to gazing at candles to energy healing to contemplative prayer to following my breath to the exotic tantra and ultimately to meditating with a mantra.

The word *mantra* comes from two Sanskrit words: *man*, which means "mind," and *tra*, which means "vehicle or instrument." So our mantra is our mind vehicle . . . our mind instrument. It is a tool to transport the mind from a state of activity to one of quieting down into stillness and silence.

Then there was the period when I first learned mindfulness meditation—the original meditation practice of the Buddha. I figured if it was good enough for the Buddha, it certainly was good enough for me! In most modern mindfulness practices, we bring our attention to the present moment. We witness our breath come in, we watch it go out. Breath by breath we observe the present moment. And as thoughts, sounds, and physical sensations come into our awareness, we do nothing with them. We don't judge them; we allow our attention to be fully on every aspect of the present moment. And throughout the practice, we simply keep coming back to the present moment—not the past, not the future—but the present inflow and outflow of our breath, where we ultimately become the silent witness to ourselves in every moment.

This is one of the most practiced types of meditation on the planet as millions of people in the corporate world, tens of thousands of children in school, hundreds of thousands of those in yoga classes, and half a billion Buddhists practice it each day. The word "mindful" has become somewhat trendy in the West over the last decade; it has even become a euphemism for wellness, sidestepping the cultish misconceptions and stigmas of traditional meditation.

Virtually every yoga class ends with some form of mindfulness meditation, lying on our back in savasana (or corpse pose), bringing closure to the class, totally surrendering to the moment, relaxing our body, and letting our mind simply drift into gratitude as all the benefits of the practice are integrated into every fiber of your being.

For many years, mindfulness practice was my primary form of meditation. But just as it was starting to become trendy, I stopped meditating.

Sleepwalking Through Life

I worked for many years in the worlds of finance and business amid the wild corporate swirl of New York City. I had even worked for a time on one of the higher floors of the World Trade Center's Tower 2, at what is now referred to as Ground Zero. But one day I realized—as my life was spinning out of physical and emotional balance—I had stopped meditating. I had replaced my 5 A.M. meditation ritual with an early morning train ride into the bowels of the World Trade Center and I had replaced my evening meditation with a double scotch. And like that . . . *poof* . . . my practice had disappeared.

Also gone were the balance and deep fulfillment of life I had felt during my meditation days. I was living to work, to fill an emptiness inside me, and stress had hijacked my body and mind. It had been a decade since I had slept through the night. Instead, I often awoke at 2 A.M. with a painful knot in my stomach that stayed there through the day and into the evening. I brought it to bed with me every night. I ate my lunch at my desk while texting on my "crackberry," chatting on my cell phone, typing e-mails, and wolfing down a sandwich . . . all in five minutes. I realized I had been doing that for almost 15 years.

Nonstop, overwhelming thoughts relentlessly raced through my head as I attempted to juggle so many different pieces of my life and found unfulfillment at every turn. I craved peace of mind. I craved a job with a purpose. I craved the depth of feeling I had known so well in my youth. I was light-years from that time. I was sleepwalking through my life. My personal and work relationships were stressed and strained. I was waking up, burning through the day, performing my "job," coming home, eating dinner, reading a book or watching TV, and passing out. My career had taken over my personal and home lives. And my life had been taken over by a zombielike autopilot existence. I felt empty, adrift from any guiding principle, deeply in pain, purposeless, and unenlightened about what my life had become and where it was headed. I started to question my accomplishments and the value I contributed to those in my life.

And so one day in SoHo, as I walked past a row of cardboard boxes where homeless people were living, a grizzled hand reached out and grabbed my pant leg. A curious, soot-covered face peered up at me and asked, "What's gonna be on your tombstone?" I stopped in my tracks (as my aimless gaze narrowed to a pinpoint, zeroing in on the man's crystalline blue eyes) and reflected on my life as his hand slowly slid down my ankle and dropped to my shoe. Face-to-face, soul-to-soul—connected in a transcendent, cosmic moment, it took my breath away. And I managed to gasp, "Oh my God!" Tears came to my eyes. We locked gazes for what seemed like eternity, and I mouthed the words to him, "I don't know." My mind was a tsunami of thoughts, memories, and desires. My gaze then passed through him . . . through everything until there was nothing. I wandered aimlessly for hours after that, his pointed words reverberating through every cell in my body. What *was* going to be on my tombstone? What *was* my purpose? I felt like a prisoner living eternally on death row, stuck in a painful purgatory with no reason for being.

My mind was overflowing with smoke-filled images of the collapse of Tower Two, just two weeks earlier. So many we knew and loved were gone and so many more we'd never get to know. For me, the psychological fallout from 9/11 drifted somewhere between emptiness, a profound sense of emotional grief, and a primal wake-up call—the deep need to live a life of purpose. But I was so far from knowing what that purpose was or having it actualized in my current trajectory. That night, as I shared my day's story with my wife over dinner, she handed me a piece of paper she had written on that very morning. She had sensed my daily pain and had explored a few deeper options for me to consider. She had written down the details of a meditation retreat in England with Deepak Chopra. She encouraged me to follow my heart. A work colleague advised me, "Jump and the net will appear." One of my yoga teachers suggested, "Quit your job today. The universe will provide." And a voice inside me said, "Trust."

I followed my heart, surrendered to this new path and jumped. I let my job evaporate into the ether. Within a week, I discovered a teacher who taught me my first meditation mantra, and one month later, I found myself in Oxford, England, learning about the concept of dharma—my purpose in life. It was there I learned that the word *guru* is a Sanskrit term for "remover of darkness," essentially one who teaches enlightenment. But no one else can actually make you "see." They can help you to awaken what already rests within you, helping access qualities previously hidden. Maybe you didn't know these aspects of yourself were even there. Maybe you did but were unsure how to access them. But once you do awaken to the stillness and silence that rest beneath the layers of activity in your daily life, you will know it's there and forever available to you to help you see clearly. Like a stormy sea that surrenders to the tranquility of a still, serene pond, in meditation the active mind progressively slows to more subtle levels of quietude. Each day, when your meditation is over, you can "listen" to life with greater appreciation and understanding and live with greater grace and ease.

Awakening to Stillness

Here's how it all unfolded. Upon hearing of my plans, one of my yoga teachers, Claire Diab, invited her friend, a meditation teacher born in India and living in London, to come across the pond for the weekend and teach me and six other students a modern translation of an ancient mantra meditation practice. During three intensive days, I learned the foundations of this timeless tool and walked through an understanding of my physical body, my subtle (psychological) body, and my causal (or spiritual) body. I then received my personal mantra based on the moment of my birth and was taught how to practically apply meditation into my daily life to ready me for the upcoming retreat.

Two weeks later, trusting in the universe to guide me to where I needed to be, I left New York City and headed off to the land of Harry Potter to spend a week with spiritual advisor Deepak Chopra. When I arrived in Oxford, I immersed myself deeply into stillness and silence along with a small group of "seekers" from around the world, looking to tap into clarity, truth, awareness, and love. So soon after 9/11, most Americans were still not flying so the majority of attendees were from England, Ireland, Scotland, and Wales, and the rest hailed from other European cities, like Amsterdam, Geneva, Rotterdam, Copenhagen, Munich, Barcelona, Istanbul, Paris, Milan, Helsinki, Prague, Brussels, and Stockholm, all speaking the universal language of consciousness! I felt right at home.

Deep, deep into meditation we went from sunrise to sunset and then after dinner. In just a few days, my soul opened wider than it ever had before, and I let go of every preconception I ever had about meditation. I surrendered to a consistent daily practice and I felt its full power. Especially in the core of my being that had been rocked so profoundly by the events of September 11. It was as if my heart was made of a soft white linen cloth that had been immersed in black India ink . . . so thick and heavy . . . so black . . . so dark and so painful. Each day that I meditated, it was as if I were draping that white linen heart through a running stream, washing it, cleansing it, purifying it of that blackness . . . a little less pain and a little more clarity. As I peeled away the conditioned layers of my life, new thoughts emerged, expanded aspects of myself awakened, and I connected for the very first time to my soul. I cried. I laughed. I tapped into the collective. I came face-to-face with my unconditioned Self and experienced the infinite one-ness of the universe. I fell in love again—with myself, with everyone, with life.

By day four, the blackness was gone. I had been meditating for more than five hours a day, and every moment felt surreal. I felt reborn. I reconnected with the tenderness of my heart, which had been closed for so many years. I awakened to a long-hidden forgiveness and made long-overdue peace with some of the deepest wounds of my past—actions I regretted, harsh words I had spoken, ways of thinking and living that had not served others, relationships that had gone undernourished or become painful, paths I'd walked that had turned into dark rabbit holes, and sweet people with tender souls along the way whom I had hurt. I began to explore my most important relationship—the one I have with my true Self—the core of my being, my pure unbounded consciousness. I found surrender. For the first time in years, I felt joy inside. I embraced detachment—trusting in outcomes rather than trying to force them. I touched a part of my being long dormant, awakening my own inner healer and I realized how easy it was for me to access the power of that Source through meditation.

But I still had so many questions, and I continued to believe the answers were out there, so on the last day of the retreat, Deepak suggested that I head off to India—the birthplace of these ancient teachings—to continue my search for the guru, someone who might have all the answers to my deepest inquiries. The vivid first impressions of my midnight landing in Delhi resonate with me still. The cabin doors opened, revealing a moonless, hazy sky. As I walked down the steps onto the runway, I took my first deep breath of India. It felt sweet . . . musty . . . humid . . . fragrant . . . ancient . . . new . . . fresh . . . sacred . . . familiar . . . and exhilarating.

As a taxi took me toward the city, the outskirts of India unfolded. Very quickly, I was in the thick of it, absorbed into the one billion-strong fabric of the magic that is India. I continued the daily routines I had learned at the Oxford retreat. I started each day with meditation, yoga, and prayer. I practiced gratitude and charity. I performed morning rituals of cleansing, bathing myself in the Ganges River in Varanasi as smoldering, cremated bodies drifted past me. I traveled east to Bodhgaya and sat under the Bodhi tree, where Buddha first attained enlightenment. I met with the *naadi*, the mystical palm leaf reader in the jungle enclave of Swamimalai, who read me the details of my past, present, and future lives scrawled in the enduring language of Old Tamil on an ancient preserved palm leaf, even revealing to me everything that had ever and would happen to me in this lifetime as well as the exact moment of my death!

In the town of Jaipur, I experienced *shaktipat*, a form of energetic awakening that blew my mind for weeks and continues to weave through me with regularity so many years later. I visited the spiritual guru Sathya Sai Baba in his Abode of Supreme Peace—the Prasanthi Nilayam Ashram—where he sprinkled me with holy ash called *vibuthi*, which he had manifested out of thin air. More than 10,000 of us sat together one morning as the sun peeked above the horizon. He taught us a heart-opening mantra and we meditated for hours rippling in and out of consciousness. I feel it now as I write these words.

Then I headed off to the Koregaon Park Ashram in Pune, founded by the magnificently irreverent and provocative swami Osho, then known as Bhagwan Shree Rajneesh. Osho had left this earthly plane of existence several years before, but it was in Pune that I stumbled on his quote, "Truth is within you, do not search for it elsewhere." But that didn't really make sense to me at the time, *so I continued to search elsewhere.*

I traveled north to Dharamsala in the Himalayas to hear the Dalai Lama speak about loving-kindness, but he was in deep meditation. (It would be seven more years before I would have the privilege to meet His Holiness and be able to truly appreciate his divine eloquence, deep compassion, and love-filled energy.) I had no planned itinerary. I simply kept following my heart and the whispers it spoke to me in my quietest moments.

Light at the End of the Tunnel

Still in search of the guru, I trekked thousands of miles south down India's belly to the Meenakshi Sundareswarar Temple in the 2,500-year-old city of Madurai. Within the vast walls of this huge ancient structure the size of a small village and honeycombed with statues, lined with shrines, prayer halls, and adorned with thousands of colorfully painted deities, a room with one thousand pillars (it's actually called the hall of 1,000 pillars and in reality only contains 985), and a sacred pond, I was squeezed among a rapturous, barefoot throng of more than 20,000 devotees of the Hindu god Lord Shiva and his wife, the goddess of compassion, Parvati.

As the waves of devotion washed through the crowd, I suddenly found myself totally alone before the holy pond, not another soul in sight! It was if the swarm of pilgrims had abandoned the city for the moment. Slowly, a figure stepped from the shadows and walked into a beam of sunlight. His silhouette had a corona around it, radiating so brilliantly that I had to shield my eyes. He introduced himself as Mr. Jinghan, a Brahmin priest who had traveled 1,500 miles south of his Punjab village in the north on a pilgrimage to meet *me*. That's right . . . *me!* To this day, I cannot explain it. But he leaned down to me, extended his hand, and in the softest and sweetest voice he whispered, "Mr. David, we've been waiting for you a very long time. Shall we sit together?"

I looked behind me to see how many of the 20,000 pilgrims had found their way into the sacred shrine. But miraculously, we were still alone. In this vast stone-encased hallway where billions had visited, prayed, and meditated over the last thousand years, there were only the two of us and the sound of our beating hearts. And without ever meeting each other before, he claimed he had traveled all this way to see me! I closed my eyes and bathed in the warm radiance Jinghan projected into the room.

We sat for a few minutes as he chanted a prayer to the Divine Mother to awaken the feminine creative power in our hearts. Within moments, his mumblings drifted into the ether, and I slipped into the gap, a place beyond space and time. The last thing I remember was feeling my heart gently crack open, a warming, comforting sensation wash over me, and then going deeper than I ever had before as everything merged into one. When I opened my eyes, I was alone. Tears were streaming down my cheeks, a profound sense of well-being rippled through me, and Jinghan was gone. As I looked around, I wondered out loud, "Was he even really here?" But then something caught my eye on the tile beneath my knee as I uncrossed my legs. Looking down, I spied a magnificent gold locket in the shape of the elephant-headed god Ganesha. The gold-faced, so-called Remover of Obstacles was suspended from a black cotton cord. Jinghan must have placed it next to my knee while I was drifting through the cosmos. I lifted it to eye level and bowed my head in reverence. Then I bent my head into it as if being anointed and slid on the necklace. Like a halo, it surrounded me and fell gently around my neck, heralding this moment of profound connection to Source.

I glanced down at my watch. Hours had passed, and the sun had drifted much lower on the horizon as the late afternoon melted into evening. Thousands of candles and butter lamps that had been invisible in the daylight suddenly bathed the room in a light show of dancing shadows and flickering images. I gazed into the vast still pond reflecting the night sky's billions of stars seamlessly melting into the tens of thousands of tiny hand-lit flames that surrounded its tranquil edges. I noticed my own flickering reflection in the belly of a silver Shiva statue that sat two feet in front of me. My amorphous rippling image reflected back at me— shrinking, stretching, distorting, expanding, and vanishing in the darkness as if I had no body; I was a vibrating mass of light. I was transfixed on my image and then I had none.

The minutes merged into hours; thousands of pilgrims trekked past me in the darkness, and sensation slowly flowed back into my body. As my awareness returned to the present moment and physical sensations returned to my body, I realized everything in the hall was framed by a radiant halo. Then I became aware of all the people in the room. Hundreds of pilgrims had poured into the room, and each of them had a radiating aura as they squeezed past me on all sides on their way to the sacred pond. I squeezed the locket in my hand, pressed it tightly to my heart, and began giggling as I recounted Jinghan's words: "Mr. David, we've been waiting for you." I slowly rose to my feet, and within seconds, I was merged into the teaming mass of devotees, physically and spiritually, as I saw them all as a reflection of my own soul . . . all divine . . . all God. It was in that moment, I first felt the tangible energy and infinite power of *the collective*, which has transformed the way I now see the world.

Vibrating from the intense rippling of the devotional intentions that emanated through the temple, I joined a wave of thousands of pilgrims traveling even farther south to the sacred beaches of Kanyakumari, at the southernmost tip of India. There we prayed to the mother goddess under a constellation-filled sky and a new moon that blanketed me in darkness as I lay in a shallow tide pool, rippling with the subtlest movements of the warm, starlit sea before us.

For five more months, I searched high and low in search of a guru to validate my transformation, chatting with roadside *rishis*, traveling from temple to temple, praying in the inner sanctums, bathing in holy lagoons, practicing yoga on moonlit beaches, receiving *diksha* enlightenment blessings, and meditating with each sun's rising and setting. Yet finding no greater truth than the timeless waves before me, I traveled east along the shore until I reached the coastal island of Rameswaram, where I literally tried to spy the mythological monkey god Hanuman, recreating the ancient tale of the *Ramayana* by leaping across the northern tip of the Indian Ocean to the island of Sri Lanka on a bridge of monkeys. But I never saw him. So I kept seeking.

We Are the One We Are Seeking

One morning, as I lay in a hammock in a tropical cashew forest in Kerala, surrounded by the most intense symphony of wild bird calls and reading from a worn copy of the *Bhagavad Gita*, I read Chapter 2, Verse 48 for what seemed like the very first and the four millionth time all at once. I found myself mouthing the words that Lord Krishna shares with the mighty warrior Arjuna: "*yogastha kuru karmani* . . . established in one-ness, perform action." And as I read, a profound and powerful message silently swept into me, beneath my thoughts and into every cell at once, cutting through the energetic curtain of forest life. All sound stopped; the cashew trees froze; the parrots became still; my body had no borders, no skin to encapsulate what I saw; the rushing sense of well-being surged into my physical body and expanded to my mind. Then came something way deeper and more profound than any thought or experience. In a flash, everything became one, and I instantly understood. How do I put it in just a few words? **The guru is inside.**

Yes, the guru is inside . . . inside each one of us! Deep . . . deep . . . deep inside, housed by this flesh casing we call a body and trapped for the span of a lifetime within the constrictions of our five senses and our mind that interprets each moment. Peel away those layers, go deep inside, and deeper still . . . and at our very core, our essence is pure, vast, unbounded consciousness. Infinite. It had been a long buildup over many years and multiple lifetimes of experience that brought me to my *A-ha!* moment. But I had touched something, connected to something, actually *been* something beyond me—something so expansive I could not fathom its edges. Yet, at the same time, I was it, and I had no edges. It was as if I had amnesia and suddenly remembered everything all at once. I describe it as finding another gear in perception, one that you always had but of which you were unaware. This shift in consciousness came to me at once like a bolt of lightning and resonates still—right now—at this very moment!

Accessing the Divine Within

What I realized that day was that we are indeed individual human expressions of the Divine universe. We absorb existence through our senses, distill it with our intellect, and what flows out is a persona—an ego—a sense of Self that individuates us from one another. It contains all the things we think we own, all the personal desires that make us unique, all the fears, hopes, dreams, and ways we define ourselves; all the attachments we have to our life—our values, beliefs, our orientation as children, parents, sisters, brothers; our personality—the stuff that makes us say, "I'm the kind of person who" thinks this, or says that, or acts a certain way, or does a certain thing. Yet, when we look to our most genuine selves, beneath the layers of the ego, the intellect, the realm of our emotions, and our physical body, we can access this Divine flow.

In fact, the answer to every question we could ever ask ourselves rests inside. We simply need to give ourselves permission to hear the answer. And how do we access the vast unboundedness of the universe beyond our conditioned existence? How do we surrender to become the calm amid the chaos? How do we reach beyond this lifetime of conditioning to experience the sweet, silent stillness that rests within? The most effective and powerful tool for expansion and transformation that I have found is the timeless practice of daily meditation.

Each of us has an innate ability to slow our minds and bodies, disconnect from activity, and visit the depths of our unconditioned Self. We are gifted with the aptitude to experience our very soul and go beyond time and space—to transcend this earthly plane of existence and then bring a little piece of tranquil one-ness back into this realm, allowing us to be happier, more compassionate, more forgiving, more creative, more intuitive, and more connected to who we are and the divinity that rests within each of us.

I almost fell out of my hammock as I leaped up in response to my *A-ha!* moment. I packed my bag, checked out of my room, walked to the bus station, traveled the 1,400 miles to Mumbai, and 25 hours later I was boarding a plane back to New York City. Intermittently throughout the 22-hour flight, I drifted in and out of meditation. One thing was clear: My life would never be the same. There was no going back. I had actually experienced universality and could not close my eyes to the infinite one-ness of the universe. And the practical lesson was even more profound. By drifting from a state of activity to a state of stillness and silence, I so easily and effortlessly accessed the realm of one-ness. And I had finally learned that by doing nothing—*no thing*—present-moment awareness will gently flow into one's daily life . . . into your waking state . . . even into your dream state.

I had finally "gotten" it. Halfway through my life, I had come to discover a part of myself that had been dormant since my early childhood. Deep, deep within, I was reintroduced to my still point—my unconditioned Self. I experienced the Universal that was within me. *I had finally found the guru!*

Tapping into Silence

Since that moment, not a day has passed when I do not dip my toes into the ocean of stillness that rests within me. Since beginning my journey, I have meditated every morning and almost every night, and my life has unfolded with purpose, clarity, deeper fulfillment, lightness, and an overall sense of well-being that flows through me in each moment. This daily reconnection has provided me with profound emotional expansion that has led me to make more conscious choices in my interactions with the world, with my friends and loved ones, and with myself.

I've learned first-hand that meditation gracefully infuses us with the inherent knowledge that in each moment, we have the ability to choose to be reflective rather than reflexive. We are not bound by our lifetime of conditioning. We have infinite possibilities in every thought, word, and action. We always have a choice. *Every moment* is a choice between a grievance and a miracle! This expanded internal point of reference creates a more open and accepting orientation to everything around me. Sometimes I see the future. Sometimes I can even hear what people are thinking. But mostly, I perceive the world coming at me in slow motion— where little overwhelms me. In fact, I seem to receive everything so slowly, that—instead of overwhelm or being manhandled by my emotions—waves of clarity unfold to cut through anxiety, anger, disappointment, frustration, and depression. I am then able to prepare my next word or action in a more thoughtful expression. I believe we all have these abilities. Our spiritual transformation is ever flowing. I don't know where mine goes from here or where it will end when I leave this earthly realm, but for now, I choose meditation and its profound daily gifts. And I encourage you to join me on this path so that your life will also unfold with magnificence!

Sharing the Gifts of Meditation

On returning from India, I immersed myself even more deeply into the timeless teachings of meditation—it was all I talked about and pretty much it was all I did! So much so that almost everyone who knew me told me that since all I ever did was meditate, I should become a meditation teacher. I listened to the constant recommendations of my friends—specifically Rookie Komitor, who had also been at the meditation retreat with me in Oxford. She told me simply, "If you really want to learn something, learn to teach it." So I complied. I reached out to Deepak and asked him for a recommendation. He invited me to come out to California and enroll in a mind-body workshop, where I would be immersed in Ayurveda—the 5,000-year-old science of life—and where he and his partner of 20 years, the famed neurologist Dr. David Simon, would be featured teachers. So I headed out to California "to learn to teach it."

I hadn't received a paycheck for six months and money was tight so I wasn't sure if investing in this course was the best use of my resources at the time; but I trusted in my heart (maxed out a credit card) and made the commitment. During that mind-body workshop, David Simon and I experienced an instant love connection. It was as if we had known each other for multiple lifetimes. We spent our lunch breaks together talking about life, love, healing, and higher states of consciousness. We could barely catch our breaths as we raced to get up to speed on each other. He wanted to know everything about me and I was so inspired by the way he spoke so softly from his heart that I couldn't stop asking him questions about his life. I had never before met anyone so egoless, so comfortable with who he was, and so articulate translating timeless wisdom into the real world. Here was this brilliant, board-certified neurologist speaking so effortlessly about the Bible, the *Bhagavad Gita*, Ayurveda, heart-healing, and meditation! He was this magnificent fusion of modern medical science and the healing arts of the East.

Each afternoon, as the workshop sessions were winding down, he would seek me out and we'd take these long, slow walks around a local golf course, which he described as "man's version of nature." We talked late into the evenings like two spiritual lovers who just can't get enough of each other. And on the last day of the workshop, I was so touched by Deepak and David's global vision of impacting a million people around the world, that I volunteered to help them raise the vibration of the center they had both created. I proposed that I would head back home to New York and advise them each week from afar. But they had another plan in mind. They asked me if I'd be willing to apprentice under them, immerse myself in the ancient teachings, and run the Chopra Center by David's side. But, I'd need to move there so I could truly "breathe the air" of that environment.

I never went back home. Instead I decided to stay and volunteer, unplug from my life on the East Coast, and in that defining moment, I moved to Carlsbad—a sunny beach town in Southern California, just a bit north of the Mexican border. I calculated that I could borrow on my credit cards for seven months of living expenses, while I apprenticed under two of my greatest mentors— and so again, I jumped—and waited for the net to appear.

Initially, because of my corporate experience, they appointed me as the COO of the Chopra Center. And one of my greatest joys was helping to build on their vision, expand the Center's global reach, and navigate their organization to a space of abundance. It had been years in the making but now I was able to use my business acumen in a cause that I felt really added value to the lives of millions around the world. But that was just the start. After those first six months, I was added to the payroll and suddenly, I had a job doing what I loved—balancing the worlds of business and wellness.

I'm often asked how I got the name *davidji*. For the first few months of my apprenticeship, David Simon and I were joined at the hip. We spent every day together talking, walking, eating, meditating, chanting, laughing, discussing the ancient teachings, and reading Sufi poetry. Wherever we went, he carried a copy of the Sufi poet Hafiz's poetry and I carried his worn copy of the *Bhagavad Gita*. We would take long walks to the beach, the botanical gardens, the golf course, and secret trails in Torrey Pines State Reserve where we would read to each other. We were inseparable and people began to refer to us collectively as "the Davids." Whenever people would address one of us as David, we never quite knew which one of us they were referring to. Back at the Center it was even more confusing, with members of the staff calling our name and both of us whipping our head around. This went on for months, and one day, Deepak and David approached me and announced that we needed to change my name. It felt like an intervention and I wasn't quite sure what they had in mind.

But in that moment, they gave me the name *davidji*. Deepak said that *Ji* was a term of endearment in Hindi and it meant "beloved." I replied, "That's so perfect! My mother named me David, because in the Bible *David* means 'beloved.' I accept!" So that day, I became *beloved beloved*! They originally spelled it DavidJi—but I changed it to all lowercase so that it would remind me to flow humility in all my interactions. And from that day, David referred to me simply as "ji."

And so, there I was in this surreal snapshot in time, the third D in the trio of Deepak, David, and davidji. At first I had to pinch myself. But then it just became the new normal. I spent every day for almost a decade working, studying, and apprenticing under them, as I simultaneously built a new infrastructure inside the organization *and* inside myself. And with each day, they encouraged me to take it deeper—teach another class, study the ancient scriptures, meditate with them, and practice more advanced techniques. My meditation practice became more grounded and my teaching became fluid. I became certified as a meditation teacher, an Ayurveda instructor, a registered 200-hour yoga teacher, and a certified Vedic Master. After my first year, they appointed me as the lead educator of the Chopra Center, and my path suddenly started to make sense. Soon I was teaching at all the workshops and leading the meditations at all the signature events.

In 2008, Deepak, David, and our tiny event team went on what David referred to as *The Spiritual Lollapalooza Tour*. Our first night in Dublin, 508 spiritual seekers filled the room, including the likes of Donovan, Gerard Butler, Fionnuala Gill, and Colin Farrell. I remember gazing out into the audience during my *Introduction to Meditation* class and repeating my *A-ha!* moment from my last day in India, "The *guru* rests inside. In fact, the answer to every question we could ever ask ourselves rests within. We just need to quiet the fluctuations of our mind so we can hear the whispers of our heart." The room went totally still and silent. The only sounds were our measured, collective breathing and our 500 hearts beating as one. Then I led the group in a 30-minute mantra meditation. The power of that collective energy was palpable. When we ended with a resounding *ommmmm*, my heart was full and my tears flowed.

It had only been eight years since I headed off on my own personal *Eat, Pray, Love* journey (without the *Eating* and the *Love*) but in that moment, all my years of study and practice made sense. I was finally living a purpose-driven life. When we returned back home, I was appointed the very first dean of Chopra Center University. In that role, I was given the opportunity to merge Deepak and David's modern translations into a recognized curriculum and take a leadership role in the process using my real-world interpretations, sacred rituals, and practical techniques.

Most people who find themselves on a spiritual path come from a place of desiring to heal themselves, even if they are unaware that is what motivates them. In time, they see that healing as so profound they can't help but share it with others. This was my journey as well. I came from a place of deep pain and overwhelming confusion. And then a spark of clarity lit inside of me, so I understand at the deepest level what you are desiring, seeking, and needing right now as you take your bold steps on the journey to the center of your own soul.

In my role as dean, I merged the vast body of knowledge I had immersed in with my business experience and my deep love for the timeless teachings to grow the University, cultivate the curriculum, and transform students into teachers of this eternal wisdom. Over those years, I dedicated each day to helping seekers understand the foundations of their practice, navigate the ancient wisdom traditions, translate theory into down-to-earth practical application, learn the myths, science, and secrets of meditation, and bring simple-to-use tools and techniques into the real world. Each year, I trained, tested, and certified five classes of Meditation, Ayurveda, and Yoga teachers, sending waves of sweet light out into the world.

The Power of a Defining Moment

In January of 2012, my dearest friend and mentor David Simon passed away after being diagnosed with a terminal brain tumor. The depth of my loss was unfathomable, incomprehensible, and left me feeling empty and hollow. Our unconditional friendship and his selfless mentorship of me that began 10 years earlier, created a defining arc in my life. He skillfully and relentlessly trained and challenged me every day to show up as my best version. And over those years, the countless private moments where Deepak, David, and I talked for hours about life, love, consciousness, and dharma are now etched deeply into every cell of my body. Those two brilliant beings of light never stopped evolving themselves, raising their own vibration, and raising the vibration of the world around them. And I was so blessed to be caught in that combined glow of Deepak's grace and David's authenticity. My unconventional 10-year apprenticeship under them taught me lifetimes of lessons. And the most profound of those was to see the best in others, to keep leading with love, and to always flow my own most authentic expression.

As we have been taught in the ancient scriptures, everything in life has a beginning, a middle, and an end. And as David Simon's physical arc in this life was ending, a new one was beginning for me. I realized to truly be my best version and step into my power, I needed to let go of one dream, and embark on another. After training more than 200,000 people to meditate, certifying more than 1,500 teachers, creating five *21-day meditation challenges*, and leading more than 100 retreats, workshops, and seminars, I realized my contribution to the Center was complete. Deepak had written more than 50 books since the day we first met; the Center was thriving; meditation and yoga were now becoming part of the mainstream culture; and a brilliant management team was in place to take Deepak's vision to the next level.

I had learned so much about the world and about myself. And yet, the emptiness inside of me was seeking to be filled with something new and fresh. The universe was calling me to evolve one more time and share this timeless body of knowledge at an even higher level. But to do that, *I needed to leave the nest and step into the unknown one more time.* And so, after weeks of deliberation, I decided to leave the place that had been my home for a decade.

Tears streamed from my eyes when I shared my decision with Deepak. My heart was so heavy considering all we had shared over our many years together. He too was grieving the loss of his partner of 20 years. But he compassionately received my news and told me that he understood my choice from a deep personal level because at a certain point in his career, he too had left the side of his greatest teacher and mentor and then followed his own dream. He lovingly reassured me that we would always be connected and I would always be a part of his family. His support helped me own my impact in that moment—and take that bittersweet leap out of the nest.

And so a month later on July 14—Bastille Day (French Liberation Day), which had also been the date I began my journey all those years before—I set out on my own to explore the world with new eyes. Twelve years earlier, I had left the safe womb-like protection of a lifelong career by following the whispers of my heart. This would be no different. The strength I had gained from that previous leap gave me the courage to step into the unknown, the uncertain, the infinite. I trusted in my decision. I trusted in the universe. And I jumped!

I didn't have a game plan in place. I just knew I wanted to help those who were struggling and suffering so I opened myself up to all possibilities.

And just as I had volunteered in my first six months at the Chopra Center, I began volunteering my services to organizations that stirred my heart. I reached out to several charities and offered to lead sunrise meditations at their fund-raisers. I offered my time and attention to hospice, wounded warrior organizations, animal shelters, and breast cancer walkathons. And then I realized I could make an even bigger difference by donating money to these charities by writing a book that would help them. *You are reading that book right now.* All proceeds I receive from the sale of *Secrets of Meditation* are donated to charity! So thank you for your contribution to this healing mission. Together we have helped the Susan G. Komen nonprofit Breast Cancer Foundation, Cystic Fibrosis Foundation, Dana-Farber Cancer Institute, PAWS Chicago, Sam Simon Foundation, LightBridge Hospice, National Urban League, Harvey Milk Foundation, World Wildlife Fund, Wounded Warrior Project, American Red Cross, the Africa Yoga Project, Kids for Peace, Tibet Fund, Rancho Coastal Humane Society, UNICEF, and the San Diego Food Bank.

It's Never Too Late to Be Reborn

I reflected back on that defining moment after 9/11, where a man living in a cardboard box had asked me, "What's going to be on your tombstone?" Back then, with so little to show for my many years in the business world, I was lost. But now I felt a sense of renewal, of purpose, of possibility. I began hosting a weekly radio show on Hay House Radio and started teaching members of the military how to heal from the stress of combat. I continued teaching mindful performance in the corporate world and began to work with cops in the U.S. and abroad and had developed an awareness curriculum for *Blue Courage*, an organization made up of current and retired law enforcement officers dedicated to restoring the nobility of policing. I started fund-raising efforts for hospice care, breast cancer research, and animal rescue, and I began recording free weekly guided meditations (there are more than 700 now), for my website and other online music sites.

Since leaving the nest, I've also trained hundreds of certified *Masters of Wisdom and Meditation Teachers* through my own teacher training program; taught thousands throughout the U.S., Canada, Europe, and South America how to share this ancient wisdom with their families, co-workers, students, and communities; created the davidji SweetSpot Community sharing the teachings with more than a million people around the globe.

My relationship with Hay House has been one of nurturing and support & I am so grateful to have merged with such a selfless organization. My online meditation video course called *The Art of Meditation* was one of the first offerings from Hay House University. And, I've been gifted with the opportunity to develop friendships with and teach alongside Wayne Dyer, Don Miguel Ruiz, Mike Dooley, Kris Carr, Barbara De Angelis, James Van Praagh, Marianne Williamson, Cheryl Richardson, and Gabrielle Bernstein. My real-world meditation tools & techniques have made it into the White House, Hollywood, Major League Baseball, the NBA, primetime TV, corporate boardrooms of Fortune 500 companies, hundreds of police precincts around the world, and even the Department of Justice. And then, my second book *destressifying* became an Amazon #1 bestseller and won the Nautilus Book Award, providing a modern translation of the ancient teachings for those new to the concept & value of the present moment. Fifteen years after I began searching for the guru, the Universe lovingly whispered back— *The guru rests inside!*

I realize this is a life journey—with no turning back. Every day since that first moment of awakening exploded through every cell in my body, I have immersed myself into the timeless body of knowledge of meditation, Ayurveda, yoga, Vedanta, emotional healing, expanded awareness and higher states of consciousness. I have sat at the feet of the masters of meditation, mindfulness, and Vedic wisdom and received some of the most powerful interpretations of these timeless teachings. And I have made my daily meditation practice a cornerstone of my life, where I have witnessed an uplifting sea change within my own being and a transformational thread of positivity woven into my interactions.

And every day, I wake up with the desire to share more with you—through guided meditations, podcasts, blogs, articles, videos, and personal transmission. Over the years, I have personally witnessed the transformation of thousands of my students as they moved from panic and anxiety to confidence and calm, from fear and anger to self-love and self-kindness, and from lost to found. My students tell me they feel a natural unfolding of deeper compassion, a greater clarity about life, a more universal perspective that weaves through each thought. My hope and intention is that you experience the same powerful transformation through the pages of this book. And I'll be right here alongside you as together we take your meditation and your life to the next level.

CHAPTER 2

WHAT IS MEDITATION, AND WHY SHOULD I CARE?

---

*"Don't ask what the world needs. Ask what makes
you come alive and go do that. Because what the
world needs is people who have come alive."*

— HOWARD THURMAN

For thousands of years, people have used various techniques to bring their minds to a quieter state of being. Depending on where in the world they have lived and what their culture or society has encouraged, human beings have come up with an extraordinarily rich array of practices for going beyond the ordinary waking state to expanded states of consciousness. Depending on the culture and religious orientation, these ritualized practices include chanting, breathing, ecstatic dancing, healing touch, listening to music, visual stimulation, and even meditating on the taste of chocolate. Each technique is specifically designed to move the mind from its current state of activity to one of present-moment witnessing awareness.

You have already experienced the phenomena of present-moment witnessing awareness many times throughout your life, but perhaps you didn't even realize it. These are the moments when you are in the "still zone." It's that moment on a roller coaster when you are screaming at the top of your lungs as your body plunges downward—or when you are playing sports and every shot you take, every move you make, is the perfect one. It's when you are giving that big presentation and rather than read some memorized script, you spontaneously seem to channel just the right words in an effortless flow. It's when you spontaneously say or do the perfect thing at the exact perfect moment, cook the most brilliant meal as if you were a culinary genius, essentially do anything to such a degree that time seems to stand still. And it's the pure joy of laughing so hysterically your belly starts to spasm. These are all examples of present-moment witnessing awareness while we are doing something, when we are not thinking for one moment about the past or reaching one second into the future.

But, when we experience that same present-moment awareness while *not doing* anything, we reach a state of *restful alertness,* and this is *the stillness zone* we experience during deep meditation—the realm of no thought, no sound, and no sensation. When you are in that space, you have essentially disconnected from all the things in your world that are in the realm of activity, and you have connected to your soul. In the language of many meditators, this is referred to as accessing the space between your thoughts—*the gap*—a space brimming with pure potential and infinite possibilities.

When you have a consistent daily meditation practice, you begin to experience that bliss more and more in your everyday life. A physiological shift occurs that grows deeper, stronger, and more profound with repetition. Like building any muscle in your body, meditation is a practice that transforms your entire physiology over time. This shift is subtle at first. Then as the process of physical and emotional softening occurs, you begin to view life in new and expanded ways. Life takes on a deeper meaning, a more universal understanding that pervades every cell of your being. The present-moment awareness you experience in meditation begins to flow throughout each thought, each conversation, each keystroke, and each breath.

In both ancient and modern writings, this change, shift, or transformation of awareness—this space of *just BEing*—has been referred to by many names, including enlightenment, transcendence, awakening, bliss, the gap, *turiya*, witnessing awareness, being in the moment, one-ness, *ananda*, and *samadhi*.

When you experience *no activity* within you or outside of yourself, you actually open yourself to realms of expanded consciousness and a *greater* depth of feeling. Levels of performance, creativity, intuition, personal growth, compassion, subtle empowerment, forgiveness, and peace of mind increase. Whether this stillness lasts for a 10th of a second, 10 seconds, or 10 minutes is of no consequence. *Touching stillness and silence—even in the smallest of doses—allows you to connect to your unconditioned Self . . . to your source.*

WHO ELSE MEDITATES?

All it takes is one meditation and you join the ranks of millions around the world who consider meditation to be a centering practice in their lives, something that connects them more deeply to their inner light. In addition to my teachers, and numerous other human empowerment leaders—such as Oprah Winfrey, Wayne Dyer, Louise Hay, Eckhart Tolle, Marianne Williamson, and Anthony Robbins—the following people have acknowledged the importance of meditation. Some have been my students, and others are simply famous meditators. We are all part of the same flow, the fabric of the collective consciousness.

Jennifer Aniston, Kristen Bell, Orlando Bloom, Cory Booker, Kate Bosworth, Russell Brand, Kobe Bryant, Gerard Butler, Kyle Cease, Leonard Cohen, Anderson Cooper, Sheryl Crow, Kat Dennings, Laura Dern, T. Harv Eker, Ralph Waldo Emerson, Mia Farrow, Benjamin Franklin, Richard Gere, Heather Graham, Ariana Grande, Tara Guber, Goldie Hawn, Phil Jackson, Kathy Jarvis, Anthony Kiedis, Annie Lennox, David Lynch, Alanis Morissette, Joel Osteen, Dr. Mehmet Oz, Gwyneth Paltrow, Katy Perry, Prince, Rick Rubin, Meg Ryan, Susan Sarandon, Steven Seagal, Jerry Seinfeld, Swami Sivananda, Howard Stern, Sting, Henry David Thoreau, Liv Tyler, Tal Wilkenfeld, Tiger Woods, and Stevie Wonder.

Of course, it's not necessary to be a celebrity or have a guru (other than oneself) to have a solid and fulfilling meditation practice. It is safe to assume that if all these high achievers meditate, chances are they share the common characteristics of people seeking balance, wholeness, healing, wellness, and the best aspects of who they are . . . their most awakened, magnificent, and Divine selves. So, let's add You and Me to that list!

The Story of You

Go back to the moment of your birth. Most likely you don't remember, but here's pretty much how it went. You emerged from the womb pure, whole, unconditioned, and perfect—with no earthly conditioning. Perhaps the doctor gently smacked you on your bottom or rubbed your chest to kick-start your first breath. From that moment on, every experience and every person that touched your world has layered and layered and layered you with messages and impressions. And you've responded with conditioning, reinforcement, and new growth . . . covering up that pure, whole, brilliant diamond in the center.

And here you are today. It's a few years later and a few million light-years from that moment of innocence, purity, wholeness, and perfection, when the light of this world first shined in your eyes. But through your meditation practice, each time you connect to your natural state of stillness and silence, you are peeling away the layers of conditioning and reconnecting to that brilliant source, dipping your toe in—dipping your fingers into that pure, unbounded, enlightened aspect of yourself.

The magnificence of meditation isn't so much the experience during the practice itself. Each time you meditate, you peel back one of these layers of conditioning, get closer to the radiance of the diamond inside, and bring back *into your life* a thimbleful . . . a teaspoonful . . . an eyedropper full of what rests at the center of your essence—pure, still, silent, unconditioned, light-filled, and universal—where you are not simply you. You are everyone and everything. You are one-ness.

Maybe that sounds a bit daunting. Maybe you just wanted to learn how to sleep through the night, have less stress, find balance, breathe easier, feel less overwhelmed, lower your blood pressure, and live a more peaceful life. You will have that too, and so much more. A regular meditation practice will very quickly give you observable physical and emotional benefits. But meditation is not like taking a Xanax to ease your worry in a moment; you meditate so you don't have the need to take anti-anxiety medication. Your calmness starts before the storm and keeps you feeling relaxed and centered even as the winds of chaos swirl around you. This sense of abiding peace and tranquility can develop pretty quickly. Meditation can help improve your physical health, your emotional well-being, and your spiritual connection with your very first experience. But it will also open up a realm of self-awareness and higher consciousness that will connect you to the more universal and divine aspects of your Self.

Exploring Your Expectations

Before every class I teach, I ask each meditation student to share why they want to learn to meditate, what they hope to experience. Here's a list of the top 20 expectations and desires that my students have shared over the years:

1. Peace of mind
2. Less stress
3. To slow down the world and stop my thoughts
4. Greater clarity or intuition
5. Less anxiety
6. Lower blood pressure
7. To breathe more easily

8. Enlightenment

9. Deeper connection to Source/Self/Spirit/God/
   the Divine

10. Emotional healing and freedom from the past

11. Awaken creativity

12. To calm the storm

13. To stop the sense of being overwhelmed

14. More restful sleep

15. Happiness

16. Deeper, more loving relationships

17. To boost my immune system

18. To ease my pain

19. To develop my ability to relax

20. To empower myself

Are there any desires on this list that resonate with you? Is there anything that you'd like more of in your life? Less of? You get to create it. It simply requires a daily practice. And I assure you that within only a few days, your life and those people in it will benefit in every moment on every level from your embracing this gentle practice.

What's the reason you want to establish a daily meditation practice? What is *your* expectation? Write it down right now under MY INTENTIONS on page 249.

And when you check back in a month or two, we'll see how you've manifested this desire in your life! I also recommend you begin using a meditation journal and that's all laid out for you on the MY MEDITATION EXPERIENCES on page 253 so you can reflect on your practice when you are not reading. Try it for a week and see how your life unfolds. Also, feel free to make notes throughout this book. Hopefully, this becomes your meditation bible that you'll read and refer back to for many years to come.

Dipping Your Toe into the Ocean of Meditation

Right now you have everything you need to meditate, so let's give it a go. First, find a comfortable place to sit—on a chair or couch, on the floor, a park bench—anywhere you will be relatively undisturbed by external activities.

Once you have found the place, get comfortable, relax into it, and simply become aware of your breath. Don't breathe any differently . . . just allow your awareness to drift to your breathing.

As you read these words, feel the air flow in and out of you. Feel your lungs stretch and relax. Feel your chest rise and fall. Breathe slowly. Now close your mouth, and gently breathe in and out, solely through your nose. Feel your belly fill as you inhale. Feel it release as you exhale. Again, don't consciously do anything to alter your breath other than closing your mouth and breathing both in and out through your nose. Just observe your breath for about a minute . . . simply be aware that you breathe in, hold it in for a sliver of a moment, exhale for a moment or two, and then hold that out for a sliver of a moment before you inhale again.

As you breathe, silently notice *I'm breathing in, I'm holding the breath, I'm breathing out, I'm holding the breath.* Maintain this awareness for the next few minutes.

Now become aware of your physical body . . . how does it feel? Are you hot or cold? Relaxed or tense? Do parts of your body hurt, and are there other parts you don't even feel right now? Notice that as your awareness drifts over different parts of your body, you become more aware of your physiology. Let's make our calves tingle right now. Feel the tips of your nostrils without touching them. Become aware of your lips. Isn't it funny how our awareness truly does dictate our experiences?

Look at your hands right now. Look at your palms. Rest them on your thighs, and feel them come to life. Out of sight, out of mind . . . but within sight, within mind. Now bring your attention to the blood flowing into your hands. Keep your focus on your palms for a minute. Now feel the blood move into your palms. Feel them begin to get warm in the center.

Where attention flows, energy goes. Do you see how as soon as you become aware of something, your mind starts to interpret your experience? Do you notice how your mind instantly wants to define it, label it, or assign it meaning? Do you see how your awareness is connected to your body as well?

Now move your awareness beyond your hands and down to your feet. Start on your right side. Flex your right foot. Wiggle it a bit. Roll your ankle around for a few moments. Now relax your foot. Feel each toe with your mind as you move your attention from each toe to the next and then from one side of your foot to the other. Feel that flow of attention move from your toes down the sole of your foot into your heel. Then move your attention slowly up the back of your calf until you arrive in your mind's eye at your knee. Now, gently breathing in and out and *using only your mind*, massage your kneecap in a circular motion and move around to the back of your knee. Now move up your right hamstring and energetically feel the front of your thigh without touching it. Let a relaxing sensation radiate from the top of your thigh. Slowly breathe in as you keep the attention on your thigh. Feel it. Close your eyes for a few moments and gently breathe. Feel it. Feel all the sensations and interpretations you are experiencing in your right leg.

Now bring your awareness to your left foot. Flex it. Wiggle it a bit. Roll your ankle around for a few moments. Relax your left foot, and feel each toe as you move your attention from each toe to the next and then from one side of your foot to the other. Feel that flow of attention move from your toes down the sole of your left foot into your heel. Then feel it slowly move up the back of your calf until you arrive in your mind's eye at your knee. Now, gently breathing in and out and using only your mind, massage your kneecap in a circular motion and move around to the back of your knee. Now move your awareness up your left hamstring and energetically feel the front of your thigh without touching it. Let a relaxing sensation radiate from the top of your thigh. Slowly breathe in as you keep the attention on your left thigh. Feel it. Close your eyes for a few moments and gently breathe. Feel it. Feel all the sensations and interpretations you are experiencing in your right leg.

Now let's bring our awareness to both feet. Wiggle them. Roll both ankles around a bit. Now relax your feet and let them melt into the floor. Now feel each toe on both feet as you move your attention from each toe to the next and then from one side of your foot to the other. Feel that flow of attention move down the soles of your feet into your heels. Remember to keep breathing as you drift to each part of your body. Then feel it slowly move up the back of your calves until you arrive in your mind's eye at your knees. Now, gently breathing in and out and using only your mind's eye, massage your kneecaps in a circular motion and move around to the back of your knees. Now slowly move your awareness up your hamstrings and energetically feel the front of your thighs without touching them. Let a relaxing sensation radiate from the top of your thighs. Slowly breathe in as you keep the attention on your thighs. Feel the energy in your thighs. Sit there for a few moments and gently breathe. Feel it.

Now move your attention to your pelvis. Sit with that feeling for a moment or two; simply observe it as you consciously move all your awareness to your pelvis. Feel the blood flow in and out of your pelvic region. Feel any discomfort you have get a bit lighter as you witness the area from the tops of your thighs to your belly button becoming more vital and warmer from the attention you place on your pelvis. Sit with this sensation for a few moments with your eyes closed.

Now drift your awareness up into your belly. Feel the blood flow into your belly. Do you see how subtly shifting your awareness has actually brought blood flow and other physiological changes to these areas? Feel the blood flow against gravity from your pelvis up into your belly.

Simply awakening the lower half of your body with your mind has brought all these body parts into your awareness. Moments ago your attention was on reading. Where attention flows, energy goes. Pretty interesting, isn't it?

Now with your breath, see if you can gently breathe and move your awareness from your belly, up your torso, to your heart. Feel the power center of your physical body—your heart—become more open and more full. Notice how right now you are able to take a deeper breath than you could before. Your rib cage can expand more with every inhale. Once you truly feel full in this region of your body, breathe in again, and as you exhale, move your attention even higher up your chest. Breathe in and pull your energy from below your heart to the area around your heart; feel the sensation in your chest. Sit with that for a few moments. Feel your heart fill with love. With gratitude. With compassion. With forgiveness. With joy. Notice as you do this a smile unfolds on your face.

Now push it up even further as you inhale. At this moment, you are experiencing present-moment awareness. As your attention goes, there you are in that moment. Not thinking about the past . . . not thinking about the future. Totally present. Totally here. Right now.

Now lift your eyes from the page after you've read these directions. Look around, and take in all your eyes observe. Don't judge; just witness, like a video camera simply absorbing all it sees in total witness mode. Take in the colors; see the depth and shade of everything around you. The shapes . . . the distances between objects, their shadows, how the light is falling, their denseness. Just stay with this for a minute or two as you receive all these waves and particles of light that you are turning into meaning.

What do you hear in this moment? Are there noises around you? Music? Sounds of nature? Sounds of a busy world? Any internal noises, like your stomach rumbling? Or the sound of your breathing?

Remember to keep breathing through your nose as your awareness heightens. Are you aware of any aromas? What is the smell of your surroundings? Keep breathing and bring your awareness to some part of your body that feels tight or heavy or constricted. It might be your heart, belly, temples, back, legs, arms, throat, or any other area. Don't do anything other than drift your awareness to that place and ask yourself how it feels. Now with your awareness on that place, breathe in deeply to the count of four. And slowly exhale to the count of four, bringing even more attention to this area. Let's do this again.

Now slowly breathe in and out three times with your eyes closed. I'll wait.

How did the experience change with your eyes closed? Did you feel a difference? Did you become aware of your thoughts? Were you thinking *more* or *less*? Did you visualize your surroundings on the back of your eyelids? Did your other senses become more aware? Did you hear better? Relax more? Did it seem comfortable or unfamiliar in any way?

And what does the area of the body you focused on feel like now? Is it a bit lighter, looser, more open? As you begin to answer this question, your mind is drifting into the past. But the present-moment awareness you experienced only moments ago is now part of you here . . . now . . . in this present moment. This whole exercise took less than five minutes. A daily meditation practice can deliver this to you in much greater doses on a consistent basis. Imagine how beneficial this could be.

Going Deeper with Your Eyes Closed

Most schools of meditation instruct practitioners to close their eyes so they will take in less activity from the visible world. We'll discuss visual meditations a bit later, but for now, let's get ready to close our eyes again. We'll be following our breath for a few moments here, so get comfortable, gently breathe, and silently notice *I'm breathing in, I'm holding it for a millisecond, I'm breathing out, I'm holding it for a millisecond. I'm breathing in . . .*

As each aspect of your breathing occurs, notice it . . . witness it . . . observe it. Feel the rising, the falling, the in, the out, the pauses—The Spaces—between each inhale and exhale . . . and keep doing so for a few minutes. If you drift away to any other experience—such as thoughts, sounds, or physical sensations (and you will)—gently return your attention to the breath and the observation that *"I'm breathing in," "Space," "I'm breathing out," "Space."* If you'd like, you can shorten it to *"In." "Space." "Out." "Space."* But don't just say it robotically; actually observe each part of your breath, and narrate the experience as you live it.

Let's meditate together using this breathing practice for three full minutes. Don't worry about timing yourself, but feel free to place a clock in front of you or look at your watch. And feel free to go longer, if you like. Simply watch your breath and surrender to the moment. Now put down your book and close your eyes. I'll wait right here.

Okay, I'm guessing you're back now. How did that feel? How do you feel now? Any changes? Thoughtfully answer these questions:

- Did the time seem longer or shorter than it actually was? Did it feel like 20 years? Or 20 seconds?

- Were you bored? Restless?

- Did you feel more relaxed at any time?

- Did you feel any settling down?

- Did you fall asleep?

- Did you become aware of your thoughts? Your emotions? Your body?

- Did you find yourself judging the experience?

- Did you feel a wave of a particular emotion or physical sensation wash over you?

- Did you experience a separation or disconnect between your breathing and your repetition of "In." "Space." "Out." "Space."?

- Did the space get longer, shorter, vanish?

- Did your awareness drift away from the breath at any time? Did you remember to gently drift your attention back to your breathing and to follow your breath?

- Did you become frustrated? Did you become lost? Did something become clearer?

- Did you see anything in your mind's eye?

- Did you notice any particular thoughts, sounds, or physical sensations that became a part of your awareness?

- Did you open your eyes to check the time or your surroundings?

- Did you see anything or feel anything that was different from what you expected?

All these sensations, emotions, thoughts, sounds, and experiences are part of meditation—witnessing awareness. You were actually just meditating! This type of meditation is known as breath awareness meditation or *mindfulness*, and you just did it. What you experienced is exactly what you were supposed to experience: drifting back and forth between your breath and thoughts, sounds, and physical sensations. And when you turn this into a daily practice, your mind calms down and finds it less necessary to engage the thoughts.

Imagine if you were receiving a text or phone call every five minutes, and your ringer was on really loud. You would notice the calming effect of turning the ringer softer, even if the calls continued. And then if you turned the ringer on silent mode, even though the calls still came in every five minutes, you would be unaware, undistracted, undisturbed. Ultimately, you'd calm down and have less anxiety or stress over the incoming messages, because they wouldn't be persistently alerting you. *Meditation helps you turn your personal ringer on silent mode to separate you from your thoughts and the external swirling of life.* It doesn't take you out of this life; it connects you more deeply to it.

Meditation actually allows you to experience yourself more deeply without the frenetic onslaught of your mind and the external world relentlessly picking at you. Everything you thought was swirling around is still out there. But now you see it differently—more consciously. It is in these moments that transformation occurs. For just a moment . . . a second . . . a minute . . . you transcend this time-bound body . . . you go beyond this ego-based mind. The experience isn't describable. It isn't really explainable. We use words like *stillness*, *peace*, or *whole*, to describe what we experience in meditation, even if just for a moment.

Giving yourself a few breaks each day from persistent activity is all it takes to create major shifts in your life. I call it taking a "time in," a term first coined by Andy Kelley, "The Boston Buddha," a meditation teacher who teaches kids in schools to connect to their own stillness and silence. The shift begins with this relatively effortless practice in which we subtly introduce stillness, which then interrupts the conditioned pattern of nonstop activity. The result is that suddenly, amid all this reinforcement of activity, there is a blip . . . a virtual millisecond of nonactivity. And it has a profound consequence. You connect to that millisecond of stillness and silence and bring it back into this world . . . into this life . . . into each thought . . . into each moment. That's the magnificence of meditation—not what happens during the meditation but what happens in every other moment of your day. It becomes a part of who you are, and it's cumulative. It builds and builds with each sunset and sunrise, with each meditation, with each new day, with each conversation, with each person in your life, with each new thought, and with each new choice.

CHAPTER 3

THE BENEFITS OF MEDITATION

"Your living is determined not so much by what life brings to you as by the attitude you bring to life; not so much by what happens to you as by the way your mind looks at what happens."

— KAHLIL GIBRAN

The physical, emotional, and spiritual value of meditation has been well documented for thousands of years. Scientists, philosophers, spiritualists, and religious leaders have heralded the power of witnessing awareness. They may refer to it as deep reflection, being present, mindfulness, contemplation, prayer, meditation, or simply relaxing, but it's all the same thing—disconnecting from the activity and drifting to the space between our thoughts. In the *Yoga Sutras*, written sometime between 200 B.C. and. 200 A.D., the sage Patanjali (who created a common thread that all schools of yoga follow) defined meditation in four Sanskrit words: *yoga citta vritti nirodha*, which means "one-ness is the progressive quieting of the fluctuations of the mind."

Over the first few days, weeks, and months of daily meditation, the quieting impact this simple practice has on your bodymind begins to express itself in each choice you make. Your shift may be so subtle that even you don't see it at first. But your thoughts, selections, decisions, and daily actions become more conscious, leading to more intuitively conscious behaviors. Then one day you realize you have a broader perspective, a deeper sense of calm, and heightened clarity . . . yes, greater creativity, expanded grace, greater ease. You realize you are making more spontaneous right choices. You realize you are being more authentic. There is greater alignment between what you think, what you say, and what you do. The world is still turning—and sometimes faster than ever—but to you, that swirl is in slower motion, like texts coming into your cell phone with a really faint hum rather than a blasting ringtone.

Over time, moving from activity to stillness during meditation translates into more conscious behaviors during nonmeditation (the other 23 or so hours of your day). Your interactions with the world shift more effortlessly from reactivity to responding, from reflexiveness to reflectiveness, from defensiveness to openness, and from drama to calm.

There's a big bonus on top of all these other nourishing aspects of having a practice. Over time, meditation quiets you to a state where you experience life with a deeper understanding of your true Self, which can open the door to spiritual exploration, connection, discovery, and fulfillment. It is along the so-called "spiritual path" that you truly can experience your unbounded and unconditioned Self—the infinite you that rests at the core of who you are underneath your body and beneath this worldly garb of titles, roles, masks, ego, and the complexities of this life.

In Part II of this book, we explore many different types of meditation. But if you simply limited yourself to only 20 minutes a day of the breath meditation we explored in the previous chapter, you would quickly start to observe magnificent, tangible changes in your physiology, emotional state, sense of Self, and sense of life. Your earthly body would be more aligned with your cosmic body. Maybe you feel it now from the short meditation we just practiced. And maybe you have never felt it before.

Regardless of the depth of your spiritual nature, simply by spending time in stillness and silence, you will become more imbued with the ability to open to greater possibilities in each moment instead of the ones you were fixed on. This creates a more universal trajectory for the rest of your life with an expanded point of view. By seeing yourself as more universal and less personal, you'll realize more options in each moment instead of seeing only the limited ones you thought you had before. Everything in your life becomes richer when you see there are lots of different ways things can play out and your previously constricted viewpoint only made you feel more helpless as life unfolded. But this tool called meditation can give you the edge you need to feel strong each day, to gain clarity, and to finally regain your peace of mind.

The purpose of a spiritual journey isn't to *change* your mind, it's to *expand* your mind to understand the true potential in each moment in your life. To discover a Self who has the ability to see more possibilities and expanded points of view—even the ones opposing yours—and then to choose creatively . . . intuitively . . . sacredly.

Evolving our Brains

Different types of meditation styles take you to different places. Some calm you in the moment, others calm you after the moment, some open you, some inspire you, some relax you, some comfort you, others transport you, and some deliver you to a life of one-ness and deeper fulfillment. This may sound like a huge leap from the few minutes of meditation you experienced in the last chapter, but the clinical, scientific proof of the power of meditation, its current trendiness, and 5,000 years of testimonials should give you the support you need right now to continue exploring.

Over the last several years, thousands of compelling scientific studies have found evidence that a regular, consistent meditation practice can offer a wide range of healing benefits. The data include hundreds of clinical studies performed by science and medical departments at major universities, research reports in such venerable sources as *The Journal of the American Medical Association (JAMA)* and *The New England Journal of Medicine*, and special features in more popular publications ranging from *The Wall Street Journal* to *Time* magazine to *The New York Times*. There is now compelling evidence that meditation is a powerful tool in managing anxiety and stress, pain relief, restful sleep, cognitive function, and physical and emotional well-being.

In the January 30, 2011, issue of *Psychiatry Research: Neuroimaging*, Massachusetts General and University of Massachusetts Medical School reported results of a clinical study that demonstrated that meditation *can* actually transform our brain. Using MRI brain scans at the beginning and end of the eight-week trial, scientists discovered that each of the 16 subjects who meditated for 30 minutes every day experienced visible changes to the physical structure of their brains. Within 56 days, each subject's MRI displayed an increase in the gray matter in the hippocampus (the part of our brain responsible for learning, spatial orientation, and memory) and a reduction in the gray matter of their amygdala (the fear, stress, and anxiety center of the brain). So if you were wondering whether the benefits of meditation will show up in your life, the answer is a powerful *yes*! In less than two months, the brain can change its physical structure and the way it's wired—all from a daily practice of 30 minutes.

A recent brain-wave study by Dr. Richard J. Davidson at the University of Wisconsin tested meditating monks (whom I like to refer to as *super meditators* since each had 34,500 hours of meditation under their belts) and non-meditating volunteers on their responses to pain and the threat of pain. Dr. Davidson monitored the brain's pain centers as he applied a heated applicator to the arms of the test subjects. As the heat was directly applied to the skin, all the test subjects responded similarly. The monitors showed their pain centers activated as the hot instrument touched their flesh. Then he changed the procedure a bit. All the test subjects were told, "In ten seconds I will apply the heated applicator." The non-meditators' pain centers reacted instantly upon hearing the words—before they were even touched! The pain centers of the *super meditators* did not respond until the heat was actually applied 10 seconds later. What's the takeaway here? The non-meditating world reacts first to the hint or projection of pain in the future and reacts as if it were feeling the pain now. The meditators stayed in the present moment longer and did not actually feel pain when the threat of pain was announced.

I find this study to be the most profound insight that we can remove and lessen suffering in our lives if we don't project ourselves into the future and manufacture potential suffering. Yet most of our life is played out in the future as our hopes, dreams, wishes, and needs, weave into expectations and we start reacting to scenarios yet unborn as if we were clairvoyant. Meditation will help you immeasurably in this process.

So the evidence is in. And, these two studies demonstrate the transformational power that meditation can have on our physical body and on our emotional response to the world around us.

Finally, after thousands of years of eye-rolling by naysayers, the value of meditation is validated scientifically in a laboratory with the most advanced technology to monitor the brain. And the results of studies like these in medical centers and institutions of higher learning continue to be published for the world to access.

Yet the most transformational results of meditation can only truly be felt by the one having the experience. That can happen with your very first meditation. And you're already there!

How Meditation Changes Our Physiology

During meditation, specific physiological shifts occur. These shifts are cumulative, and over time, they can transform the way our bodies and minds balance themselves and integrate with each other. The most powerful proof that meditation changes the bodymind lies at the very core of our DNA, in a primal survival response we all have shared for millennia: the fight-or-flight response.

THE FIGHT-OR-FLIGHT RESPONSE

As human beings evolved more than 20,000 years ago, we were hardwired with a self-preservation reflex—a powerful survival mechanism woven into our DNA—known as the fight-or-flight response. It was first described by American physiologist Walter Cannon in 1929 and explains what happens to our body's most primal brain functions when we sense a threat to our physical body—essentially how we react when something crosses our perceived boundary of safety. When we perceive a life-threatening situation, we react in the moment and choose one of two basic paths of survival: to fight or to run.

Essentially, it works like this: Imagine you're hunting and gathering in a jungle during prehistoric times, when you hear a saber-toothed tiger make a loud hiss. On perceiving this threat, your body's limbic system (which controls emotion, behavior, memory, and your sense of smell) immediately responds via your autonomic nervous system, a complex network of endocrine glands that automatically regulates your hormonal chemistry and metabolism. The autonomic nervous system also performs functions like the unconscious licking of your lips, the consistent blinking of your eyes, sneezing, and other functions you usually perform automatically to stay in balance, without conscious awareness.

THE BODY REACTS TO A THREAT

On hearing the saber-toothed tiger, your sympathetic nervous system (which is the part of the autonomic nervous system that regulates all our body's functions) rapidly prepares you to deal with what is perceived as a threat to your safety. It essentially says, "There's a good chance you will become this predator's dinner, but if you fight or run away, you could live." It then goes on a lightning quick mission to help you achieve that goal. First, you begin to perspire. Your limbic brain knows that if you do end up fighting or fleeing, you will most likely overheat, so the fastest way to bring your temperature down is by automatic sweating.

Next, your hormones initiate several metabolic processes that help you cope with sudden danger. Your adrenal glands release adrenaline (also known as epinephrine) and other hormones that speed up your breathing, spike your heart rate, and elevate your blood pressure, quickly driving more oxygen-rich blood to your brain and to the muscles needed for fighting the saber-toothed tiger or for running away.

All of this happens before you've had an intellectual conversation with yourself about the impending danger. In fact, the threat could be real or imagined, but if the limbic brain perceives it, you will automatically respond in seconds *as if the threat is real*.

These self-preservation processes are all triggered by the same part of your brain that regulates hunger, thirst, sexual arousal, fear, and sleep. Your energy soars as the stress hormones adrenaline and cortisol surge into your bloodstream. At the same time, your pancreas secretes a hormone called glucagon to immediately raise your blood sugar with the equivalent sugar kick of you eating several candy bars at once.

As these physiological changes take place, your senses become heightened, your heart starts racing, and all distractions, pain, thoughts, and internal conversations leave your awareness as your focus becomes concentrated on one single goal: survival.

Your bodymind starts sending very clear messages to different cell clusters and organs throughout your body: *We don't need to be thinking about growth*, and your growth hormone secretion shuts down; *we don't need to be thinking about sex*, and your sex hormone levels decrease; *we definitely don't need to be thinking about fighting germs right now*, and your immune system is suppressed. The blood flow to the largest organ in your body (your skin) is also reduced and the blood in your digestive system leaves and heads to your arms and legs so you can better fight or better run. With your mind and body in this temporary state of metabolic overdrive, you are now prepared to respond to a life-threatening situation. And this will most likely be the most stressful and intense fight of your life. Your bodymind knows this and is preparing you in milliseconds.

What happens next is truly amazing. The solid parts of your blood—your platelets—begin to plump up and get stickier. Your bodymind is preparing to fight whatever life-threatening entity is out there, so your blood begins preparing to clot in advance of your being cut!

Because of its enormous influence on emotions and memory, the limbic system is often referred to as the "emotional brain." It's also called the "old" or "early" mammalian brain, or paleo-mammalian brain because it emerged with the evolution of our warm-blooded relatives and marked the beginning of social coop-eration among all animals. But fast-forward 20,000 years to the present-day reality, and there aren't too many saber-toothed tigers out there. In fact, unless you're defending your country in a war zone or in a life-threatening line of work such as firefighting or law enforcement, the daily need for the rest of us activating our fight-or-flight mode is a rarity.

This is what happens to your body during the Fight-Flight response:

- An increase in blood pressure, and stress on your heart

- An increase in your stress hormones (adrenaline, cortisol)

- An increase in your blood sugar (glucagon tells the pancreas to slow insulin production)

- A decrease in blood circulation especially to your digestive tract

- A decrease in your growth and sex hormones

- Suppression of your immune system, and

- An increase in the thickness and stickiness of your blood.

We can look at these as the seeds of illness because they lead directly to the following diagnoses: *coronary heart disease, anxiety, addictions, diabetes, gastrointestinal disorders, infections, cancer, strokes,* and *heart attacks.* Modern science is slowly discovering that chronic stress impacts the brain as well. Clinical trials on mice have demonstrated that these stress hormones affect our dendrites—the signal receivers and senders on nerve cells—by shrinking them, which impedes the easy flow of the information they are transmitting. When this occurs in our hippocampus, it challenges our memory and learning ability.

Stress: How We Respond to Unmet Needs

The fight-or-flight response is referred to as a stress response. The term *stress* is short for *distress*, a word evolved from the Latin word *stringere*, meaning "to draw tight or pull apart." In English, it was first used centuries ago to describe hardship and affliction. In the 1930s, Hungarian endocrinologist Hans Selye popularized the theories of stress leading to disease and 45 years later authored the classic *Stress Without Distress* in which he first introduced the concept of eustress or good stress. Eustress is where you respond to a stressor such as a challenge with positive feelings because you feel it will bring you personal growth, deeper fulfillment, or lasting satisfaction. When you are competing at sports, exercising, riding a roller coaster, watching a scary movie, working on a project that has meaning to you, or are challenged out of your comfort zone, the stress that results is eustress. According to the newest scientific research on stress, when we interpret a given situation as:

- Finite—having a beginning and an end
- Challenging rather than threatening, and
- An opportunity to learn or grow.

Our body then perceives the experience as nourishing and this type of stress has been proven to build resilience, increase wound healing, and strengthen us emotionally. But when our interpretation is that of feeling threatened in any way, Selye's research shows the stress hormones secreted can have a degrading impact on the body.

In your most stressful moments, it can sometimes feel as if you are being pulled in a million directions emotionally, physically, mentally, spiritually, and in all the other aspects of your life. David Simon taught me a pithy definition of stress: *how we respond when our needs are not met.* For most people, this occurs between 8 and 15 times each day. For example, you order what you think is the simplest dish on the menu, and it takes the longest to come out. And when it does, it's cold or not what you thought you ordered. A conversation doesn't go the way you planned. The phone rings, and it's him; the phone rings, and it's not him. Someone cuts you off on the highway. You have a one o'clock lunch date, and you rush to get there on time only to have to wait 30 minutes for your friend to arrive. You stub your toe. Your computer freezes up. Your TV show doesn't record. You're hoping to hear news that never arrives. You hear something else that makes you change your plans. You expect something to happen, and it doesn't, or it does but doesn't play out exactly as you had scripted it. You mis-speak or do something that just doesn't feel "right."

Each day we experience small disappointments and larger expectations not being met.

Whenever your needs aren't met, you have the potential to respond in many ways. When you respond reflexively instead of reflectively—acting out a conditioned pattern or automatically fighting or fleeing instead of choosing a more intuitive or enlightened response—you lower yourself to your most primitive state such as the fight-or-flight response, which is hardwired into your DNA.

For thousands of years, great scientists and philosophers alike have agreed that it's not what happens to you but how you respond to life that determines your emotional and physical health. You can express your disappointment in many ways—from barking at someone to storming out of a discussion to rolling your eyes and taking a breath. But what happens to all these unmet needs, big and small? Each time your needs are not met and you react to this stress with disappointment, your heart beats faster, your breathing speeds up, your immune system shuts down, and your platelets get stickier. How long do you think this can go on before these primitive interpretations and reactions lead you to experience disease in your bodymind?

Over time, unrelenting chronic stress can lead to emotional, physical, or sexual dysfunction, increase your chances of getting sick, and may manifest as chronic illness such as irritable bowel syndrome, fibromyalgia, lupus, Crohn's disease, migraine headaches, and even skin disorders like psoriasis.

16 SECONDS TO CLARITY

Think of a current situation in which your needs are not getting met. Most likely this involves another person (or even yourself) who has disappointed you with a certain behavior or the lack of a behavior you desire.

Close your eyes, and see that person in your mind's eye. What feelings do you have for this individual? Why are you angry or disappointed? What did they do or not do? Maybe this person is you. Are you holding a grudge against yourself or someone else? Feel all the physical and emotional waves that flow through you when you put your attention on this person and this issue.

Since hopefully you're not facing a physical threat at this very moment, it would be impossible for your body-mind to invoke fight or flight in the physical sense. But you are capable of deploying an emotional fight-or-flight response called the *reactive* or *ego response*.

How we respond—essentially, what we do—with our feelings ultimately determines our emotional health. What are you doing with your feelings about the person you're thinking about? Repressing them and withdrawing? Holding on and strategically lashing out with resentment? Letting them drive your thoughts and build the drama? Consider the long-term consequences of not having your needs met and the toll it can take on you emotionally, psychologically, and physically.

So right now, you probably are experiencing some irritation, discomfort, or annoyance regarding this person or situation. Let me show you an amazingly powerful exercise that I have taught to members of the military, law enforcement, and people in high-pressure situations to move beyond stress. With the vision of that person or situation still in your mind's eye:

Right now take a long, slow deep breath in . . .

And watch the breath as it moves into your nostrils . . .

Witness it as it moves into your sinuses . . .

Observe it as it moves into the back of your throat . . .

Into your chest . . .

And down into your belly . . .

And hold it there.

> And watch it as it sits in your belly . . .
> And witness it . . .
> Observe it.

Now gently release that breath and feel it start to move up your chest and watch it as it moves into your throat . . .
Back into your sinuses . . .
And observe it as it releases out through your nostrils . . .

Now hold the breath out and watch it as it starts to dissipate . . .

Observe it . . .

And witness it as it dissolves into the ether . . .

Now breathe normally.

That was 16 seconds. Four seconds in; four seconds of holding the breath in; four seconds out; and four seconds of holding the breath out. Now do it with your eyes closed and watch your breath the whole way. I'll wait right here.

How do you feel? If you were playing along, for those 16 seconds you were not focused on the irritation or irritating person. Your attention was not in the past, nor was it in the future. Your awareness was in the present moment. And in the present moment there is no fear, no sadness, no anxiety, no worry—no anger or irritation. There is only the now. And you get to step into this moment with less emotional turbulence, less constriction, greater calm, and greater ease.

In 16 seconds, we stopped the flow of stress chemicals and hormones that was starting to trickle through you. We stopped emotional fight or flight in its tracks! The next time you are on a line, stuck in traffic, faced with a disappointment, or sensing the surge of chemicals and hormones starting to hijack your emotions, practice *16 seconds* and you will very quickly come back to your center. This simple present-moment-awareness tool has helped hundreds of thousands of people be the calm amidst the chaos, the stillness inside the storm, and the best version of themselves at a time when they'd otherwise say the words they'd regret, or do the thing they wished they hadn't.

Emotional Charge and the Ego Response

Since this form of the fight-or-flight response is more emotionally based, we respond with emotional charge rather than punching someone or running away; we bark back or shut down. It's still a very primitive response, and we use it when our ego, rather than our life, is threatened. When our actual flesh is threatened, fight or flight kicks in. When our sense of Self (our ego) is challenged, the ego response is the most common biological response. This is what you were starting to feel as you envisioned the irritation in your life, or "crossing the mine field." This is the realm of *I, me, mine*—our magnificent ego, our sense of Self, our sense of ownership of people, things, and experiences. When that ownership is questioned or one of our boundaries is challenged or attacked, we lash out to defend it or shut down in resignation.

The ego response has the whole spectrum of fight or flight woven into its emotional expressions. The fight version of the ego response may manifest as reactive, angry, argumentative behavior. The flight version of the ego response can take the expression of emotionally shutting down or withdrawal, such as refusing to converse with someone or giving only terse replies.

Think of a time you were having a heated discussion and found yourself reacting with anger, raising your voice, or even barking at another person. And at some point, most of us have reacted with the emotional version of the flight response as we walked away, shut down dialogue, or hung up on someone. It's the classic "talk to the hand" directive of walking away from a conversation. More extreme forms of flight are expressed through escapist behaviors, such as substance abuse, excessive television viewing, gambling, or Internet addiction.

Men and women tend to deal with stressful situations differently. While this is a broad generalization and exceptions naturally exist, men are more likely to respond to an emergency or perceived threat with a response such as aggression (fight), while women are more likely to respond with the response of fleeing (flight). But because everyone has both masculine and feminine aspects, in any given moment, a man may flee a situation or a woman might react with aggression. Recent studies have found that in addition to the fight-or-flight response, in a threatening situation, women are likely to use a third strategy, known as the *tend and befriend response*, finding ways to defuse the crisis by enlisting cooperation. In 12-step programs and recovery circles, the freeze response (a form of flight) has also emerged as a common withdrawal alternative to fight and flight.

The physiological and emotional responses to stress are well documented. And it's pretty obvious that if we respond with an ego response to every need that's not met, we will certainly die sooner or live a more painful life. Fortunately, meditation offers a tool that helps reverse the impact that fight-or-flight and ego responses have on our minds and bodies. Meditation can unravel the cellular damage that stress has caused and alter our DNA hard-wiring of the fight-or-flight response. Just a few years ago, a group of scientists—Elizabeth H. Blackburn, Carol W. Greider, and Jack W. Szostak—discovered that our chromosomes are protected by long, threadlike DNA molecules called *telomeres*, which carry our genes from one cell to the next. Their research also revealed the existence of an enzyme called *telomerase*, which lubricates and lengthens our telomeres. They won the Nobel Prize in Medicine for discovering that *the length of each telomere and the amount of telomerase covering each one determines the very health of our cells as they are created.* As lower levels of stress hormones are introduced into our system through a daily meditation practice, damaged telomeres mend, and our immune function rises. Emotionally, we start to respond more intuitively and less reactively, releasing us from the prison of conditioned ego responses. In time, we will be moved from an existence of conditioned, limiting beliefs to a more unconditioned life of infinite possibilities.

The Restful Awareness Response

When we meditate, our body's chemistry changes. In fact, we experience the opposite of the physiological effects produced by the fight-or-flight and ego responses. We are less inclined to perspire, our breathing and heart rate slow, our body's production of stress hormones decreases, our sex hormone production increases, our growth hormone levels are elevated, our immune system strengthens, and our platelets become less sticky as blood flows more easily throughout our entire body. As these physiological shifts to our physical body occur, our mind calms, anxiety lessens, stress seems to shed, and there is an emotional shift in how we respond to unmet needs. This state of restful awareness can last for a moment or through the entire meditation. But the beauty of this process is that restful awareness continues to benefit our bodies even after our meditation session. As we meditate on a regular basis, we slowly and gently shift our automatic response mechanism to a more unconditioned one.

In restful awareness, we move through situations with greater grace and ease. We're less impulsive and more intuitive. We're making more conscious choices, because we intuitively know the highest choice in that moment—the one that honors our Self and the person we are interacting with. The one that elevates both of us to the highest plane of existence, the one that comes from a heart filled with compassion, forgiveness, and a desire for peace.

The more time we spend in the state of restful awareness, the more we are open to multiple interpretations of a situation or scenario throughout the rest of our day. We become less attached to our previous interpretations, and our need to defend them feels less urgent. We see the bigger picture rather than the more narrow view we once had. Over the first few weeks of daily meditation, this expanded awareness weaves itself intermittently through all our interactions. As we continue to regularly meditate and spend time in stillness and silence, each day becomes more comfortable, *restful awareness becomes more and more our natural state*, and greater clarity begins to unfold. It becomes less important to defend our point of view because we see greater possibilities. Then creative solutions start to emerge to once-daunting challenges, and constrictions magically open up.

We become more alert, more creative, more intuitive, and more relaxed. We start having anxiety-free days, and stress becomes more manageable. And our first response to unmet needs is no longer the ego response. Our more common response to an unmet need starts to be one of restful awareness—of silent witnessing before we act out old, conditioned response patterns yet again. This "new" state could also be called *restful alertness* because our senses are heightened and we begin to experience a new lightness of being. Little things don't irritate us or knock us off course as easily. Experiencing greater peace of mind throughout the day is also very common, as is more restful sleep, better digestion, and an entire new level of vitality. We are slowly returning to equilibrium—to wholeness!

Many of my students tell me 30 minutes of meditation is more restorative to them than 30 minutes of sleep and several studies now seem to confirm that. If you have an irregular or abnormal sleep pattern, it can normalize in just a few days after you have gotten comfortable with your new meditation routine. Of course, if the thing that keeps you awake is a deeper emotional constriction or pain, meditation will help to relieve the acuteness of the pain. However, only a commitment to deeper self-discovery, emotional release, and emotional healing work will relieve the emotional pain at the core of your insomnia.

Releasing Stored Emotional Pain

To uncover, mobilize, and release this dormant, emotionally toxic plaque, I recommend a doctor-designed emotional healing process. Two programs with which I am intimately familiar are the Hoffman Institute's *Quadrinity Process* (which I attended in 2006), developed by Dr. Robert Hoffman, and the *Awaken Your Inner Healer* program, which I developed as a fusion of my training at the Hoffman Institute and Dr. David Simon mentoring me to be a facilitator in emotional healing processes. The Hoffman Quadrinity Process is designed to help people identify their emotional pain, mobilize it, release it, and then heal their wounds. Essentially, deconstruct your emotional Self and then reconstruct it with less baggage, less conditioning, and less anger. The Hoffman Quadrinity program was particularly helpful to me in seeing my story as an excuse for not making conscious choices in the present. Once you can step out of victim mode and take ownership of your life, you can write the next chapter in which you've chosen lightness over baggage, forgiveness over resentment, compassion over blame, and more conscious choices over conditioned ones. My *Inner Healer* program guides you on a journey into the depths of your soul to awaken your magnificence beneath all your baggage, loosen your grip on it, and free your soul. *But, if you are in deep emotional pain right now, don't let it fester. Reach out to a psychologist or psychiatrist in your local area and get help.* No one needs to live in acute emotional pain, and working with a therapist, support group, or an emotional healing program can help you lighten your load. It's impossible to do this deep work and not feel a bit lighter, and that lightness only increases with a daily meditation practice.

I have found these emotional healing processes to be powerful pathways to forgiveness, compassion, growth, and self-love. They allow you to experience a better version of yourself. In essence, lightening my load has unlocked a spiritual doorway that expanded my understanding of meditation as a process of surrender. And that powerful energy of stillness then translates into my daily life. I no longer find it necessary to try to be in control of every moment. *Sometimes it's okay to set your course, engage your intention, lean in the direction of your desires, take your hands off the wheel, slide over into the passenger seat, and let the universe do the driving.*

Spiritual Benefits of Meditation

The spiritual aspect of meditation has long been misunderstood. And, this is one of the main reasons why mainstream culture has not been more open to embrace the practice. Even the definition of spirituality differs from person to person. Each of us is seeking a reconnection to the whole, to our Source, to God, to our most divine version. We each choose the most resonating path to understand and express the bigger, more profound, universal concepts of life, death, pain, love, truth, bliss, and purpose. Some people don't care about these things, because their awareness has not drifted into these concepts at this point in their lives. Ultimately, each of us will walk through these experiences and face these questions. So even if someone is not currently engaged in this conversation, simply having an awareness of these natural life principles invokes an understanding that there is something bigger, more expansive, more knowing, and more intelligent than we are. We could call that entity a universal being. Never born and never died. Existing in every moment and connected to all things simultaneously.

In Vedanta, the ancient Indian philosophy of self-realization, there is a school of thought known as *Advaita* (pronounced *add-veye-ta*), a Sanskrit term for "non-duality." According to Advaita, one-ness is the only reality. Everything else is an illusion, known in Sanskrit as *maya*. The philosophy states that our ignorance of our one-ness is the cause for all suffering in the world. Only through the direct knowledge of this one-ness (actually experiencing it) can true liberation occur. In Sanskrit, this liberation is called *moksha* (*moke-sha*). Understanding that all existence is non-dual—not two things but *one* pure whole—is the path to moksha. Meditation gently guides you to that space.

Most of us grew up in homes where we were introduced to an all-knowing, all-seeing, infinite being known as God. How else can finite flesh beings such as us, with limited tools and a limited understanding, ingest such a beyond-this-realm concept as one-ness? There needs to be an almighty essence that embodies all the characteristics of one-ness so we can better understand them—a sort of guide between us and one-ness. Most of us have a similar understanding regarding our own personal God's nature. Essentially, this being created everything; is infinite, immortal, omnipresent, spans the existence of time and, therefore, is timeless; controls or influences everything; is everywhere at once or has demigods or avatars who can be anywhere; is capable of resurrection and rebirth; can be worshipped and appealed to; and has the ability to craft what we would consider miracles.

Even if you weren't brought up in a formal religious or spiritual tradition (if you are an atheist you can still meditate and receive all the benefits) it is still likely that you believe there is some form of intelligence beyond ours. So whether your orientation is toward the Divine, a god, multiple gods, or a higher power, we define our personal understanding of this universal nature as *spirituality*. *Essentially, spirituality is the journey we take in each moment from our most individual Self to our most universal Self and then back again, integrating a bit of that divine magnificence back into our flesh-encased human form. From constriction to expansion!*

When our mind analyzes this being or power, we see this omniscient, omnipotent, infinite God or spirit at once in everything and yet separate from us and the world. Vedanta would say this separation exists only on the surface, only in our mind. *Deeper below the surface, our mind, body, and spirit are all the same things— pure, unbounded consciousness—one-ness wearing different disguises.* According to Vedanta, liberation lies in knowing the reality of this one-ness and experiencing spirit through varying aspects of study (*gyan*), devotion (*bhakti*), selfless service (*karma*), and practice (*raj* or the royal path).

Two of the practices of the royal path that most directly connect us to spirit are meditation (restful awareness) and yoga (body-centered restful awareness). The path to this understanding of spirit is a deeper understanding of who we are, what we really want in life, and why we are here. This has been referred to as the expansion of consciousness—moving from a constricted, conditioned space where we define ourselves as the roles we play in life and the things we own (essentially, our positions and our possessions) to the more expansive perspective of who we are, how we are connected to everything, and what we came here to do. Essentially, *you are not in the universe, the universe is in you*!

CHAPTER 4

HIGHER STATES OF CONSCIOUSNESS

"Who you are cannot be defined through thinking or mental labels or definitions, because it's beyond that. It is the very sense of being, or presence, that is there when you become conscious of the present moment. In essence, you and what we call the present moment are, at the deepest level, one."

— ECKHART TOLLE

As more academic institutions and medical centers perform research on the impact of meditation on the brain, the body, and our emotional responses to the world around us, additional physical and mental benefits are being acknowledged by the scientific and medical communities. Almost every week, a new study peels away a layer of the unknown regarding the interplay between our mind and the concepts of self-awareness, decision-making, and our emotional triggers. A topic, however, that still remains in the fuzzy area is the concept of *consciousness*, a word whose definition has evolved over thousands of years depending on the interpreter.

We speak of consciousness generically as *awareness* and sometimes as the truest understanding of our *reality*. And, we know that subtle shifts in our consciousness alter the very interpretation of our reality. We all see the world through very personal filters that put a spin on everything we hear, see, say, and think. As we digest each moment through a dynamic interplay of everything we've ever experienced and everything we currently experience, we translate the world in our own individual way projecting that onto everything and everyone around us. For example, we can wake up in a positive mood, filled with vitality and gratitude, and our world feels shiny, supportive, and nourishing. Suddenly, we receive unsettling news, and we can shift into anxiety, frustration, and sadness. And then everything starts coming through the lens of those emotions, moods, physical feelings, and perspectives. These are the nuances of consciousness as we "yum" or "yuck" every moment and every experience.

Yet there are three common states of consciousness or awareness that every being on the planet experiences every day:

1. **being awake**—we are aware of ourself; we think of our self-identity in terms of "I"; and we are very aware of our thoughts.

2. **being in deep sleep**—we are in a state of restful *dullness*; our mind is not aware of our physical world or our thoughts, yet our brain is actively restoring our mindbody system, healing tissues, secreting hormones, nourishing the physiology, and actively consolidating memories.

3. **dreaming**—our mind is active and filled with thoughts; we are unaware of the current reality outside of the dream state; we think of our self-identity in terms of "I."

Every day of our life is spent moving between these three states of consciousness. But, if you meditate, there are actually more states available to you.

The Fourth State of Consciousness: Glimpsing the Soul

According to the ancient teachings of Vedanta, there is a "higher" state of consciousness beyond the first three—a state where our mind has fully quieted down into silence and our senses have become still. This is a state of BEing beyond this physical world of form and phenomenon—state of restful awareness. We can access this state of consciousness through meditation—or as the ancient sage Patanjali defined it: *the progressive quieting of the fluctuations of our mind*. And the more you meditate, the more this state of consciousness becomes available to you. For new meditators, this is where you experience your soul for the very first time. Where we sense something deeper and more profound. And for those with an established practice, this is the doorway to our deepening connection to Source, to the Divine, to Spirit. In Sanskrit, one of the names for this state of consciousness is *atma darshan*, translated literally as *viewing the soul*. As we meditate, we drift back and forth between our waking state filled with thoughts, sounds and physical sensations to this blissful state of restful awareness— occasionally glimpsing our soul . . . and then back again . . . gently ebbing and flowing like the tides.

Another Sanskrit name for this fourth state is *turiya* (which literally means *the fourth* and is pronounced *toor-ya*). And in this state of restful awareness, we are awake but at rest. This is distinctly different than simply being awake because in our typical awake mode, we are in activity. Our senses are activated, our mind is running on autopilot, we are actively thinking, listening, typing, driving, eating, loving, speaking, and, most importantly, we are DOing. When we are in this fourth state of consciousness, our mind is awake . . . even alert, but we are in a quiet, restful state able to just BE rather than DO.

In our modern culture, it was the Maharishi Mahesh Yogi who first named the fourth state *Transcendent Consciousness* and then shared a fifth, sixth, and seventh state of consciousness with the world. According to his teachings, once you have glimpsed your soul, as you continue to cultivate your meditation practice and find comfort in this state of restful awareness, you are able to experience even higher states of consciousness. And as these higher states of consciousness awaken inside of us, the world outside of us opens to a transformational evolution. Maharishi referred to these higher states as:

5. **cosmic consciousness,**

6. **god consciousness**, and

7. **unity consciousness.**

THE SEVEN STATES OF CONSCIOUSNESS

1. Waking

2. Deep sleep

3. Dreaming

4. Glimpsing the Soul, Transcendent Consciousness, or Turiya

5. Cosmic Consciousness or Witnessing Awareness

6. Divine, God, or Love Consciousness

7. Unity or One-ness Consciousness

After you have spent six months meditating every day (for 30 minutes, twice a day), you will have spent more than 180 hours in stillness and silence. That's 648,000 seconds of simply BEing without DOing! Over the course of those six months, you will have fallen asleep in meditation, had over half a million thoughts during your practice, drifted in and out of consciousness, shrunk your amygdala, increased the size of your hippocampus, and transcended reality as you once knew it. You will have totally established a solid foundation to move fluidly through higher states.

But way before that, (in a matter of days) your own consciousness as you now know it will begin to dramatically shift. Your internal reference point for all experiences will shift from body, mind, and ego, to the observer of body, mind, and ego. And this will open you to **the fifth state of consciousness**, known as *Cosmic Consciousness or Witnessing Awareness.*

Consciousness in Motion

In this fifth state of consciousness, you move through life as the silent witness. Over time, you stabilize this state of consciousness and you see your soul in every moment! This is the state where you realize, "I am not my thoughts"; "I am not my body." You truly grasp the concept that you are not in the universe; but, rather, the universe rests inside you! You experience the physical world at the exact same moment you experience the non-local domain, the realm of the unmanifest. You see finite and infinite simultaneously. You witness your physical Self from the standpoint of your deeper all-knowing Self. You show up fully present in all your encounters *outside* of meditation. You start seeing multiple aspects and perspectives simultaneously in challenging situations because you are a dispassionate on-looker. Your intuition becomes more crystalized. You start to notice that you allow situations to unfold rather than trying to force them, you let others finish their sentences, and you see the bigger picture in every moment.

This higher state of consciousness begins to manifest in your relationships as you are more accepting, truly listening, and more able to receive. You even begin to see yourself in deep sleep and your dreams become more lucid. And it is in this state of consciousness that your fear of death melts away because you truly understand the concept of timelessness. That you are not this physical being separate from the world but rather that the world is within you. The hallmark of *Cosmic Consciousness* is the cultivation of your ability to stay in the state of atma darshan *outside* of meditation when you are in activity, *glimpsing the soul* in every moment.

God in Every Moment

Over time, as you refine your witnessing awareness in the fifth state, an even more subtle expression of consciousness unfolds, known as *Divine or God Consciousness*. This **sixth state of consciousness** expands its witnessing beyond the Self and reveals aspects of reality that you never thought were possible. The manifest and the unmanifest domains of reality begin to blur into one another—with love being the thread that connects them. Your personal awareness actually transcends the surface of objects and situations outside of yourself as you see the true depth of existence . . . the Truth in all things—an essence of the divine creator in every person, every flower, and every gust of wind. You begin to hear beyond what your ears are capable of, see beyond what your eyes tell you, and feel without actually touching the object you are sensing. This was the state of consciousness that the English poet William Blake must have been describing when he wrote:

> *"To see a World in a Grain of Sand*
> *And a Heaven in a Wild Flower,*
> *Hold Infinity in the palm of your hand*
> *And Eternity in an hour."*

In this sixth state of consciousness, empathy takes on a new definition, as the boundaries between your own body and mind become porous extending into your environment and even into others. Compassion flows openly into you, and through you into every crevice outside of you. A clairvoyant sense of expansiveness unfolds through each moment. You begin to experience the world through your heart and gratitude ripples through every thought, word, and action. This sixth state of consciousness has also been referred to as *Love Consciousness* because, in this state, you effortlessly fall in love with everything and everyone. You are humbled and awed by the beauty and magnificence of every atom in the universe. Some modern Pentecostal Christian philosophies refer to this state of conscious as having the *Holy Ghost Power* where Jesus has been activated within you, coursing through every fiber of your being. But Divine Consciousness has nothing to do with religion. It's simply a state of consciousness in which you see the fingerprints of the Divine (your higher power, or a divine creator, or your understanding of a compassionate God) in every aspect of your world.

As I journeyed through India, *Divine Consciousness* kept unfolding with every new encounter I had. My heart was so full that I saw kindness in the hearts of beggars, grace in the eyes of thieves, and tender devotion in the austere grimaces of holy men. At a certain point, two chefs I befriended in Sri Lanka told me, "Mr. David, you fall in love too easily." I smiled, hugged them, and said, "Thank you. That's very sweet of you to say." At another point in my life, I might have been defensive or embarrassed or tried to play it down; but, in that moment, my vulnerability felt like an open invitation to the Divine. My soul felt naked to the world and I felt happy about that.

In 1974, when Mother Teresa said, "I see God in every human being. When I wash the leper's wounds I feel I am nursing the Lord himself. Is it not a beautiful experience?" she was clearly living in a state of Divine Consciousness on the path to Sainthood.

And when you live your life in a constant state of Divine Consciousness, that becomes the platform for the seventh state of consciousness, known as *Unity or One-ness Consciousness*, where the individualized Self that witnessed everything in *Cosmic Consciousness* is no longer separate from anything. There is no separation between you and the world outside of you, no distinction between you and God because he, she, it has merged into you, no thin line between you and divine spirit. You are now one with the Universe. As the ancient Vedic texts teach us, *Ayam atma brahman*—my soul (atma) and the Universal spirit (brahman) are the same (ayam). In *One-ness Consciousness*, there is no separation between anything.

The Snowflakes of Our Life

In science and mathematics, there is a concept known as *Fractal Theory*. Fractals are the seeds of everything in existence and fractals holds the key to how a pattern will continue to unfold. Fractals exist everywhere around us, especially in nature. There's actually a mini-ocean inside each drop of water in the ocean. And yet the drop is its own individual expression at the exact same time that it is the one-ness of the ocean! To better understand the concept of fractals, think of a snowflake. Contained in every cell of the snowflake is the same exact geometric pattern that we see when a snowflake lands on our palm. And, although every snowflake is unique, the tiny crystal structure that rests at its very center is repeated again and again and again in every miniscule cluster of frozen water throughout the entire flake as it grows.

Ocean waves, a nautilus shell, crystals, the rings of Saturn, a fern, a heartbeat, a head of broccoli—even a tree—all spring from the very first seed that began the pattern. And there is truly no cellular distinction or separation from the very first fractal of that entity and the much larger expression of that fractal. This is *One-ness Consciousness*. When you realize simultaneously that *you are* the drop of water in the ocean AND *you are* the ocean! In this state of consciousness is there is no personal Self. There is only the ONE, the Universal Self, which knows only one-ness.

The concept of "I" can't exist when you experience existence as one-ness because there is no Self and nothing outside of Self to compare itself to. When we are truly one with the Universe, we don't have a sense of individual existence so we can't even say to ourselves, *"I've* merged with the Universe" because there is no "I." The term "I" is a conversation our ego has with itself and there is no ego in one-ness because there is no Self! In a true state of Unity or One-ness Consciousness, there is no *A-ha!* moment because *you are the A-ha! moment.* So experiencing this state of consciousness is not the finish line of spirituality. It's simply the beginning or *the fractal of deeper understanding.*

This explanation of higher states of consciousness is not a roadmap to enlightenment but, simply an understanding of what can occur in the process of self-realization. Once we begin our journey of meditation, we see that all these states of consciousness are available to us, and we will experience flickers of each state depending on our background, our life tendencies, our perspective in a given moment, and our ability to surrender to the present. We will just BE. There is no true spiritual hierarchy. *Our aim is not to try to achieve* a specific state of consciousness. We can't will our way into expansion; it only unfolds as we surrender more and continue to evolve as tender, open, trusting and expansive Beings.

Discovering Our True Self

Most people embarking on a new meditation practice are often seeking more from life or from themselves. As they begin to explore their thoughts, dreams, and daily choices, an awareness settles in that they are not their thoughts or their body, but that they are more than that—they are pure, unbounded consciousness sealed in a flesh casing for the span of a lifetime. That perspective changes everything because it means that in any moment anything is possible. Previous patterns, ruts, conditioned responses, thoughts, and behaviors start disintegrating, becoming less conditioned as they are bathed in droplets of our unconditioned Self.

The purest, most defenseless and unconditioned aspects of ourselves begin to take hold in our daily routine, and then they weave themselves into our physiology. With each meditation, you move deeper into the most universal, infinite expressions of your being which rest at your very core: your unbounded, uncondi-tioned Self.

As you continue to meditate, your very foundation expands. If your starting point for all things is at a higher level, everything that flows from that point on vibrates at a higher frequency. You see the world differently. You recognize that everything is Spirit and we are all connected. *Each of us is simply a wave in a vast ocean that contains billions of waves. As waves in this sea of one-ness, we occasionally pop up to individuate ourselves. But just like any wave on the ocean, after we have crested, we collapse back into the one-ness of the unified surf.*

I believe that one of the biggest reasons meditation is not more prevalent is because it's impossible to convey the transformational nature of the practice. People try it and if they don't have an *A-ha!* moment or achieve enlightenment in a week or a month, they abandon the practice. You are obviously on the path to enlightenment. From this moment forward, you don't need to worry about what higher state of consciousness you are in. Osho, the great philosopher and guru, is known to have said, "Enlightenment is finding that there is nothing to find. Enlightenment is to come to know that there is nowhere to go." You don't need to be a guru, yogi, or believer in any one philosophy or religion to incorporate this capability into your life. You just need the willingness to try it. So what's the best path? In the next few chapters, we explore a variety of meditation practices from traditions throughout time and cultures throughout the world. As you practice each one, see what resonates most, practice it, and live the benefits!

PART II

MANY PATHS TO ONE-NESS

There are literally thousands of schools and philosophies of meditation, each with a unique technique or way of helping to experience present-moment awareness. I celebrate them all, and this book honors every tool, technology, and body of knowledge that can help you quiet the fluctuations of the mind and achieve deeper meaning, purpose, peace, and fulfillment in your life. I personally have explored many different schools of meditation, and I've practiced several for as little as two months and some as long as 15 years. Since 2002, I have meditated usually two times a day for 30 minutes, and often more if I am teaching a class or leading a retreat. Meditating with a group is a unique experience because you receive all the individual benefits of meditation as you additionally experience the energy of the collective. And you can pretty much meditate for hours because you have the support of the group doing it as well. That's why meditation workshops and retreats powerfully amplify our personal *and* universal connection.

The concept of "rounding" is practiced in many meditation retreats. You meditate in rounds of 20 or 30 minutes and then stop and bring your attention back into your body through yoga, breath-work, or dance. Then, at the peak of your activity, you stop, settle in, and go back for another session of meditation. At some of my retreats and teacher trainings, the rounding can go on for hours each day. And very quickly, this realm of stillness and silence permeates everything you do, from washing your face to practicing yoga to chewing your food to interacting with other beings. Just imagine what it's like when all the activity you thought was so critical to your existence is replaced by stillness and quietude.

After several days of this level of practice, the layers of your conditioned Self begin to peel away. By spending hours in the stillness and silence of your own purest essence, you come closer than you ever have to experiencing your own soul. And then you realize that everyone around you is going through the same thing. This experience is described in spiritual circles as being "naked"— when all the layers of your conditioned life have been peeled away and nothing but your soul remains.

The combination of different types of meditation, group meals, energy work, chanting, dancing, lectures on the soul, teachings from the Vedas, and group interaction interweaves the physical, emotional, and spiritual components of meditation into a very personal journey, traveling from your most ego-based, individual Self to the most divine and cosmic aspects of your universal Self. Some people want to be in a giant hall surrounded by 500 other meditators because it allows them to be anonymous. Having attended hundreds of these experiences, I often prefer smaller more intimate groups under 30 people. To me, they feel safer, more personal, more comfortable, and more heart-based. But it's totally a matter of personal preference in a given moment. When the time is right (and you will know when that is), treat yourself to an intimate meditation retreat that speaks to you. In just a few days, you will experience a powerful transformation rippling through every cell in your body. And if you are already a meditator, and want to deepen you practice or learn how to share the teachings with others, I encourage you to consider my *Masters of Wisdom and Meditation Teacher Training*, where you then become part of a community of meditation teachers around the planet from all walks of life.

You may never attend a meditation retreat, but you have the ability to receive the same transformational benefits at home by truly living this experience with a commitment to daily meditation practice. The key is to *do* it rather than try to figure it out intellectually. The Third Zen Patriarch, Jianzhi Sengcan, also known as Seng-t'san, confirmed this in his Zen poem *Xinxin Ming* (Hsin Hsin Ming), "The more you talk and think about it, the further astray you wander from the truth. Stop talking and thinking, and there is nothing you will not be able to know. To return to the root is to find the meaning, but to pursue appearances is to miss their source. At the moment of inner enlightenment there is a going beyond appearance and emptiness."

These words may sound New Age-y, but he wrote them 1,500 years ago. And if you think about it, very few moments in our lives go by in total stillness and silence. In virtually every moment of your life, whether you are sleeping, dreaming, or awake, you are in activity. Even when you have the chance to be in stillness and silence, most likely you choose activity.

How long are you comfortable doing nothing before you reach for your device, check in on social media, turn on music, check your e-mails, or reach for some distraction? These are all expressions of activity, and most of us stay in activity all day long until our bodymind collapses at night in sleep in order to rejuvenate.

When you are in a deep state of rest, when you are sleeping or dreaming, these are known as dull states, or states of restful dullness. There is still activity in every moment of dreaming sleep, such as rapid eye movements and physical experiences emanating from the depths of your dreams. And in deep sleep, when there is stillness, it is not the alert stillness you experience when you are in meditation; it is dull stillness.

Of all the practices and behaviors I have explored, meditation is the easiest and most effective for engaging in present-moment witnessing awareness in a state of stillness and silence—pure restful awareness in an alert state—and ultimately, unity of your physical Self, your emotional and egoistic Self, and your spiritual Self.

There is only one stillness and silence that rests within you, there is only one universal force that flows through everything, and there is only one present moment. Yet there are so many ways to access it and become aware of it—following your breathing, using a mantra, contemplative prayer, physical forms of meditation that use the senses, and communing with nature. There are walking, dancing, lovemaking, and even smoking meditations popularized by Osho.

The chapters in *Part II: Many Paths to One-ness* walk you through the most common techniques and accessible practices so that you can get a sense of what each feels like and gravitate toward the one that most resonates with you. I have explored all the following meditations, ultimately finding most comfort in *Nakshatra (BirthStar) Mantra Meditation* as the easiest method to ritualize on a daily basis and, therefore, the most powerful practice for me. However, it took me many years of serial meditating—dabbling, immersing, stopping, starting again, being distracted, immersing again, stopping, using meditation to cope with crisis, starting again, and stopping a third time—before I finally gathered all this experience to master *BirthStar Meditation* and make it part of my daily routine. I'm hoping to help you arrive at your own practice less circuitously.

When most people think of meditation, they think of someone chanting *"Om"* either out loud or repeating it silently. This practice is known as mantra meditation, and I'll go more deeply into it a bit further on up the road. But first, join me as I share with you the many forms that I have been fortunate to experience over my meditating lifetime. Some may resonate with you more than others; some may be more practical for you to practice than others. Yet recognizing the various ways to quiet the mind's fluctuations to achieve stillness and silence in your life can be an amazing gift that connects you more deeply to this precious existence of ours on planet Earth.

CHAPTER 5

SECRETS OF BODYMIND MEDITATION

"A moment. The moment of orgasm.
The moment by the ocean when there is
just the wave. The moment of being in love.
The moment of crisis when we forget ourselves
and do just what is needed."

— RAM DASS

Let's begin with one of the easiest and most scientifically sound meditation techniques and the one that first made me aware that meditation can be a valuable life tool: *biofeedback*. Biofeedback is the process of becoming aware of various physiological functions by monitoring them so that you can influence, alter, and/or control them. Over time, you can train your sympathetic nervous system to be less reactive to stressors and to recover more quickly. Through the practice of biofeedback, you can influence your pulse rate, breath, muscles, brain waves, perception of pain, and other bodily functions.

Typically, in biofeedback, you observe your progress on a computer monitor, and as you get closer to your targeted pulse variance, breathing flow, and brain-wave frequency, you see the changes on the screen. Biofeedback is used to manage stress, lessen anxiety, regulate blood pressure, improve physical performance, ease headaches, and heighten mental acuity.

Early in my meditation journey, I enrolled in a research study to explore the mind-body connection. It focused on measuring and monitoring my biosignals as I performed various actions to lower them. Biosignals are the electric currents produced across a group of cells, a specific tissue, or an organ such as the brain, heart, or skin. Energy runs through us and so do measurable amounts of electricity and magnetic pull. Modern science has even observed and measured the electrical currents and biosignals that plants generate. The goal of biofeedback is to monitor your biosignals so closely that you can adjust and alter them as they are occurring.

You can do it right now. Instead of breathing regularly, inhale very slowly through your nose to the count of four.

One. Two. Three. Four.

Hold this in to the count of four.

And now exhale through your nostrils to the count of four.

Now hold that out to the count of four.

Continue this process eight more times. This should take you about a minute and a half. I'll wait.

Most likely you've slowed your breathing to less than 10 breaths per minute, slowed your pulse by 20 percent, lessened your anxiety in this moment, and reduced the moisture that your skin exudes when you are overexcited or stressed. You are calmer now than you were only two minutes ago. If we chose to, any of us could formally monitor these biosignals to track our progress. The traditional biosignals monitored in biofeedback are the EKG (electrocardiogram), EEG (electroencephalogram), HRV (heart-rate variability), and GSR (galvanic skin response). The HRV measures the time or interval between each beat of your heart. Strangely enough, consistency between beats of your heart is not the goal; rather, having some form of variation in the beat-to-beat interval is the sign of a healthy heart. Infinite possibilities exist even in your heartbeat!

The GSR detects increased levels of perspiration generated by our autonomic nervous system and is used in traditional lie detection processes when one is hooked up to a polygraph. In addition to becoming more conductive during the telling of a lie, our skin also perspires when we experience anger, fear, pain, surprise, sexual feelings, and emotional arousal. The use of lie detector tests in court cases remains questionable, but the truth about lie detectors is that they do reveal certain involuntary responses to stressful situations, such as increased skin conductivity and breathing rhythms. But they don't always mean that someone is lying.

The Body Never Lies

In every moment, our biosignals reveal our true emotional state, yet very few people around us can see them. Our mind sends signals to our body, which then reacts spontaneously, creating the perfect feedback loop. We wear our emotions on our bodies and ultimately in our bodies. David Simon often said "90 percent of our physical toxicity is emotionally derived." There are even those who specialize in the study of human emotions by interpreting facial expressions. One of those is Dr. Paul Ekman, a psychologist who can determine with near certainty whether a person is lying based on small visual clues known as micro expressions. Ekman established that the face has 43 distinct and involuntarily muscle movements that create thousands of expressions, including the seven basic human emotions of anger, contempt, disgust, fear, happiness, sadness, and surprise. It was Ekman's work that was the inspiration for the TV show *Lie to Me*, starring Tim Roth as the micro-expression expert Dr. Cal Lightman. This level of research and understanding was in its infancy when I entered the biofeedback study many years ago. It was a six-month study that had fairly rigorous controls, especially for a second-year college student—no alcohol, no drugs of any kind, and no mind-altering substances for half a year! Weekly blood and urine tests kept the participants true to the process. Every other day for six months, I visited the clinic for 90 minutes, first slowing down for a half hour to establish a baseline and then plugging into an EKG through a skin-conductivity cuff with 10 rubber finger thimbles that connected my internal electrical circuit board to the computer's motherboard for an hour.

In front of three lab techs in white coats with clipboards, I performed exercise after exercise, using my mind, my breath, and my heart. I stared into a dashboard that integrated several moni-tors and dials, including one that showed me my blood pressure. I learned to lower the numbers on command, starting with a basic BP reading of 160/120. Within a few months, I dropped it down to 100/60, which is about where my blood pressure reading has stayed since then.

As the months passed and we approached the end of the study, I had to proactively increase my resting pulse after it plummeted below 50 beats a minute for a few weeks. I found myself becoming light-headed in elevators and airplanes. To regain my equilibrium, I began to secretly reverse my intentions during each day's testing, and all my numbers began to rise, making me look like an unsuccessful test subject. I ultimately revealed to the clinicians that biofeedback worked so effectively that I had to elevate my blood pressure to keep from passing out.

They kicked me out of the study!

Exploring the HeartMath Technique

In recent years, I have experimented in biofeedback using a program developed by the Institute of HeartMath, in which you attach sensors to your fingers and breathe in various depths and frequencies to create what's known as coherence—a highly efficient physiological state in which your nervous, cardiovascular, hormonal, and immune systems are fully aligned and working together in a balanced and harmonious state. The state of coherence is very similar to what athletes refer to as being in "the zone." Everything is in total alignment, with effortless ease.

In the HeartMath program I used, the process started with a black-and-white picture on the screen that slowly transformed into color as I achieved deeper and deeper states of relaxation. As I went deeper into a state of coherence, more vivid and colorful aspects of nature emerged from the background—a waterfall, a rainbow, bunnies, and deer prancing through lush, green forests. The more I got into the zone, the more the colors flowed. This positive reinforcement subliminally helps lower activity levels while in a state of rest. But in order to get feedback, you have to be paying attention in some way—and that's not my ideal method of connecting to stillness and silence.

Biofeedback's Continuing Evolution

Over the last few years, as technology has advanced, biofeedback monitors and feedback mechanisms have become affordable and almost gamelike in their look and feel. They have entered the mainstream meditation world marketed primarily as stress management tools. Biofeedback has evolved to include more brainwave monitoring using sensors that now rest gently on your head or behind the ears. The newest software now allows you to see real-time results and, through training and practice, change your brainwave patterns through a similar process known as neurofeedback.

One of the more popular biofeedback products that I have played with is MUSE, the brain-sensing headband which costs a few hundred dollars. The plastic headband rests its sensors against your forehead and is held in place by wrapping behind your ears. Then using the Muse app on your phone or tablet, you close your eyes, plug in your earbuds, and listen. Muse gives you feedback about your meditation in real time by translating your brain signals into the sounds of wind. When your mind is calm and settled, you hear calm and settled winds. When your mind is active the winds will pick up and blow. So you can throttle yourself back and forth to achieve your desired results.

After each session, Muse will show you how your brain did from moment to moment through a series of graphs and charts. You can save your results, monitor your progress over time, earn points to unlock new features, and receive guidance on how to improve future scores.

Although I have occasionally enjoyed the practice of biofeedback and its visible physiological results, I find it to be a highly physical form of meditation. I am always aware that I am in feedback mode and meditating for some result. As a goal-oriented individual using a goal-oriented product, I consistently found myself focused on seeing how much I was moving the dials or how much time I spent in relaxation mode. Although biofeedback slowed my breathing and my heart rate, and I ultimately dropped my resting pulse rate down to 45 beats per minute, I never truly felt stillness or silence. When using biofeedback mechanisms, you experience relaxation, but don't feel fully connected to any state of one-ness. I often felt like I was part of a lab experiment where I already knew the outcome. I will always probably test the newest tool out there, but I am more a believer in the "no equipment necessary" philosophy.

CHAPTER 6

SECRETS OF VISUAL MEDITATION

"Sometimes I think all my pictures are just pictures of me. My concern is . . . the human predicament; only what I consider the human predicament may simply be my own."

— RICHARD AVEDON

In my early twenties, I met a woman who was really into candles—an innocent pioneer in the realm of natural candlemaking, which is now a global, multibillion-dollar business. She had developed a recipe with a soy base that contained essential aromatic oils, and as the wicks burned, they unleashed a magnificent primal aroma that awakened and healed. At times, she ringed her entire house in row upon row of these intoxicating candles, and we would sit in the dark and stare at the hundreds of flickering golden dancers that surrounded us. We did this for as long as the candles burned—sometimes with music playing and sometimes just sitting in stillness and silence. The hypnotic attraction of the flames would ultimately pull me in, and I would feel a sort of high as I floated into the light and eventually merged with light itself, feeling my body become porous and my individuality unfold into something bigger than me . . . beyond me . . . everything and nothing at once, BEing the moment.

It was years later, in an Ashtanga Vinyasa yoga class, that I first was taught to use this focusing technique as part of a yoga *asana* (pronounced *as-ana*), which literally means *sitting down* or *seat*, but which we most often translate asana as pose, posture, or position. The technique was called *drishti* (also spelled *dristi*), and in Sanskrit, it means "insight, wisdom, intelligence, or point of view." During yoga practice, the drishti serves both as a way to move beyond this local realm of space and time—beyond your normal vision, beyond physical balance and equilibrium—and as a metaphor for focusing consciousness toward a vision of one-ness. It's a form of meditation in itself.

Drishti Meditation

When using a drishti during yoga practice or open-eyed meditation, you softly focus or gently gaze at some concentrated point while keeping your attention directed within. The drishti point can be a candle flame or the edge of your nostril, your third eye (the point between your eyebrows), your navel, or some point in the distance. Drishti isn't about the external object you are focusing on. The purpose is to draw your consciousness away from the distractions around you to a single focal point—a point from which your concentration is ultimately directed inward. In yoga, drishti is a point of focus where the gaze rests during poses of flexibility, balance, or strength. Focusing on a drishti aids concentration since it is easier to become distracted when the eyes wander all over the room. You can actually stand on one foot for longer if your attention is locked on a fixed point in the distance.

In certain styles of yoga, each asana has a specific drishti, which also aids in alignment. For instance, in the yoga asana called *parvatasana*, also known as mountain pose or downward facing dog, your legs and arms create an A-frame, with your butt sticking high in the air, pulling up to the sky, and the drishti is your navel. In the yoga asana called *utthita parsvakonasana*, or extended side angle pose, you lean to the side, with one hand on the ground supporting you, and your drishti is upward toward your other hand, which is raised and extended, guiding your head up to the sky. You look to your raised fingers, which ultimately become the sky, which ultimately become one-ness.

It was legendary teacher and yogi Sri K. Pattabhi Jois who first introduced the soft gaze drishti practice to the Western yoga world 75 years ago, teaching students to direct their awareness to one of nine points of focus on the physical body as they moved through the 28 asanas or poses of the practice. The ashtanga yoga tradition, popularized in America by guru Jois, describes nine classic drishtis and emphasizes a fixed gaze with soft eyes.

They are:

1. Tip of the nose

2. Third eye

3. Navel

4. Thumbs

5. Hands

6. Big toes

7. Far to the right

8. Far to the left

9. Up to the sky

Let's experience these drishtis right now.

Take a deep breath in, hold it for a few beats, and then slowly let it out through your nostrils. Keep breathing at this same pace. Long, slow, deep inhales.

After you've done this a few times, drift your gaze to the tip of your nose. Feel your eyes cross and relax. Do this for a minute or so.

Now bring your awareness up to your third eye, located in the middle of your forehead, a bit above your eyebrows. Feel your eyes open and close. Stay in this space for a few minutes.

Now bring your attention to your navel. Look within. Keep your eyes in a soft gaze. Stay here for a few moments.

And now gently drift to your thumbs—no thoughts but your gaze for a few moments.

And now expand your awareness to include your whole hand. Keep breathing . . . long . . . slow . . . deep breaths.

Now drift your gaze to your big toes. Wiggle them to bridge the energetic distance between your physical and astral toes.

Now without moving your head, drift your gaze all the way to the right, almost trying to see your right ear. Keep your gaze soft, and keep breathing.

Now move your eyes as far as they will gaze in the other direction.

After you've gazed left for a minute or so, bring the gaze to center, and raise your eyes up to the sky.

When you've done that for a minute or so, close your eyes, and just sit and let that process settle in.

How do you feel? Any different?

As with many forms of meditation, drishti meditation involves deep focus and concentration. In contrast, in the practice of Nakshatra *BirthStar* Mantra Meditation, one does not focus or concentrate, which I find liberating. But focus and concentration can be powerful tools in yoga practice because they allow you to move beyond your physical body to the drishti. And when you are in a state of body-centered restful awareness, the drishti ultimately becomes you, beyond space and time. It's a beautiful and deeply centering and unifying experience.

Sri Yantra Meditation

Similar to the act of drishti, *Sri Yantra Meditation* is another popular form of visual meditation. It is rooted in India's Vedic and yogic traditions.

For thousands of years, people have meditated by staring into the devotional labyrinths of Buddhist mandalas and Hindu yantras in order to achieve higher states of consciousness. These are visual representations of the journey of evolution, usually depicting a deity or a dot (referred to as the bindu) in the center that acts as the source of one-ness. Around this central focal point are ever-opening concentric circles (*mandala* is a Sanskrit term meaning "circle"), other geometric shapes, and depictions of nature or holy scenes.

The Sri Yantra took this devotional art to a new level in the 8th century as one of the first nonreligious geometric depictions of this sacred journey. *Sri* (also spelled *shri* and pronounced *shree*) is Sanskrit for "wealth" or "abundance"; in this case it means "most revered." *Yantra* is a Sanskrit word for "vehicle" or "instrument." So the Sri Yantra is a revered visual instrument that uses the mathematical proportions known as the golden ratio. The scientific proportions used to create such structures as the Parthenon, and the Great Pyramid at Giza are based on the same naturally occurring sacred ratios we witness in the development of pinecones, ferns, succulents, and nautilus shells. (Remember all that stuff about fractals?)

The sacred geometrics of the Sri Yantra depict a pure visual expression of the journey of existence, expanding from the cosmic one-ness (the source) to multiplicity (our personal expression of the universe) and then back to one-ness, all the while providing that very experience of one-ness. It is a meditation in itself.

Using what is now referred to as mathematical psychology, the ancient artisans of the Sri Yantra applied such scientific techniques as the Fibonacci sequence, which is the mathematical representation of the sacred ratio. The simultaneously static and dynamic interplay of all the elements of the Sri Yantra—squares, circles, "perfect" triangles, lines, and a point—depict the process of evolution (growth away from the source) and involution (coming from multiple layers back to one single source) in the form of a visual meditation. It has often been referred to as a visual representation of the vibration *Om* (said to include all the vibrational tones of the planet) and honors the power of masculine and feminine energy rather than the figure of a god or goddess.

Because it is a visual representation of the vibration *Om*, the Sri Yantra is considered the most powerful yantra for meditation for the fact that, first and foremost, it is a silent vibration—the unstruck bell! And that silent focus on the object of your attention disconnects you from all other activity and takes you on a journey into one-ness, where all your desires will be fulfilled. Meditating on the Sri Yantra is essentially a visual interplay and fusion of duality—the manifest world of form and phenomena, with non-duality—the formless unboundedness of the unmanifest world.

The Sri Yantra is formed by nine interlocking triangles that surround and radiate out from the central point that then creates thirty-four individual triangles. This centering point, known as the *bindu*, is the junction point between the physical realm and its unmanifest source and represents the universe in all its abundance. Four of the larger triangles point upward, representing Shiva, or masculine energy. Five of the triangles point downward, representing Shakti, or feminine energy. Thus the Sri Yantra also represents the union of masculine and feminine divine energy.

Since the Sri Yantra is composed of nine triangles, it is often known as the *navayoni chakra* (in Sanskrit *nava* means "nine," and *yoni* refers to female womb as the source of all life, and *chakra* means "wheel"). Together, the nine triangles are interlaced in such a way as to form forty-three smaller triangles in a web representative of the entire cosmos or a womb symbolic of creation. This is surrounded by a lotus of eight petals, a lotus of sixteen petals, and an earth square resembling a temple with four doors that face all four sides representing north, south, east, and west.

The Sri Yantra is also known as the *nava chakra* because it can also be seen as having nine levels. These levels, displayed in all traditional Sri Yantras, start from the center and radiate outward from:

1. *Sarva Anandamaya*, composed of a point or *bindu*

2. *Sarva Siddhi prada*, composed of 1 small triangle

3. *Sarva Rogahara*, composed of 8 small triangles

4. *Sarva Rakshakara*, composed of 10 small triangles

5. *Sarva Arthasadhaka*, composed of 10 small triangles

6. *Sarva Saubhagyadayaka*, composed of 14 small triangles

7. *Sarva Sankshobahana*, comprising an 8-petal lotus

8. *Sarva Aasa Paripuraka*, comprising a 16-petal lotus

9. *Trilokya Mohana* or *Bhupara*, comprising a square of three lines with four portals

To perform a Sri Yantra meditation, sit down comfortably at a table or desk. Prop up the yantra one to two feet away, directly in front of your gaze, or watch it on a monitor. (Visit the Meditation Room at **davidji.com** for a full-page, full-color Sri Yantra, and a Sri Yantra audio meditation where I will guide you through the process.)

Once you are comfortably set in front of your Sri Yantra, read the directions below and feel free to gaze at the image on the page.

As you look at the yantra, allow your eyes to focus on its center. This dot in the center is called the bindu, which represents the unity that underlies all the diversity of the physical world. Now allow your eyes to see the triangle that encloses the bindu. The

downward-pointing triangle represents the feminine creative power, the womb of all creation, while the upward-facing triangle represents male energy, movement, and transformation. Allow your vision to expand to include the circles outside of the triangles. They represent the cycles of cosmic rhythms. The image of the circle embodies the notion that time has no beginning and no end. The farthest region of space and the innermost nucleus of an atom both pulsate with the same rhythmic energy of creation. That rhythm is within you and without you.

Bring your awareness to the lotus petals outside the circle. Notice that they are pointing outward, as if opening. They illustrate the unfolding of our understanding. The lotus also represents the heart, the seat of the Self. When the heart opens, understanding comes.

The square at the outside of the yantra represents the world of form, the material world that our senses show us, the illusion of separateness, well-defined edges, and boundaries. At the periphery of the figure are four T-shaped portals, or gateways. Notice that they point toward the interior of the yantra, the inner spaces of life. They represent our earthly passage from the external and material to the internal and sacred.

Now take a moment to gaze into the yantra, and as if in slow motion, let the different shapes and patterns emerge naturally, allowing your eyes to be held loosely in focus. Gaze at the center of the yantra. You are gazing on perfection: the golden ratio. Pure balance and equilibrium. Let's drink it in. Without moving your eyes, gradually and very slowly begin to expand your field of vision, lingering over each layer as you expand your vision. Continue slowly expanding your vision until you are taking in information from greater than 180 degrees.

Notice that all this information was there all along, but because you were fully present, you just became aware of it as it unfolded. This is akin to the unfolding of your life's journey . . . from the one source to individuation, ever evolving, changing, *shifting, transforming, and moving outward in so many different directions.*

Now slowly reverse the process by gently drawing your attention back in. Slowly move from taking in everything around you, and begin to narrow your gaze. Move your awareness slowly back to the yantra's four gates, and stay there for a few moments. Then ever so gently, move deeper into the yantra. Drift your soft gaze slowly back through each circular channel of lotus petals and triangles and ultimately back to the bindu— back to the source. Take a few minutes to do this.

This process of moving back to the bindu is called "involution"—moving from multiplicity, our multidimensionality back to one-ness as you drift your awareness back into the center of the yantra, layer by layer.

Don't feel the need to stare at the yantra beyond a comfortable amount of time; 5 to 15 minutes is perfectly acceptable; there is no need to overdo it. Whatever length of time *you* are comfortable with should work. And now go through the process of evolution and involution.

After you have gazed at the yantra for a few minutes, gently close your eyes for between 5 and 25 minutes, and let the yantra unfold in your mind's eye. This practice of letting the yantra unfold within you is a powerful part of the meditation, as the stored geometric images drift you back and forth between DOing and BEing. The patterns of creativity represented by these primordial shapes express the fundamental forces of nature that flow through existence and through you. When you are done with both parts of the meditation, feel free to just sit and slowly let the subtle nature of what you just experienced ripple through your thoughts, your being, and your breath. Notice how you feel. Notice the volume and the activity levels of the world around you and then become aware of the world within you. Just witness yourself through the whole process. And breathe.

Always remember to be gentle with yourself, and take a few minutes (or longer if possible) to sit quietly before you resume physical activity. The trancelike effect of the Sri Yantra meditation can carry over into the next few hours of your day, so make sure not to drive or operate heavy equipment immediately following this or any form of meditation.

After practicing yantra meditations, you will lose the feeling of separation between the yantra and your Self, essentially disconnecting from the concept of separateness itself. You will experience one-ness when you cannot differentiate whether you are in the yantra or the yantra is in you. Note: Doing the meditation isn't going to put you in a permanent state of psychosis, make you unable to distinguish boundaries, or unable to live in the daily world.

The yantra meditation is not meant to replace your daily practice but can be inserted at any point in your day. It will act as a complementary practice to whatever other form of meditation you are engaged in. Drishti meditations are powerful experiences and can help progressively slow the fluctuations of the mind, while providing glimpses of spiritual awakening. Yet receiving visual images and activating your powers of focus are still *activities* that keep one rooted in the physical and subtle realms of activity! So let's keep exploring other forms of meditation so you can taste even more subtle experiences.

CHAPTER 7

SECRETS OF SOUND MEDITATION

*"Why are there trees I never walk under but large
and melodious thoughts descend upon me?"*

— WALT WHITMAN

Every life form on this planet expresses itself through sound. Every animal has a distinct voice, from the basso profundo rumblings of elephants and the full-mouthed roars of lions to the squeals and caws of finches and exotic parrots. Gargantuan whales and their smaller dolphin cousins ripple their magnificent songs through the depths of the sea, while mice squeak, lizards hiss, weasels whimper, owls hoot, and wolves howl to each other across the miles.

Sound can bring us to the present moment. It can also drift us into the past and sometimes even into the future for short bursts of time. The world around us calls out in myriad voices: the ocean churns and shouts even as it caressingly laps at the shore; trees creak and moan as they bend and sway in the gusting wind, their branches shaking their leaves like maracas; fields of flowers sing in unison; even the thousands of blades of grass in every front yard and backyard bow and reach for the sky as they subtly chant their whispering chorus.

The whole planet is in song, and hearing it is simply a question of the tool we use to listen—our ears, our eyes, our hearts, our skin, our bones, our minds, our souls. When we can elevate a particular sound until it is the loudest vibration in our awareness, that can become our meditation. But just as the Sri Yantra meditation is not meant to be a replacement for your daily meditation

practice, sound and guided meditations are meant to be a complement to your daily practice.

Guided Meditation

I love guided meditations. I have experienced deep healing and
powerful *A-ha!* moments listening to guided meditations. Some
can be effective in helping you train your mind and body. Many
athletes use guided meditations and visualizations to reinforce
and fine-tune an experience they would like to replicate, such as
running the big race, hitting the perfect golf shot, mastering a
penalty kick, defying gravity on a skateboard or snowboard, or
swinging a hockey stick just before the puck arrives. By picturing
the process and desired outcome over and over in your mind, you
become primed for when the event actually takes place. Under
basketball coach Phil Jackson, the Chicago Bulls and the Los
Angeles Lakers meditated their way to multiple championships,
and football coach Pete Carroll helped the Seattle Seahawks
visualize and meditate themselves to the Super Bowl.

Less popularized are the meditations and visualizations
for nonathletic activities, such as relaxing the body before and
during an MRI, a medical procedure, or the often anxiety-filled
process of giving birth; releasing stress before and during a
plane flight; preparing for a difficult conversation; lessening and
releasing physical pain stored within the body, delivering a speech
or presentation, and doing deeper emotional work to release
experiences that no longer serve you.

There are guided meditations that bring you into the present
moment by taking you out of your past, out of your future, and
out of your head by using words, sound, and music to take you
on a journey of empowerment, acceptance, emotional healing,
or peace. *Come Fly With Me*, my album on stress-free flying, was
developed after several of my students revealed they were horrified
to fly on airplanes and were in emotional pain in the days and
weeks leading up to the flight—from packing to checking in to

boarding and especially during takeoff and landing. Now they, along with tens of thousands of airplane passengers, have a tool to help them move through these constrictions without the emotional turbulence.

Throughout the years—starting when I received a bootleg audio copy of Ram Dass reading passages from *Be Here Now* to my freshman immersion into Zen philosophy, when Alan Watts guided me through a journey from my head to my soul—I have experienced powerful breakthroughs and expansions of awareness through guided meditations.

My deepest past-life regression was a guided meditation at my very first retreat. It only lasted an hour, but it felt like centuries had shifted as I journeyed back to yesterday, and then last week, and then last month, last year, 10 years ago, 20 years ago, into the womb, and then beyond the womb into my previous life!

It was unbelievably transformative. And yes, I had drifted away to someplace in the ether. But it was not a meditation of stillness and silence. My hearing was activated; I was very subtly paying attention to the guide's words. My mind was engaged. It felt a bit like sleepwalking. As long as we are listening, we are consciously activating attention and intention and maintaining a foot in the realm of activity—the realm of the conditioned world.

Depending on what you need at a particular moment in time, guided meditation can move you, open you, ready you, soothe you, or heal you. But it cannot replace the extended periods of time you spend in *unguided* meditation, *unless* it contains periods of absolute silence with no words or music. That is why all my guided meditations have always had at least 5 to 30 minutes of pure silence woven into them. I'll start the meditation with background music to help you settle in and then guide you into a particular teaching or visualization. But then we journey *together* in silence so that you can truly connect to the stillness and silence that rests within you and awaken the space that connects us to each other. In that space, you are no longer listening; you are truly surrendering to just BEing.

Guided meditations are a powerful initiation for those who want more peace and relaxation or less anxiety and stress. Many of us began with guided meditation because it's a gentle way to test the waters without being frightened away by concepts of spirituality, mantra, or extended sitting "doing nothing." Ten years ago, after taking a training with Stephen Covey, I latched onto his idea that doing anything for 21 days makes it a habit. So I created this concept I named *the 21-day meditation challenge.* I recorded three weeks of guided meditations and boom! Thousands of people signed up for the journey. Then I recorded another one and over 25,000 people signed up. And then I recorded a third one and over 50,000 people registered for the experience. The feedback was so overwhelming that David Simon and Deepak joined me on the next few challenges.

In 2007, while David Simon was writing his seminal book on addiction with Deepak, he revealed to me that his research had led him to believe that it was in fact *40 days* of practice that ingrained new behaviors rather than 21 days. To a certain extent it burst my bubble. But then I stumbled upon the 13th-century Sufi poet Rumi's quote, "What nine months in the womb does for an embryo, 40 early mornings will do for your growing awareness." Those words went straight to my heart, and I fully embraced the power of 40 days instead of 21.

Several weeks later, I was invited to record my first 40 consecutive days of guided meditation for a program called the *Winter Feast for Your Soul,* and I was given creative control over every meditation. I wasn't sure if people would be willing to hang with me for that many days, but I was so excited to lead a 40-day journey, I dove in. The response was off the charts! More than 20,000 people downloaded the meditations and more than 90 percent hung in for the whole 40 days. I received thousands of e-mails from all over the world from people whose lives had been so radically transformed that I offered it again the following year and then a third time, releasing what I believe to be the most powerful guided meditation creation I've ever conceived—*40 Days of Transformation.*

Since January of 2012, I've sent out a free guided meditation to my community every weekend, recorded an additional guided meditation on my weekly Hay House Radio show *LIVE! from the SweetSpot*, and released more than 500 additional meditations. Every one of these guided meditations incorporates 5 to 30 minutes of silence, so you can truly experience the scientific, physical, emotional, and spiritual benefits of a real meditation—and truly cultivate your practice in the process. I've also developed a free online meditation resource center on davidji.com for the readers of this book called the *Meditation Room*, which includes meditations, timers, videos, downloads, tips, and additional tools to help you destressify.

So many of my students with strong and consistent mantra practices began their journey simply by hearing a guided meditation in a yoga class, on a CD, a download, a stream, or on their iPhone!

WHEN TO USE GUIDED MEDITATIONS

If you have a dedicated meditation practice, any other meditative or spiritual practice, including guided meditations, will be heightened by the power of you spending time each day in stillness and silence. Use your daily practice to complement any other guided, energy, or silent meditation you wish to add to your day. I recommend to my students that they meditate twice each day, following their breath or using a mantra once in the morning upon waking and again in the afternoon or early evening. Between these sessions, they can use other meditation forms they desire, such as a daily guided meditation session, a midday pranayama or breathing session, or an evening chakra tuning before bed. And I have received so many e-mails from people who use the *40 days of Transformation*, as their daily practice, starting again every 40 days. They like that I ring a chime at the 10-, 20-, and 30-minute mark so they can sit for as long as they like. They've locked in their practice and they are comforted feeling like they are meditating with me and thousands of other people around the world every time they begin their practice.

In Chapter 16, we'll go deeper into how to ground your daily practice and create an effortless meditation ritual so don't worry about that now. Keep exploring with me.

The power of any other meditation you do rests on the consistency and frequency of your daily meditation practice—the bookends of your day.

The Sound of Bowls

Beyond the sound of the human voice speaking words with all their meaning and our conditioned associations, non-vocal vibrations can be very powerful objects of attention in meditation. They also have an energetic aligning power as they flow through every cell of your body. Since the time of Buddha, practitioners have used gongs, chimes, crystal bowls, metal bowls, drums, and other natural vibrations to induce states of transformation and meditation, essentially using sound to take you into stillness.

The most enduring vibration creators are the bowls of Tibet and Nepal, which are traditionally made of an alloy known as *pancha dhatu* (meaning "five tissues or layers") or *panchaloha* (meaning "five metals"), a combination of copper, tin, zinc, iron, and a precious metal (usually either gold or silver). The craftspeople who make five-metal bowls especially cherish iron from meteorites.

To "play" a bowl, a padded mallet is tapped on the lip, edge, or side of the bowl creating the first vibration. To expand the sound, the mallet is ever so gently rubbed clockwise in a wandlike fashion, around the outside of the bowl—like stirring a pot of soup (except on the outside)—to tease out the single vibration into a chorus of harmonies. Tibetan metal bowl masters place an "orchestra" of bowls in front them and move around the floor tapping, stirring, blowing into the bowls, gonging, and coaxing waves of vibrations into a powerful healing symphony.

The power of these multiple-metal blends lies in the fact that each metallic compound vibrates at a different speed, creating multiple harmonies and polyphonic waves of sound that ripple through your body. Other metal percussion instruments—such as cymbals, tingshas, gongs, and chimes—can also create this vibrational experience.

Rubbing a mallet over a *crystal singing bowl* is akin to rubbing your finger over the rim of a wine glass to create a ringing sound. Imagine a bowl 10 times the thickness of a wineglass and made up of crushed quartz instead of crystal or glass. The bowl's shape and consistency allow the vibration to echo endlessly in a very specific key, creating the sound of a choir—hence the term "singing" bowl.

Most crystal singing bowls are made of quartz crystals with physical properties that cause them to amplify, conduct, and transform energy. This is why even today, quartz is used in computer chips, TVs, microphones, and watches. To craft a singing bowl, a master crystal-glassmaker shapes crushed quartz into a bowl whose size and design create the desired vibration—a particular musical note, or a combination of notes in a certain key—that aligns with a specific energy center in the body.

The Healing Power of Sound

Whether metal or crystal, the bowls' vibrations resonate beyond the ear's ability to receive sound. It is the whole body that resonates, not simply the eardrum. So when a pure vibration ripples through every cell in your body for a few seconds, then minutes, then longer, a natural state of cellular alignment occurs. The beauty of sound waves is that they rise, fall, and ripple into more subtle states of silence and that gently coaxes your body *and* mind into deeper states of stillness and silence.

This sound experience is less a form of meditation and more like a healing aural massage that creates a trancelike state temporarily disconnecting you from your thoughts, any other sounds, and, to a certain extent, your own body. The vibrations can continue rippling through your body for days, and the nurturing power of sound healing on a physical and emotional level is profound.

I have found that listening to bowls is most powerful for me after I have performed some emotional clearing or emotional release work that leaves me in a tender and vulnerable state. To have those sweet, safe sound waves ripple through me, gently caressing my wounds, and leading me into silence, is one of the most healing experiences in life. The master Tibetan bowl player Damien Rose is a dear friend of mine. His albums *Liquid Bells Singing Bowls* and *Calm* are powerful journeys into silence through the transformative power of sound. Damien also performed live on my first guided meditation album, *Fill What Is Empty; Empty What Is Full*, bringing tears to my eyes with his devotion to this sacred art. You can feel his heart going into each vibration on the tracks that feature his acoustic healing bowl sounds, especially through the guided *chakra meditation*.

Sound therapy is a core part of learning and healing. At all my signature meditation and healing immersions, as well as my Teacher Trainings, we often have a session known as the Gandharva Sound Bath. In Hindu mythology, Gandharvas were celestial musicians who performed exquisitely pleasing music for the gods at their palace banquets. They also acted as intermediaries, who flew through the sky, carrying messages between humans and the gods.

Perhaps you've seen pictures of these Gandharva Sound Bath sessions on my website, where we all lay down on blankets, our heads facing the Master Sound Healer as we surrender to the magical, hypnotic tones of sonic crystal or Tibetan bowls and experience powerful vibrational healing. After just a few moments, we melt into our blankets, and I guide the group in opening our energy fields as the vibrations permeate every cell in our being.

The Gandharva Sound Bath is a deeply meditative experience and for hours after the experience ends, the vibrations continuously return you to the present moment. Even days later, you continue to feel the vibrations ripple like waves lapping the shores of your bodymind. And the effect they have on the brain simply through the healing power of sound is irrefutable. But unless you hang out with me every week, live with a healing arts musician, or learn to play bowls, this type of meditation cannot realistically become part of your daily routine.

Sound and its subtle rippling is recognized as a powerful tool that can paradoxically can take us deeper into stillness and silence. So that I can access the power of sound at a moment's notice, I recorded a loop of *OMs* and bowls that I play if I'm having a particularly turbulent day. Closing my eyes and listening to this crescendo of all-consuming vibrations always brings stillness to my being and a smile to my face. Scientifically, the vibrations move through every aspect of your being, creating a sort of coherence that delivers equilibrium into each cell. At a certain point, the outside world is saying *"Om,"* and so is your inner world. You can stream it in *The Meditation Room*.

The Science of Sound Waves

Thousands of people use non-musical sound-wave frequency recordings to meditate, and many have found this to be a very positive practice in their lives. Over the last 20 years, I have had many sound-wave frequency meditation sessions that created deep states of relaxation for me and moved me into deep stillness. I have been part of several studies in which I was hooked up to biofeedback monitors that showed as I listened to sound-wave frequencies through headphones, my brain waves slowed, creating a deeper state of relaxation. In fact, modern science has confirmed that specific sound-wave frequencies create specific brain-wave patterns. However, given the current limitations of scientific understanding, there is the obvious assumption but not yet *conclusive evidence* that particular brain-wave patterns indicate a specific state of consciousness.

Advocates of this school of meditation point to evidence that playing a specific sound-wave frequency can create a certain brain-wave pattern in your head, which then reflects a certain state of consciousness. Essentially, play the sound wave, and the brain responds accordingly and attunes. And so it would logically follow that once you're attuned, you will experience the intended brain-wave state of consciousness of the wave being heard. For example, gamma waves have long been associated with states in which one takes things less personally, senses the dissolution of one's ego, or has an overwhelming feeling of universality or one-ness. So logic would conclude that by playing gamma waves, one would experience the characteristics of those universal states. There are several studies that either point to this correlation or imply it. Since science has not yet figured out how to determine *the state of consciousness* in someone else's brain or mind, there is currently only anecdotal evidence that this technique has scientific validity. Yet thousands use sound waves to meditate, and many have found this to be a very positive practice in their lives.

Over the last 20 years, I have had many sound-wave meditation sessions that created deep states of relaxation for me and moved me into deep stillness. I have been hooked up to biofeedback monitors to determine that my brain moved even deeper, reflecting theta waves, but again, determining that I achieved a specific state of consciousness is difficult. Here's essentially how it works.

Beta Waves

In our normal waking state, our brain produces beta waves. In fact, we pretty much live our waking lives in beta state—a state of waking alertness characterized by busy or anxious thinking and active concentration. When the brain is in the beta state, also known as beta rhythm, its frequency can be recorded on a brain-wave monitor known as an electroencephalogram (EEG). The frequency range of beta waves is 13 to 30 cycles per second. You don't have to memorize that; it's purely for comparative purposes as we explore other brain-wave rhythms, and you can view the following chart, which shows all the waves and frequencies.

Alpha Waves

When we are relaxed, the rhythm of our brain waves slows down. As the activity slows to a frequency below 13 cycles per second, we enter a brain rhythm known as alpha state. This is defined as an intensely pleasurable and relaxed state of consciousness associated with deep physical and mental relaxation. On an EEG, the alpha state is defined by a pattern of smooth, regular electrical oscillations in the brain that occur when a person is awake and relaxed. In contrast to the more active frequency of beta waves, alpha waves, also known as alpha rhythm, have a frequency range of 8 to 13 cycles per second.

During a sound-wave frequency meditation, as we move from the beta brain-wave state of normal waking consciousness to the slower brain-wave pattern associated with our alpha state, one can sense a powerful shift to a more surrendering state of consciousness expressed through physical relaxation and emotional openness. This is typically the state that our brain exhibits during meditation.

Theta Waves

Once the alpha state is achieved, some people choose to stay there as an antidote to stress or a method to calm themselves when they are experiencing agitation. Others, having experienced the relaxation of the alpha state, choose to drift deeper still. In some of the more popular sound-wave frequency meditation techniques, the premise is that we can drift even deeper into stillness by further slowing the sound waves, thereby inducing the brain to slow its activity and create theta waves. Theta waves, which are thought to move even more slowly than alpha waves, are produced in the frequency range of 4 to 8 cycles per second.

When the brain is in theta rhythm, the sense of openness we experience in alpha expands even further to a state of more holistic or universal awareness. In theta state, we experience a state of suspension. Like the gentle tides of the surf—moving in, hesitating for a moment, and then drifting out—we drift back and forth from activity hovering over the line into stillness. Of course, we can never be aware of that deep stillness until we drift back to the alpha state and then we have a comparison point. We've all experienced those surreal moments just before we've drifted into sleep that seem dreamlike even though we're not really sleeping. This state is known as theta rhythm, and the ability to hover there for a few moments or minutes is akin to consciousness surfing, riding the edge, hanging on the precipice between the uplift of the wave and the churn of surf only inches below, being in total stillness in the midst of activity and witnessing it. When we meditate regularly, our brain experiences a more consistent pattern of theta rhythm.

Delta Waves

At the slowest end of the brain-wave spectrum are the delta waves (0 to 4 cycles per second), which we experience in deep sleep, also known as slow-wave sleep. At this low frequency, we can experience what is known as lucid dreaming, where we are the witness to our dreams, simultaneously experiencing ourselves as both the subject and the object of the dream. In fact, as our understanding of low-frequency brain waves has evolved, it has led to several theories about meditation and brain-energy consumption.

Gamma Waves

Gamma waves are a pattern of brain waves with a frequency range of 80 to 100 cycles per second, much higher than the beta waves of our waking state. According to current research, gamma waves appear to reflect the harmony or synchronization of various interconnected neural networks within you: essentially, your brain at peak performance. So even though the frequency range is at the high end of the sound-wave spectrum (five to seven times faster than beta waves), the brain is in an optimal receptive state to push the boundaries of awareness as it accesses information in new and different ways.

Although at opposite ends of the sound-wave activity spectrum, both delta and gamma wavelengths have been thought to harmonize states of euphoria and even deeper one-ness by briefly putting the brain into a state in which it is highly receptive and totally aware while it consumes power at an infinitesimally low rate. This has been referred to in the scientific community as the "zero power hypothesis," and this is what is happening when you drift "into the gap" in meditation. In short, it's a state in which you have disconnected from brain activity and are using close to zero brainpower. Some researchers believe that in this state, you become less of yourself and more of your *Self* as you move further from your personal brain activity and the concepts and perspectives of an individual, and closer to a more universal and expanded perspective.

Brain Waves and Their Connection to States of Consciousness

While we cannot determine an individual's state of consciousness by simply observing them, scientific analysis tools such as EEGs can help us understand the presumed state of consciousness. The following chart illustrates the correlations.

Wave	Wave Frequency, cycles per second	Presumed State of Consciousness
Delta	0–4	Deep sleep/subtle witness to dreams
Theta	4–8	Universal or witnessing awareness
Alpha	8–13	Awake and relaxed
Beta	13–30	Active waking state
Gamma	80–100	Expanded/unity awareness/ universal cognition

A compelling study on the effects of long-term meditation on the brain was carried out at the University of Wisconsin by the neuroscientist Richard J. Davidson. Published in 2004 in the *Proceedings of the National Academy of Sciences*, the study investigated the brain-wave patterns of eight Tibetan monks. The monks were hooked up to EEGs with more than 250 sensors, meditated on "unconditional compassion" as the object of their attention, and then had MRI brain scans. The monks, who were handpicked by His Holiness the Dalai Lama, had undergone training in the Tibetan Nyingmapa and Kagyupa traditions of meditation and had spent an estimated 10,000 to 50,000 hours in meditation, over time periods ranging from 15 to 40 years. A control group of 10 student volunteers with no previous meditation experience were also tested after one week of training. Davidson and his researchers found that meditation activated the brain waves of the monks in significantly different ways than those of the volunteer students. During meditation, the monks produced much greater and more powerful gamma waves than the students, who showed only a slight increase in gamma-wave activity. But even the behavior of the waves was different, moving through the monks' brains in a more coordinated and organized pattern than in the students' brains. It's also important to note that the monks who had spent the most years meditating exhibited the highest levels of gamma waves. Equally significant is the fact that even when the monks were not meditating, the gamma signal in their brains stayed active. Their brains were actually different from those of the students, with stronger waves associated with problem solving, consciousness, and perception.

The Adaptable Brain

The Davidson study also demonstrated that the mental training and neural coordination a meditation practice (and presumably other disciplines) delivers can itself change the inner workings and circuitry of the brain in the area that is thought to control our focus, memory, learning patterns, and our perception of consciousness. Davidson's study clearly revealed a strong correlation between higher mental activity, a sense of heightened awareness, and gamma waves. While scientists used to believe that the brain was hardwired at a young age and couldn't create new neurons or new neural paths, an abundance of research that includes many studies on meditation has now proven that the brain is incredibly adaptable and dynamic and can change throughout one's life, a quality known as *neuroplasticity*.

Researchers at Harvard and Princeton have begun testing some of the monks who participated in Davidson's study, looking at different aspects of their meditation practice, including their ability to visualize images and control their thinking. Davidson's vast research (which I elaborated on in Chapter 3) has sparked others to explore these concepts. Neuroplasticity is now being scientifically observed in the brains of those just starting a meditation practice!

A 2016 Carnegie Mellon University research study led by Dr. David Creswell, associate professor of psychology in the Dietrich College of Humanities and Social Sciences, demonstrated that meditation fundamentally alters the brain network functional connectivity patterns very quickly, reducing stress and the inflammation it causes throughout the body.

Instead of using monks as test subjects, the randomized control group was made up of 35 unemployed, job-seeking, stressed adults who were exposed to either an intensive three-day mindfulness meditation retreat program or a relaxation retreat program that did not have a mindfulness component. Published in *Biological Psychiatry*, the study showed that mindfulness meditation training, compared to relaxation training, reduces Interleukin-6, an inflammatory health biomarker, in high-stress, unemployed adults.

All the participants completed a five-minute resting state brain scan before and after the three-day program, and provided blood samples right before the study began and at a four-month follow-up. The brain scans on the test subjects showed that mindfulness meditation training reduced inflammation and increased functional connectivity in the dorsolateral prefrontal cortex. This is the part of the brain responsible for impulse and emotional control, flexibility of thinking, working memory, planning, and prioritizing—the skill sets that those who thrive in the workplace require. Those who instead received the relaxation training did not show these brain changes. According to Dr. Creswell, "mindfulness meditation training improves your brain's ability to help you manage stress, and these changes improve a broad range of stress-related health outcomes, such as your inflammatory health." While relaxation is soothing and restorative in the moment, we now know that just a little bit of consistent meditation makes you a better decision-maker, provides clarity, and helps you in the workplace.

While many advocates of sound-wave meditation state that listening to a specific vibration creates certain brain-wave patterns that reflect a certain state of consciousness, it is, in fact, currently impossible to determine the state of consciousness in someone else's mind or brain. That could change next week, but for now, it's all up to interpretation.

Sound-Wave Audio Technology

There are many sound-wave technology companies that have introduced lower or deeper carrier frequencies such as delta waves and high-quality gamma-wave audio recordings to induce meditation. Many of my students began with one of the sound-wave meditation technologies and then moved on to mindfulness or a mantra practice. But they took their first step into meditation because listening to sound waves seemed like an easy method.

I have experimented at length with many wave frequencies to move me from one brain-wave state to another. I have experienced many deep sessions where theta and delta waves were played through headphones or speakers for hours. In 2005, David Simon and I experimented for three consecutive months using theta-, delta-, and gamma-wave recordings during our daily meditations. We experienced very deep relaxation, intense meditations, and some powerful releases. And on *Journey to Infinity*, my Ayurvedic sound healing album with *SacredFire*, we embedded sound waves into the first few guided meditations using binaural beats to quickly calm your mind and get you into the meditation groove.

Many of my students who began meditating using sound now prefer a daily practice that they can do without additional equipment, one that offers them opportunities to drift into unity consciousness on their own. But for those who want to have meditation done "to" them or who are looking to take a first step, sound-wave practices can open your eyes to the possibilities and, in the process, offer some very cool experiences.

CHAPTER 8

SECRETS OF ENERGY MEDITATION

"You have become so overflowing with love, with compassion, and you want to share. It happens at the fourth center, the heart. That's why even in the ordinary world people think love comes out of the heart. For them it is just hearsay, they have heard it; they don't know it because they have never reached to their heart. But the meditator finally reaches to the heart."

— OSHO

Throughout time, many have meditated using their connection to the energy centers in and outside of the body. There are hundreds, if not thousands, of ways to awaken, harness, release, and connect to your own energy through meditation. The most popular and most pervasive is the chakra meditation known as chakra tuning or chakra toning. I took my first step into that realm more than 15 years ago, when I stumbled into what I thought was a simple hatha yoga class that turned out to be a two-hour chakra awakening session. In that class, I learned that according to ancient Vedic wisdom, there are seven major energy centers in the body. These are known as chakras, a term that derives from the Sanskrit word *cakram*, meaning "turning" or "wheel."

What Are Chakras?

The traditional Indian healing system known as Ayurveda teaches that the chakras are the energetic junction points connecting our local domain world of form and phenomena with the nonlocal realm of the unmanifest. The ancient Vedic texts of the later Upanishads, a core philosophical scripture of Hinduism, state that there are 108 chakras in and outside of the body. There are seven main chakras within the body that are said to be the core energy centers. They radiate like wheels of light outward from a point on the physical body and through the layers of the subtle body (mind) and causal body (spirit) in an ever-increasing, fan-shaped or heart-shaped formation. These points are thought to be the focal points for the reception and transmission of our vital life force energy, known as *prana* in Sanskrit.

The seven main chakras are aligned in a column that begins at the base of your spine and extends to the top of your head. They're located symmetrically up your body, each spaced a distance of approximately seven fingers from each other, which is one hand width and two additional fingers from the tailbone to a bit below the navel, to the center of your chest behind your abdomen (called the solar plexus), to your heart, to your throat, to the third eye (an inch or so above your eyebrows), and then to the crown of your head.

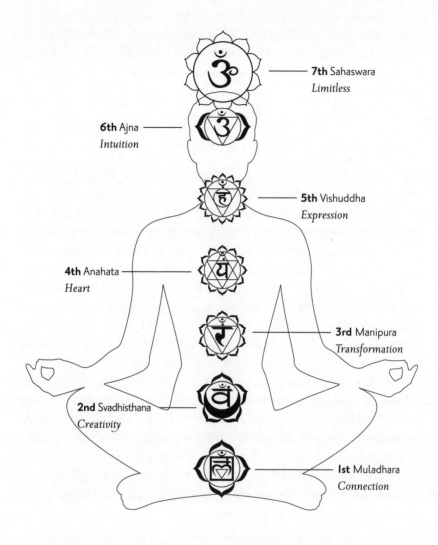

7th Sahaswara
Limitless

6th Ajna
Intuition

5th Vishuddha
Expression

4th Anahata
Heart

3rd Manipura
Transformation

2nd Svadhisthana
Creativity

1st Muladhara
Connection

In addition to the Vedas, other wisdom traditions from Asia, the Middle East, and even North America have integrated the chakras into their cultures. For example, the heart-expanding philosophy of Sufism rooted in ancient Turkey and Persia refers to four of these chakras as having powerful personalities. Accordingly, in these traditions, the navel chakra is called the "Self"; the heart chakra—"Secret"; the throat chakra—"Mysterious"; and the crown chakra—"the Teacher." The Hopi Indians of North America also speak of these same four chakras and describe them as being located on the crown of the head and in the regions of the throat, heart, and navel.

The Colors and Vibrations of Chakras

Each chakra has a specific color associated with it, as well as a vibrational mantra that opens or tunes the energy flow in each of our energy centers. This tuning is similar to opening up additional lanes on a highway. When the traffic has broader bandwidth, it can flow more easily and quickly. The world-renowned Plant-Spirit medicine healer, Karla Refoxo, spent many years living in Nepal exploring the origins of the ancient chakra practice. She worked with the indigenous people of Kathmandu to craft handmade chakra amulets that were then blessed by the living saint Mata and charged with healing energy. I am a fan (and wearer) of her powerfully charged amulets designed to awaken blocked energy in specific chakras. Chakra meditation is powerful because it opens you up to a more universal flow at the level of your personal physiology, your emotional state, and your spiritual awareness. Let's explore each of the seven main chakras in a little more detail to set the foundation for the meditation. In the Vedic tradition, they start with the most earthbound and weighty and move upward to the more subtle, getting lighter and lighter until they reach the state of pure ether.

First Chakra

The first chakra, also called the root or base chakra, is known in Sanskrit as the *Muladhara* (pronounced moola-dara). This is your personal connection to groundedness, stability, connection, and community, and therefore it is the heaviest of chakras. This foundational chakra is the platform for everything we create in the physical world. The root chakra is located at the tip of the tailbone and is essentially your contact point to the earth when you sit on the floor or ground. This is the site of your physical connection to the world. Traditionally, the Muladhara is associated with the color red. During a chakra tuning, this root is where the foundational flow of all the universe's energy enters you. So the flow of anything from the unmanifest, the unseen, the unbirthed, or the infinite enters here. The vibration or mantra for the first chakra is *Laam*.

SECOND CHAKRA

The second chakra, also called the sacral or sex chakra, is known in Sanskrit as the *Svadhisthana* (pronounced svah-dee-shtana) chakra. This is your personal connection to creativity—your own and that of the universe. It is located three fingers below your navel. Traditionally it is associated with the color orange. The most powerful energy on the planet is creative energy. And it is the energy of birthing that transforms the unmanifest into the manifest, thought into action, concept into product, idea into utterance, and desire into fulfillment.

When the second chakra is balanced, you are full of possibilities. You move in the direction of your dreams, and you know that you are deserving of them. The vibration or mantra for the second chakra is *Vaam*.

THIRD CHAKRA

The third chakra, also called the solar plexus chakra, is known in Sanskrit as the *manipura* (pronounced monny-poora). This chakra moves you forward and helps you follow through in the direction of the seeds you've planted in the fertile ground of your second chakra. The manipura is located in the center of your chest at your solar plexus, a few inches below the joining of your rib cage. This is essentially the center of your body, where your emotional and physical digestive fires burn most brightly. This radiating power plant moves you toward your target and awakens your personal, internal strength to achieve your intentions and desires. Traditionally it is associated with the color yellow. This chakra has also been referred to as the sun or *Surya chakra* (*surya* means "sun" in Sanskrit), because the golden yellow sun that radiates from the solar plexus is ever evolving, metabolizing, and transforming us in every moment.

When we harness the energy of the solar plexus chakra, we find empowerment and transformation. The vibration or mantra for the third chakra is *Raam.*

Fourth Chakra

The fourth chakra, also called the heart chakra, is known in Sanskrit as the *Anahata* (pronounced anna-hatta) chakra. This is your personal connection to love, compassion, empathy, forgiveness, and peace. The Anahata is located near your physical heart, in the center of your chest. You can place your hands on your heart right now and breathe in and feel the love flowing in and out of you. That's your Anahata—your true Buddha nature. Traditionally, it is associated with the color green.

The world could always use a bit more love, and *each of us* could also always use a bit more love. We never can have enough. If we could open our hearts even a little more each day, we would be happier, and those around us would feel that shift and share that energy. You actually can make a difference in the world each day by simply loving a bit more than you do right now.

To get the love flowing, you need to love yourself first, which is difficult for many of us. What's the challenge? We have built barriers to receiving love. We tell ourselves, "I'm not worthy," "I don't deserve it," or, "Others deserve it more than me." Or sometimes we simply feel "less than." When we awaken our heart chakra, love radiates around us, to us, and out into the world.

If we are going to share our gifts with the world, we need to fill ourselves first. It's similar to when you board a plane and the flight attendant says something along the lines of, "If the cabin decompresses, oxygen masks will drop down. If you're traveling with a child, please make sure you put the mask on yourself first before you place it on the child." Take a few minutes right now and practice the heart sutra meditation on page 123. You will absolutely feel a shift.

The vibration or mantra for the fourth chakra is *Yaam*. Several Sanskrit scholars have also said the vibration can be pronounced as *Yum*.

Fifth Chakra

The fifth chakra, also called the throat chakra, is known in Sanskrit as the *Vishuddha* (pronounced vi-*shoo*-da) chakra. This connects you to expressing both your personal Self and your most universal Self. It is located at the center of your neck in the middle of your throat. Traditionally it is associated with the color blue.

The throat chakra is where we communicate, emote, and give ourselves permission to express. Congestion in the throat chakra is often a sign that you are repressing some aspect of yourself, not willing to admit something to yourself, or that you are withholding permission from yourself to do something. This is the chakra that is the last doorway to the lighter, higher chakras and the more ethereal nature of Self. Before there can be a growth breakthrough or a step into the next chapter of your life, you must give yourself permission to move forward in some way—something you have long denied or repressed.

When this chakra opens, you have truly given yourself permission to let the universe work through you. You are willing to let your voice be heard! The vibration or mantra for the fifth chakra is *Haam*. Some scholars also pronounce this mantra as *Hum*.

SIXTH CHAKRA

The sixth chakra, also called the third-eye chakra, is known in Sanskrit as the *Ajna* or *Ajana* (pronounced *ahjj*-na) chakra. This is your personal connection to source, insight, and intuition, essentially the doorway to what the 9th-century sage Adi Shankara referred to as the "causal realm." It is located in the middle of the lower forehead, between your eyes and up a bit.

Traditionally, the sixth chakra is associated with the color purple. Throughout time, in many different cultures, there has been a distinct relationship between the third eye and mystical or spiritual properties. It is considered the connecting point between your personal Soul and the universal Spirit—essentially where all your discernment and intuition rests.

In her classic book *Babel*, Patti Smith, the singer, songwriter, laureate, spiritual warrior, and rock 'n' roll goddess, eloquently described the magic of the third eye in this excerpt from her poem about the most famous ninja to ever have lived, Sandayu the Separate:

> Sandayu enters. He bends down and carves an eye in the smooth forehead of his smiling wife. Hand in hand they walk through the garden. Then she blinks, then focuses on the face of her husband, sweet light of nostrils, he is seen at last! Thus found he laughs and shakes the sky. He is no longer Sandayu the Separate but Momochi, carver of the third new eye.

The vibration or mantra for the sixth chakra is *Shaam*. When we awaken this chakra we begin to really *see*, and make more conscious choices.

SEVENTH CHAKRA

The seventh chakra, or crown chakra, is known in Sanskrit as the *Sahaswara* (pronounced sah-ha-*swa*-rah) or thousand-petaled-lotus chakra. This is your connection to the unbounded, infinite, expanding flow of the universe. It is located at the crown of your head and is often depicted in art as the Hindu deity Shiva, spouting the Ganges River from the top of his head. Traditionally, it is associated with the color white or ultraviolet—beyond the spectrum of all colors.

This is the chakra in which everything that has just flowed through you flows back out into the universe. When one has limiting beliefs, opening up the crown chakra provides you access to the entire universe of possibilities. This is you in your most universal state, surrendering your individuality and ego for cosmic consciousness and moving from multiplicity into one-ness. The vibration or mantra for the seventh chakra is *Om*.

There are some schools of chakra practice that use the vibration *Om* for the sixth chakra and teach that the vibration of the seventh chakra is beyond sound. Please feel free to follow the practice that feels most comfortable to you.

CHAKRA TUNING

To activate, open, release, or expand your chakras, you "tune" them by bringing your awareness to them, envisioning the color of the chakra, connecting to its particular intention, and then repeating the vibration or mantra associated with the chakra. I'm most familiar with the practice of starting from the root and working your way up through the chakras. In other traditions, such as Reiki energetic healing, practitioners are known to perform their tuning starting at the crown chakra and moving downward.

LIGHTNESS AND THEN INTEGRATION

The most common process of chakra practice is to move from the root to the crown—the most dense to the most subtle manifestations of your being—opening your energy pathways first in your heaviest, most physical, and most deeply grounded aspects of your existence and then moving upward to ever-lighter expressions of your being. In many practices, you then weave your way back down from the crown to the root to integrate the lightest parts of you back into your more dense chakras. *Yogastha kuru karmani. Established in one-ness perform action.* This attunement will open all your energy centers as wide as possible and then flow this energy at every level back through your energetic essence. The result? An openness, coherence, and lightness of being that floats through your physical body, your emotional, psychological, intellectual realms, and your soul.

Over the years, I have recorded many chakra meditations, and several can be found online. On my first album *Fill What is Empty; Empty What is Full*, I created a healing chakra meditation called "Heal Your Body" that uses the chakra mantras and additional vibrations to take you to a deep place of physical and emotional healing. On *Guided Affirmations, Channeling the Universe through the Chakras*, I was inspired by the artisanship of Karla Refoxo's Tulku Chakra Amulet Collection and the affirmations she has woven into the charged chakra amulets she creates in Nepal.

In that 20 minutes of "energy meditation," you open each chakra, and as you tune each one through the power of affirmations, you access the universal traits in each energy center to empower yourself. There are many other resources that can offer you a chakra meditation that lasts from five minutes to an hour. Whatever you choose, I encourage you to explore some form of chakra practice to experience a unique and healing opening.

Sutra Meditation

Sutras are mantras with meaning and we often refer to them as affirmations. *Sutra* is the Sanskrit word for "stitch" or "suture" and is similar to a stitch binding two pieces of skin or cloth. In the realm of meditation, affirmations act as sutras to connect your world of space and time to the world beyond space and time . . . from your physical realm to the ethereal, astral realm . . . from the local domain to the nonlocal domain . . . from the manifest realm to the unmanifest. Back and forth and back again.

This is akin to flowing on an energy highway, where the chakras are the tollgates you gently open with your present-moment awareness. At each junction, subtly repeat the sutra as it weaves itself between the local and nonlocal realms. Then move your awareness to the next chakra and drop another sutra, let it resonate for a few minutes, and move to the next chakra and drop another sutra there. You continue until you have done this for all seven chakras. This powerful ritual of first going into silence for 30 minutes creates the perfect pathway through which your energy effortlessly flows within you and without you as you sit in stillness.

THE HEART SUTRA MEDITATION

In my album *Journey to Infinity*, I created a soothing Heart Sutra meditation called *Shanti: Peace and Protection*. My collaborator on those 102 minutes of blissed-out musical mantra meditations is the Canadian sound-healing duo *SacredFire* made up of the brilliant musician Dean Richards and the voice of an angel, MJ Vermette. MJ chants the ancient *Shanti Mantra* (the prayer of peace and protection) as I whisper in the background, "Gratitude, Trust, Love, Peace." I encourage you to download this 9-minute heart sutra meditation. But you can also practice this powerful meditation the next time you meditate. Here's how it works: After you have meditated for anywhere from 5 to 30 minutes, gently drift your awareness to your heart, envision a green color, and silently repeat, "Gratitude, trust, love, peace."

In your mind's eye, envision dropping the sutra into your heart as if you were dropping a pebble into a still pond. The ripple will start to fade out at the 5-second mark and turn back to stillness at about 10 seconds. Let the sutra slowly ripple until it stops (about 10 seconds). For example, silently repeat gratitude (let it ripple for 10 seconds), then trust (10 seconds), then love (10 seconds), then peace (10 seconds). And do that four times. The slow rippling acts as a timer, readying you for dropping the next sutra. Doing the complete set of four sutras four times takes less than 3 minutes.

Let's try it now.

Bring your awareness to your heart. Envision a green color in that area. And now, very slowly, silently repeat with your eyes closed: gratitude, trust, love, peace; gratitude, trust, love, peace; gratitude, trust, love, peace; gratitude, trust, love, peace. Then just sit for a few moments, and let that settle in. When you notice that you've drifted away to thoughts, sounds, or physical sensations, very gently drift back to *gratitude, trust, love, peace.*

How does that feel? Do you feel any different? If you can tack this ritual onto the beginning or end of your morning meditation, within days your heart will begin to open a little bit more. You will feel a greater sense of compassion, be more forgiving, and flow with a lighter sense of being. And you will actually experience greater gratitude, trust, love, and peace throughout your day!

You can perform the heart sutras (see the previous sidebar) as part of your daily practice, and your life will begin to become happier and more loving. What you think, you become. And the heart sutras are powerful affirmations to evolving you to a life of greater love and compassion. Simply go into meditation, and after you have been in stillness and silence for 20 to 30 minutes, stop repeating your mantra or following your breath. Then just float for a bit. And when your heart and soul are as defenseless and vulnerable as they can be, silently repeat *gratitude, trust, love, peace.*

Gently drop each sutra like a pebble into a still pond, and allow the ripple to be effortless. Gratitude . . . trust . . . love . . . peace . . . And do that four times.

For the high achiever in you, I've developed another practice that you can use with all the chakras. We use one affirmation for each chakra and silently repeat it four times and then move to the next chakra and do the same until you have moved from the root to the crown. After seven days of meditating and then dropping sutras, you will be able to calmly meditate in the middle of New York City's Times Square! Everything you desire will start to unfold effortlessly in your life.

The effectiveness of the sutras is most powerfully activated when they are dropped into stillness and silence. That is the most fertile soil for intentions to sprout in. For the full impact of the sutras, I recommend that you append this heart sutra practice to the end of your daily meditation practice. Do this for a week, and your life will change. You'll never want to stop.

Let's get a sampling by performing the chakra sutra meditation right now. For this meditation, feel free to sit comfortably in a chair and read it to yourself. Once you have gotten comfortable with how it works, feel free to lie down.

THE CHAKRA SUTRA MEDITATION

Start by taking a few long, slow, deep breaths in and out. Once you feel you have settled down a bit, close your eyes for a moment, and envision the chakras in their special places within your body and glowing the color associated with each energy center. See all seven of them radiating: the root . . . red; the second chakra . . . orange; the solar plexus . . . yellow; the heart chakra . . . green; the throat chakra . . . blue; your third eye . . . purple; the crown chakra . . . ultraviolet . . . an opalescent white light. Now gently bring your awareness to the base or root chakra (Muladhara) chakra. Its color is red and the vibration is LAAM. As you envision the energetic flow and the color, silently say the sutra I CONNECT . . . I CONNECT . . . I CONNECT . . . I CONNECT . . . *and after you have let* I CONNECT *ripple, chant the vibration out loud.*

Laam. Laam. Laam. Let's settle in for a few moments and just breathe.

We've just awakened our energy of connection, grounded-ness, and stability. This foundational energy must be strong to act as the platform for all energetic flow throughout the body. With each beat of your heart, feel the strong, red pulse of the Muladhara, channeling the energy of wholeness, stability, and balance. See yourself as a conduit for the life force. You are a vessel of connection. You are a channel for this flow of chi, qi, or prana. It journeys through your energy centers, strengthening with each pulse as it moves in you, throughout you, through you.

Next, bring your awareness from your tailbone to a place a few inches below your belly button. This is the second or navel (Svadhisthana) chakra. This is your center of creativity, of birthing new healing aspects of your Self. This is where your nourishing decisions come from. This is the font of all your creative energy.

Its color is orange, and with each breath, you can feel the orange expansion of your Svadhisthana chakra. The vibration is VAAM. *As you envision the energetic flow and the color, silently say the sutra* I CREATE . . . I CREATE . . . I CREATE . . . I CREATE . . . *and after you have let I CREATE ripple through you, chant the vibration out loud.*

Say it out loud with me slowly. Vaam. Vaam. Vaam. Let's settle in for a few moments and just breathe. Radiating out and through each cell, this is the energy of awakening, birth, growth, expansion, and nourishment. This energy center acts as the fertile soil for the birth of infinite possibilities and the pure potentiality of creation from nothing. You are a conduit of creativity.

Now bring your awareness to the solar plexus chakra, the center of your torso. In Sanskrit, it's known as the manipura chakra. Its color is yellow, like the sun, and the vibration is

RAAM. *As you envision the energetic flow and the color, silently repeat the sutra* I TRANSFORM . . . I TRANSFORM . . . I TRANSFORM . . . I TRANSFORM . . . *and after you have let I TRANSFORM ripple through you, chant the vibration out loud.*

Say it out loud with me slowly. Raam. Raam. Raam. Let's settle in for a few moments and just breathe. We've just awakened our energy of forward movement, of seeing things through, of getting it done. This is the chakra of our inner fire (Agni). This metabolic energy must be strong to consume all emotional and physical ingestions, cook them, transform them, access what nourishes us, and let go of what no longer serves us. With each beat of your heart, feel the strong, yellow fire of the manipura.

When the inner fire of manipura chakra is weak or blocked, we may feel tired, frustrated, and withdrawn. We're scared to take risks and confront people or issues. We don't have enough energy to plant and nourish the seeds of our intentions and desires, so they are unable to germinate and flourish.

By strengthening the power of our manipura chakra, we nourish the inner fire that burns away whatever is no longer serving us, including limiting beliefs, ideas, and memories. This will allow your life energy to flow freely so that you can experience the joyful energy that fuels all your intentions and helps you realize your deepest dreams and desires. You are a conduit of transformation!

Now move your awareness from your solar plexus to your heart (Anahata) chakra. This is where your ability to be peace, love unconditionally, trust in the Divine, and, most important, to forgive reside. This includes not just forgiving others but forgiving yourself as well.

Its color is green, and with each breath, feel a green pulse of pure love wash through your body. The vibration is YAAM. As you envision the energetic flow and the color, silently repeat the sutra I LOVE . . . I LOVE . . . I LOVE . . . I LOVE . . . *and after you have let I LOVE ripple through you, slowly chant the vibration out loud. Yaam. Yaam. Yaam. Let's settle in for a few moments and just breathe. You are a conduit of love,*

*compassion, forgiveness, and peace. Feel these universal char-
acteristics flow through you. You are a conduit of love.*

*Next, drift your awareness to the throat (Vishuddha)
chakra, located in front of your neck. It governs your expression
and your ability to give yourself permission in all areas of
your life. This chakra is associated with the dream state of
consciousness, but more importantly, it is your voice in the
world. Its color is deep blue, and the vibration is HAAM. As
you envision the energetic flow and the color, silently repeat the
sutra I EXPRESS . . . I EXPRESS . . . I EXPRESS . . . I EXPRESS
. . . and after you have let I EXPRESS ripple through you, slowly
chant the vibration out loud. Haam. Haam. Haam. Let's settle
in for a few moments and breathe. We've just awakened our
energy of communication and expression. Constrictions in
this area often prevent us from clearly expressing ourselves to
others, and a total constriction indicates that you haven't given
yourself permission to speak. The Vishuddha must be strong
so that all the energy created in the body has a place to express
itself. You are a conduit of expression, translating the Universe
into your own individual voice in words and actions.*

*Next, move your awareness from your throat to the spot
right between your eyebrows and an inch up. This is your third
eye (Ajna) chakra. It sits in the middle of your forehead and
connects you to insight. We have two eyes looking out and one
divine eye looking in. The ajna chakra helps you make choices
that are aligned with your higher power. This is the chakra of
judgment, discernment, and intuition. This is your conscious
choice maker.*

*Its color is purple, and the vibration is SHAAM. Opening
this chakra will help you make better decisions. As you envision
the energetic flow and the color, silently repeat the sutra I SEE
. . . I SEE . . . I SEE . . . I SEE . . . and after you have let I SEE
ripple through you, slowly chant the vibration out loud. Shaam.
Shaam. Shaam. Let's settle in for a few moments and breathe.
We've just awakened our energy that connects us to true sight
and insight! You are a conduit of divine vision. The ajna must*

be open to have unencumbered clarity, to see into the future, and to allow us to trust the universe.

Now shift your awareness from your third eye to the crown of your head. This is known as your crown (Sahaswara) chakra—the thousand-petaled lotus. This is your connection to the universe—to the infinite . . . to Spirit . . . to Source. When this chakra is open, all aspects of your existence become unified and liberated. You truly merge with the Universe.

Its color is pure white, ultraviolet light, and the vibration is Om. *As you envision the energetic flow and the color, silently repeat the sutra* I TRUST. . . I TRUST . . . I TRUST . . . I TRUST *. . . and after you have let I TRUST ripple through you, slowly chant the vibration out loud. Om. Om. Om. We've just awakened the energy that connects us to pure, unbounded consciousness. This is where your soul merges with the universal Spirit. Let's settle in for a few moments, just breathe, and allow the merging.*

Once the Sahaswara chakra is wide open, the energy of the universe can freely flow in, out, and through the body from the tailbone to the crown. By chanting all these vibrations, you have opened and aligned your energy centers. There still may be some congestion and some constriction, so perform this chakra tuning with regularity and your healing will accelerate. Right now, let's activate our body's own natural healing properties by feeling the sacred energy flow through from the root to the second chakra to the solar plexus to the heart to the throat to the third eye to the crown. When the constrictions have been opened, the energy effortlessly flows through you on a journey of reawakening your wholeness.

Just sit and take a few moments to witness your bodymind. Notice what you feel and how you interpret it. You may want to journal or simply let the awakened energy flow continue to reverberate. Whatever you choose to do, always be gentle with yourself after you've meditated or performed a chakra tuning.

With your eyes open or closed, sit for a few moments, and let the stillness and silence settle in. Don't leap up to answer the phone, and don't feel the need to end the meditation until you are ready. For energy meditations or chakra tunings, listen to your bodymind, and don't drive or operate heavy machinery immediately following the practice.

You can perform chakra tuning any time by closing your eyes, putting your attention on each chakra, and bringing an intention to it. This can be in the form of chanting, speaking, whispering, or silently repeating an affirmation (I am creative, I am worthy of love, I am whole, and so on), a mantra (om mani padme hum, aham brahmasmi, so hum, etc.), sutras (gratitude, trust, love, peace), or the sounds of each chakra (Laam, Vaam, Raam, and so forth). Just the simple act of combining (1) single-pointed attention on your chakras and (2) the subtle intention to open and receive will bring an expansion into your energetic relationship with the world.

CHAPTER 9

THE FIVE SECRETS
OF THE SWEETSPOT

"Your beliefs become your thoughts; Your thoughts become your words; Your words become your actions; Your actions become your habits; Your habits become your values; Your values become your destiny."

— MAHATMA GANDHI

Now that we've gotten comfortable using affirmations and sutras, I'd like to share with you a powerful set of tools that I use *right after I meditate* to provide me with an evolving foundation for reflection, growth, and deeper understanding. Essentially, I have crafted my own set of personal sutras from the myriad translations of the teachings of the Old Testament, the New Testament, the Buddhist treatise of the Dhammapada, and the ancient Vedic texts known as the *Upanishads*. I use these sutras every morning in a process that is akin to planting intentions like seeds in the fertile soil that rests within. By implementing this post-meditation ritual over the past few years, I have had a transformational shift at my core and learned to make more conscious, nourishing choices in my life. I refer to this set of meditation tools as *the Five Secrets of the SweetSpot*.

Here's how it works. After I have sat in stillness and silence for about 30 minutes, I drift my awareness to five personal expressions of the universe that I would like more of in my life:

- Patience

- Acceptance

- Defenselessness

- Compassion, and

- Abundance.

And I repeat each like a sutra—over and over and over for about a minute and then drift to the next. Sometimes I find myself in thought and then I'll gently drift back to the sutra and begin repeating it again. Sometimes I get lost among the sutras. That's okay. It's sort of fun. When it happens, I'll smile and start again with whichever sutra appears in my awareness first.

I have found that silently repeating these sutras after coming out of stillness and silence is a gentle process that eases my transition from a state of restful awareness into more active awareness. One powerful, tangible result is that these affirmations ripple through my awareness all day long and before, during, and after every interaction I have with the world outside of me—especially in all my interactions with humans and animals. I also believe that placing my attention on five principles that will help me grow and will lead to a better life for me and everyone I touch. Whatever happens, it's five minutes of connection to principles that I honor as core to a life of happiness.

Each of these "Secrets" also provides the perfect closure to my morning meditation practice and have helped me to evolve my transition into waking state. And at the deepest level, they connect me to more universal aspects of myself so that I can more fully experience life outside of meditation. In their most essential way, the *Five Secrets of the SweetSpot* express the qualities I would like more of in my life. Let me explain further:

Patience. The ability to be physically, emotionally, and mentally restful yet alert while your senses ingest, your mind absorbs, and your intellect digests, and then to intuitively act from a space of stillness. Patience is not about being dogged in any sense of the word;

hence it is not about patiently persevering. It is about surrendering to see what will unfold in a detached way . . . orienting yourself *away* from the Self filled with expectations *to* the *Self* who is the witness of the magnificent unfolding of life. Repeating this sutra has allowed me to become a better listener.

Acceptance. *The state of being open and receptive at the intellectual and heart level so that whatever arises is welcomed and appreciated.* Acceptance is truly welcoming something into your being as a friend would invite another friend into his heart, with arms wide open, owning every moment of the experience. Accepting is different from tolerating, which is more like allowing something to enter your space rather than inviting it in. Do you see the subtle difference? Repeating this sutra has allowed me to be more open-minded to others' points of view and receive love without resistance.

Defenselessness. *The state of universality when there is no need or urge to defend or promote yourself.* When you are defenseless, nothing can be taken *personally* because there is no person or ego to defend. Being *defenseless* is not about being weak, and it's not a state that can only be experienced in meditation. It's about not feeling the need to impose your will, your personality, your persona, or your point of view on something. It's trusting so completely that you realize *tat tvam asi*—"you are that"—every face you see is a reflection of yours and ever thing you see is an expression of you. You have no sense of I. You are simply the pure witness. Repeating this sutra has allowed me to be more vulnerable and more secure.

Compassion. *True compassion is the ability to be sympathetic and empathetic, as well as have the desire to alleviate another's pain and suffering.* Beyond living life at the level of "Do unto others as you would have others do unto you," compassion looks to heal others even in instances when you would not heal yourself. There are many people we like, even love, yet the depth of our compassion for them is shallow. Perhaps fear, jealousy, resentment, guilt, or anger color our perspective and each carries with it a certain attachment that prevents true compassion.

There are many people and things we think we love, but often it is because of our current relationship to them. Most likely, if the relationship changed, so would your feelings about those people or things. For example, let's say you "love" your boss and he treats you really well. But, if your boss fires you today, your feelings about him or her would change. You might not be as forgiving of previous actions you blessed because of your "attachment" to him. You might even say that you don't like him anymore since you were fired. If your partner, fiancé, lover, or spouse came home today and told you they were leaving the relationship, you might not look upon them with the same level of forgiveness, support, and sweetness as you did previously. Most likely, that's because you have more attachment to them rather than compassion for them. Or perhaps you are confusing loving-kindness with a more attached definition of love.

How can we know if we are feeling compassion about something and are not simply attached? In the examples above, the moment the relationship changed between you and your boss or you and your partner, most likely so did the level of *rooting* for that person. You stopped feeling the way you had. True compassion is independent of attachment. Imagine if our compassion could transcend our relationships and the attachment we have to them—pure sympathy, pure empathy, and pure desire to help others heal. Repeating this sutra has allowed me to be more empathetic.

Abundance. The perspective in which you realize that you are an expression of the expansiveness of the universe. When we look to our most genuine selves—beneath all life's drama, and the moment-to-moment conditioning we have self-imposed—we see that we are rich in every way. We are open to wealth consciousness. We are unconstricted, ever evolving, and pregnant with possibilities. When we look really deep, we see that the fear, lack, and poverty consciousness we embrace are indeed self-imposed or projected upon us by what we read, what we hear, and what we see, but that's not who we are. We are open conduits for the magnificent flow of the abundant cosmos. We are designed to experience our most expanded universal aspects of Self. Repeating this sutra has allowed me to feel more worthy in my smaller moments without resisting out of fear.

Acknowledging these five characteristics as part of who I am right after I have quieted my mind for 30 minutes allows the seeds of these affirmations to settle into the stillness of my heart and flow through my day with greater grace and ease. It's one thing to plant a seed in turbulent soil; the results are somewhat predictable. But planting seeds in fertile, rich, still soil provides an entirely different experience.

As the remnants of the vibrations of those words continues to ripple through my being at the most subtle level, they flow into every fiber of who I am—my words, my thoughts, my deeds, my beliefs, my stillness, my silence, my pure unbounded consciousness . . . my essential being. And they become more of me as I open my eyes after each meditation.

How to Use the Five Secrets of the SweetSpot

Practicing any regular meditation ritual that includes sutras will gently infuse you with a subtle awareness of whatever affirmation you choose. And if there are values that you currently find more relevant to you right now, then feel free to use those as *your* Secrets of the Sweetspot. I've used *Surrender, Acceptance, Forgiveness, Abundance, Love.* And *Stillness, Clarity, Kindness, Courage, Peace.* And, of course, *Gratitude, Trust, Love, Peace.* You'll find over time you want your awareness to be on certain values or characteristics that you want more of or that you wish to enhance. So allow this practice to evolve as you evolve.

Start with the Sacred Reflections

To start the process of loosening your grip on the universe (HA! As if you really have a grip on anything), always start your meditation with a few slow, long, deep breaths using your nostrils to carry the air in and out. And then begin to watch your breath as it flows. After about four rounds of this slow, gentle breathing, where you witness your breath move in and out of your body, you'll feel yourself start to settle down. You can then begin your formal practice with any questions or any prayer you feel like starting with. In my classes, we often begin by asking ourselves a series of questions known as *The Sacred Reflections: What am I grateful for? Why am I grateful? What does my heart long for? What is the essence that rests at my core? How can I help others doing what I love?* Don't worry about coming up with answers. The point is to simply ask each question over and over and then move to the next. Sometimes answers will flow. Other times, there will be no answers. Keep repeating the questions. Even if nothing flows back in the moment, the answers will begin to come to you in your waking state outside of meditation.

By asking these questions, listening to answers, and letting go of outcomes *The Sacred Reflections* set the table for your meditation practice. There is no need to bring the questions or answers into your mind during the meditation. They are already a part of who you are. As you expand in consciousness, the cosmic dialogue will continue to expand within you. You will gain clarity into who you are and how you flow your essence into the world, your heart will expand exponentially, and you will discover your purpose for being here. (Remember: Don't bring any thoughts, concepts, ideas, plans, or expectations into the meditation. Let it all go before you begin your formal practice.)

These are some of the deepest questions you can ask yourself, which is why we do nothing with the information that comes to us during meditation. That's simply a process for establishing your dialogue with the universe, and making the soil more fertile. It's outside of meditation, when the seeds you've planted are growing, that insights begun to unfold.

Creating Your Ritual

What are the questions that are important to you? Write them down, explore them before meditating for a solid week, and you will feel them unfold in your life. (Remember: Don't bring these questions or their answers into your meditation.) After you have asked and answered (and sometimes there will be no answers) all these questions, simply release them. You can add emphasis to your letting go of them by physically releasing them. Take a long, slow, deep breath in and as you exhale, release them out into the universe.

Then meditate using whatever technique resonates with you most.

After meditating for your desired time, when you are in the most relaxed state possible, drift your awareness to The Five Secrets of the SweetSpot and effortlessly repeat each sutra for about a minute—patience, acceptance, defenselessness, compassion, abundance. After you've allowed abundance, the last sutra, to ripple into stillness, sit in silence for a few moments. Then seal your meditation by chanting *Om*, the universal vibration that heralds our one-ness. Let that settle for a few moments, slowly open your eyes, raise your hands to your heart, and bow to all your fellow meditators around the world who shared this collective consciousness with you. Then simply move into the rest of your day. You'll notice a perspective shift within two meditations!

The Five Secrets of the SweetSpot

1. Patience
2. Acceptance
3. Defenselessness
4. Compassion
5. Abundance

The Sacred Reflections

1. *What am I grateful for?*

2. *Why am I grateful?*

3. *What does my heart long for?*

4. *What is the essence that rests at my core?*

5. *How can I help others doing what I love?*

Using the Five Secrets of the SweetSpot *as Your Sacred Reflections*

Since infinite flexibility with your practice is so important, there's a way to merge your *Sacred Reflections* question-asking process **with** the *Five Secrets of the SweetSpot* sutra practice. The beauty of using a sutra format is that it is simple, straightforward, and easy to remember. The advanced version of this teaching is moving from a one-word sutra to a more formal question directed *at yourself.* Using the question format will invite you to go even deeper into the sutras and be even more introspective regarding your internal levels of patience, acceptance, defenselessness, compassion, and abundance. This in turn will begin to manifest in your waking state! I encourage you to try it both ways. (Whatever works!) Whichever method you decide to do, always settle in first for a few minutes. Ever so gently witness your breath as it moves in and out of you. Then, instead of asking the *Sacred Reflections*, use the sutras of *the Five Secrets of the SweetSpot* in the form of questions. Here's the process:

1.) Patience

First I ask myself *"How I can infuse myself with greater patience?"* Then I walk through a few situations and relationships in my mind in which I could be a bit more patient. This is where the stillness and silence that happens in my meditation integrates into my real life. Patience is a virtue, and when I am out of balance or overheated physically or emotionally, that virtue is usually in short supply.

Next, I walk through a few situations and relationships in my mind in which I could be a bit more patient—conversations or interactions where I was curt or short or bored or not fully present. Situations in which I left behind emotional toxicity rather than nurturing nectar because I was impatient. Then I see how I could change that—not go into the past but rather create the future!

We all have the ability to witness more and react less. By bringing your awareness to the concept of patience before and after meditation, you will be able to see yourself being patient (or not) as it's happening in the middle of a word, a thought, or an action. This is one of the keys to emotional intelligence—being able to receive information and process it without emotional charge. This will allow you to flow more easily with incoming information and respond with spontaneous right thought, word, or action.

2.) Acceptance

Next, I ask, *"How I can **accept** more?"* And I'll envision a situation in my life where I am resisting accepting something—maybe a material thing, maybe a potential experience, maybe a point of view. Perhaps I am in denial about my personal interpretation of that situation and I am refusing, repressing, or resisting seeing it in another light. Then I open myself to the other point of view and remind myself of the sutra *tat tvam asi—I am that*. Whether THAT is someone or something I adore or I detest, I am that! Everything I point at is a reflection of all my physical and emotional energy. Everyone is my mirror. Everything is what I love, hate, embrace, and resist. I must own them all. Things I resist are more manifested in my life because of the attention I place on resisting rather than accepting. How can I not accept that? How can I not accept me? How can I not allow acceptance to wash over me?

If it is a situation that I have been resisting, I ask if I am procrastinating or stalling. Am I putting off taking responsibility for issues that disturb my consciousness—unresolved issues of life, love, health, fulfillment, money, purpose? Am I ready to accept that everything in my life is exactly as it should be? I have the present moment to make amends and write the next chapter of my life. But to do that, I need to turn the page and know that the ink is dry. I must own my past. I must own the impact I have had. *I must accept that this moment is perfect* because every moment and every choice and every breath *that has led us to this very moment* is perfect.

3.) Defenselessness

The next question I ask is, *"Is there something I am **defending** right now? What is it I am defending? And why?"* Exploring the ego and examining the things you defend as one of the first things you reflect on in the morning can be very illuminating. After you've meditated, you will move into the day in a less defensive and more expansive space. Asking questions about what you defend will open you to aspects of yourself that others see but you are otherwise blind to—subtle defenses that only bubble up in the quiet moment they are questioned.

Why are we defending? What are we defending, really? Isn't this just a way for us to publicly or privately display our strength or power? Or to disguise our fear, our weaknesses, or our insecurities? When we defend, it's our chance to exhibit our knowledge of things we think we know or show our grasp of some information. And in most cases, it makes us even more rigid in our opinion. Yet, as the Buddhist nun Pema Chödrön teaches, "The truth you believe and cling to makes you unavailable to hear anything new."

Are you trying to hold on to something that perhaps no longer serves you? Maybe once it did, but now it doesn't. Or perhaps you're trying to put your mark on something that doesn't inherently bear your name. Like a dog marking its territory, you defend a piece of real or virtual turf. Maybe it was something you once prized, but now you don't see the value or thrill or importance of it anymore, yet you still defend it *to protect your past decisions*, your ego, your sense of Self. Don't worry, being defenseless is not about being weak. It's about being passive. Water is never weak; it is divinely passive. That is when we are at our best—when we are like water, surrendered, flowing effortlessly, passive, not weak . . . defenseless.

And throughout the day, let defenselessness ripple through your every thought, every word, every deed. Even when you become frustrated, angry, or aggravated in some way or you're struggling to get your point across, realize that through being defenseless, you can learn more about your universal Self, your cosmic being, your relationship with those in your life, and your soul, your atman. Others are more likely to listen to what you have to say when you don't feel the need to defend.

4.) Compassion

Next, I ask, *"How can I be more compassionate?" "Who do I have compassion for?" "Who do I not have compassion for?" "Why don't I have compassion for them?"* The world could be a very different place if people—all people—practiced just a bit more compassion, which I define as *a deep awareness of and empathy for another's suffering coupled with the wish to relieve it.* A compassionate person cultivates awareness for spotting the unique gifts and qualities that make each person special. A compassionate person sees the Divine in every set of eyes it gazes into. By seeing people in their most godlike state regardless of what else is going on, whether they are feeling full or at their lowest ebb, it is possible to help them restore their self-belief by keeping a firm, clear vision of their goodness and special talents.

Osho has often said that on the scale of love, sex is at the very bottom and compassion is at the very top. Thich Nhat Hanh, the Vietnamese Buddhist monk, teacher, and philosopher has said, "We practice in this way until we see clearly that our love is not contingent upon the other person apologizing or being lovable." And Albert Einstein is known to have said, "Our task must be to free ourselves . . . by widening our circle of compassion to embrace all living creatures and the whole of nature and its beauty."

Compassion is the doorway to freeing ourselves from our own suffering. When we can see ourselves in everyone else, we are able to see god within ourselves and the Divine in others. This is a one-ness that can permeate every moment.

5.) Abundance

The last questions I ask myself before going into meditation are, *"How much can I expand myself beyond my self-imposed limitations?" "How wide can I open my heart?" "How vast is the realm of spirit that flows through me?" "How can I grow beyond my limiting beliefs?"* If my goal is to be the best version of myself, better than last year, better than yesterday, better than five minutes ago, I can only get there by dying to the past and growing into the future regardless of how painful I imagine the process to be.

Can I open my heart so widely until it flows into my cosmic essence, bypassing my mind, my intellect, and my ego? How gently can I surrender to the practice to lead me into one-ness and into contact with my most universal Self? How open am I to expanding from individual to universal? And how can I open myself more readily, more easily, and more innocently to my understanding and surrender of ego, letting go of the need to apply meaning, my meaning, to every thought, sound, and physical sensation? How abundant can I become in this moment?

So when we use the *Five Secrets of the SweetSpot* as our *Sacred Reflections*, we always begin by asking questions and listening for universal answers. Sometimes answers will flow; other times, there will be no answers; and sometimes weeks from now an answer will flow to you in the least likely of circumstances. But simply asking a few questions establishes your dialogue with the universe. These are deep discussions and transformative conversations to have with yourself and the all-knowing unknown.

Asking these questions—even if there are no answers—plants very powerful seeds that ripple deep inside at the cellular level. Remember, where attention goes, energy flows, and simply placing your attention on the *Five Secrets* (or any five qualities you choose to evolve in your life) will have a transformational effect on your day when you come out of meditation. Your thoughts will be sprinkled with aspects of the Five Secrets, your words will begin to change, and your behaviors will see a subtle shift—*simply by asking the questions* and then letting them go.

That is the key. After we have sacredly reflected on these five aspects of your being, we take a long, slow deep breath in release all the questions and all the answers, and then begin meditating. If the conversation sparks up again in your meditation (and it will), ever so gently drift your awareness back to the object of your attention.

Let's stop reading for a few moments and experience the process of asking questions, waiting for answers, and then going into meditation with the *SweetSpot Sutra* meditation.

The SweetSpot Sutra Meditation

For this meditation, we'll practice *the Five Secrets of the SweetSpot* by asking a few sacred questions, letting answers flow, and then releasing all the questions and answers out into the cosmos, letting the universe work out all the details. Then begin repeating our mantra. The silent mantra we will use is *I AM*, which comes from the root of the verb *to be*. *I AM* is a state—you aren't actually doing; you are simply being.

We'll spend about five minutes total on this pre-meditation process. It goes like this: say the word *patience*, first out loud, then whispered, then repeat it once silently to yourself. Then we'll ask the question "Where could I use more patience?" etc.), close our eyes, wait a bit in silence for answers (or no answers), take a deep breath in, release whatever answers have come, and then move to *acceptance* and perform the same process, and so on. When we have asked, answered, breathed, and released for each of *the Five Secrets of the SweetSpot*, we take a deep breath in, release all the questions, answers, thoughts . . . whatever came . . . and let it all go.

It does not matter whether answers flow or not. All that matters is that you place your attention on these aspects of yourself. After about five minutes of this sutra practice, let go of all that you were thinking.

At that point with all the thoughts and intentions released into the ether, we close our eyes and begin silently repeating *I AM* over and over. When you notice you've drifted away from *I AM* to thoughts, sounds, or physical sensations, just gently drift back to *I AM*. Your meditation will be a gentle drifting back and forth between thoughts, sounds, sensations and *I AM*.

So let's begin by saying each Secret, first out loud, then whispered, then silently. Next, read the corresponding questions and close your eyes for a minute or two and let answers flow. Then open your eyes, move to the next set of questions, close your eyes, wait for answers, and so on. Let's begin by first taking a deep breath in, holding it, and letting it go. Now breathe normally and begin:

Patience: How can I be more patient? Is there something happening in my life in which I could use more patience? Is there an issue in which I could benefit from another's patience? (Ask and wait for answers for about one minute.)

Acceptance: How can I be more accepting? Is there something happening in my life in which I could use more acceptance? Is there an issue in which I could benefit from another's acceptance? (Ask and wait for answers for about one minute.)

Defenselessness: How can I be more defenseless? Is there something happening in my life in which I could use more defenselessness? Is there an issue in which I could benefit from another's defenselessness? (Ask and wait for answers for about one minute.)

Compassion: How can I be more compassionate? Is there something happening in my life in which I could use more compassion? Is there an issue in which I could benefit from another's compassion? (Ask and wait for answers for about one minute.)

Abundance: How can I be more abundant? Is there something happening in my life in which I could use a deeper sense of abundance? Is there a constriction that is limiting me? Is there an issue in which I could benefit from another's sense of expansion? (Ask and wait for answers for about one minute.)

Now drift your awareness to your heart or your solar plexus and plant a few intentions . . . whatever seeds you came up with. Whatever came up over those five minutes, plant those intentions deep within the fertile soil of your heart, or your transformation center in your solar plexus. Now take a deep breath in, feel them nestle themselves into the soil, and let go of all the questions, answers, and thoughts that you were just immersed in.

You have now connected with your own understanding of the Five Secrets of the SweetSpot. You have connected with your own ability to invite more patience, acceptance, defenselessness, compassion, and abundance in your life. You have planted it all within.

Now make sure you have let go of all those questions and all those answers or no answers (remember: it's about your attention and your intention, not about any answers that arrive or don't arrive) and begin repeating the mantra I AM. Slowly, repeat it out loud five times, then whisper it five times. And then begin repeating it silently to yourself without moving your lips or tongue. It's just a faint idea; it's not a clear pronunciation. You are not enunciating, you are passively listening to it.

As you continue to repeat it with less and less effort each time, surrender to the mantra. Don't try to pronounce it perfectly. Don't even say it . . . simply listen to it. It will change and get fast or slow, loud or faint, or become jumbled, distorted, or invisible. However it changes, be unconcerned and keep following it. Don't try to control it. Very shortly, sensations will drift away.

This is just about the point in the process where the control freak in us may start to give up or try to make the experience happen. Hang in there. Continue to repeat the mantra and feel the comfort of drifting back to it when you find yourself in thoughts, sounds, or physical sensations. I AM. I AM. I AM.

Start with 10 minutes and every few days add a few more minutes to the practice until you have reached 30 minutes. But for now, open your eyes after 10 minutes. Use the alarm on your cell phone to time yourself. Always feel free to chant Om to herald your universality before you open your eyes to end the practice.

You can do this for as little as 5 minutes or as long as you'd like up to 30 minutes. Longer than that is unnecessary unless you have drifted away and totally lose track of time. But don't feel the need to push beyond half an hour; after that you start to daydream. If you have the desire to meditate longer than this, try breaking it up into two rounds of 25 to 30 minutes.

Keep surrendering to the mantra and to the experience. It is as if you were in a new world and all you can do is observe it. Witness it. Receive the experience—don't feel the need to create the experience. You have all your other waking hours to create your life. Here in this moment where there is no agenda, and no trying, and no doing, and no reward for effort, rather than trying to make something happen, ALLOW it to happen. Allow it to unfold without imposing your rules. Let the universe bathe you with grace and ease. If you let it, it will all happen gently and tenderly. So don't feel the need to force or concentrate. That's all part of the *doing* mind-set. And if you're doing anything, you're doing too much. If you're trying anything . . . you're trying too hard.

The Secrets of the SweetSpot and the *Sacred Reflections* are the stepping stones to an effortless daily practice and the building blocks for living an expansive life. Of course, you can begin your practice with any ritual that feels comfortable. What are the questions that are important to you? Write them down and explore them before meditating for a solid week and you will feel them unfold in your life.

CHAPTER 10

SECRETS OF SENSORY MEDITATION

"We should be blessed if we lived in the present always, and took advantage of every accident that befell us, like the grass which confesses the influence of the slightest dew that falls on it; and did not spend our time in atoning for the neglect of past opportunities, which we call doing our duty. We loiter in winter while it is already spring."

— HENRY DAVID THOREAU

Sensory meditation focuses on taking in the world around you through your body and celebrates being present to a particular sensory experience. Sensory meditation uses one or several of the five senses—listening to sounds, soft gazing, inhaling aromas, feeling with your hands or other body parts, and tasting—to fully experience the present moment. By allowing the sensations of a particular sensory organ to become the object of attention, the messages transmitted by our other sensory organs just drift away. The sense becomes an overt conduit for all information coming into your body, and all your thoughts melt into the precious present moment as it unfolds.

Through this practice, you can learn how to develop a deeper awareness using your senses. In time, this awareness will offer you insights into an aspect of yourself that rests beneath your senses—your energetic Self—known in Sanskrit as the *pranamaya kosha*. Literally, *prana* means vital energy, *maya* means illusion, and *kosha* means layer. This aspect of yourself is the illusionary layer of vital energy!

We've already explored the secrets of sound and sight meditation in a specific practice, yet we have the ability in every moment to simply witness through our ears and eyes and experience the same object with new eyes and new ears! Take a few moments for the next few days and stop . . . look around . . . fix your gaze on something either very familiar or something totally unfamiliar and stay with it for several minutes. Keep using it as a drishti, and immerse into its being with a soft gaze, merging yourself into its shape, texture, pattern, structure, color, thickness, density, relationship to things next to it, and its essence. Additionally, over the next several days, do this with sounds you hear. You can use only sounds of nature—birdcalls, the rustling of leaves in the wind, rain falling, dogs barking, the splashing of ocean waves. Or allow any sound to become the object of your attention, including train whistles, car horns, leaf blowers, plane engines, and highway traffic. They are all simply vibrations.

"Clarity. Clarity of vision.
What you've been looking at from the
wrong angle and not seeing at all."

— THE EDGE, U2

Aroma and tasting meditations are more like experiential immersions rather than meditations, but they can be a sweet doorway to present-moment awareness. In aroma meditations, the object of your attention is your nose and the gentle breath that wafts into your nostrils. This inhalant can be anything: the earthy aromas of a pine- or cedar-filled forest; the intense, snaking smoke ribbon of incense; the subtle, intoxicating fragrance of essential oils; the salty mist of the ocean air; the aromatic bouquet that lifts off a copper karahi sizzling a curry; even the comforting first whiffs of our morning coffee brewing.

Secrets of Aroma Meditation

Our connection to smells and their meanings are carved into our nervous system. Olfaction is our most primal sense and in a nano-second can trigger memories of our grandmother's freshly baked cookies, our grade-school teacher's perfume, or the musty cabin of our childhood summer camp. And we can also use distinct aromas to fully enter the present moment for short periods of time.

In an aroma meditation you can immerse yourself in one scent or in a series of aromas so you can better experience the depth of a particular smell by comparing it to another. This process awakens aspects of your nasal receptors that you may not have experienced before. And it will consistently provide you with short bursts of present-moment awareness, though rarely one-ness.

The nose is so delicate that after extended periods of aroma immersion, our sensors become saturated, and we start to hit a sensory threshold. The complexity of that first inhalation becomes more subtle, and the intensity can only be recaptured after stepping away from the aroma for a while and letting our smelling ability "recharge." Another way to do this is to experience a flow of multiple smells, such as diverse and aromatic spices, herbs, or oils. But even with changing aromas, very quickly you hit the saturation point, and one smell bleeds into another.

At my first Ayurvedic cooking class, our chef cooked us through a guided meditation of all the spices used in his *masala*, a word that means "mixture" in Hindi, Urdu, and Bengali. Six of us sat in front of his cooking island, and he poured the raw ingredients one by one into our palms as we inhaled with our eyes closed. Then he poured the same ingredient into a sauté pan over a high flame and toasted it so the nutty, sharper quality of the spice filled the air. Next, he added a splash of oil and the aroma changed one more time, becoming sweeter, richer, and in some cases, cloying. He proceeded to guide us in this awakening the senses meditation with a magnificent spice parade of white peppercorns, cloves, malabar leaves, pippali (long pepper), black cumin (known as *shahi jeera*), cumin seeds, cinnamon, green cardamom, nutmeg, star anise, and coriander seeds. With our eyes closed, we simply breathed first the raw, then the toasted, and then the sautéed spice. We sat and breathed with big smiles on our faces as the atmospheric quality of the room and our consciousness transformed with each spice, generating a new wave of aromatic awareness.

Secrets of Tasting Meditations

After we had been enticed with the spices, we dined on one of the most delicious meals I have ever tasted. The depth of flavor in each bite carried with it the subtlety of each phase of the spice's evolution within the cooking process. In its final form as a masala, each spice had its own flavor as well as its interplay with each of the other spices and the merged flavor! With each bite . . . with each inhalation . . . I was so absorbed into the moment that time stood still. Every time I dine on Indian food (which sometimes is weekly), I experience a precious waft of that present-moment awareness infused with an aroma that carries with it the laughter and bliss of that meditation. Our senses of taste and smell are so primal, they can instantly transport us back to the moment and we will experience the same physiological sensations and emotions that we did the very first time. Whenever I smell any of those raw spices, I smile and feel comforted.

You can eat mindfully pretty easily no matter what you eat or where. Try it at an upcoming meal—truly savoring each bite, each chew, and each swallow. I encourage you to eat one meal a week in silence with no TV, no talking, no music, no reading material—just you and the food before you.

The challenge of quickly overloading a sense organ is also true for tasting food, which is why champagne meditations and chocolate meditations have become so popular. You have to take baby steps, slowly savoring each inhalation, taste, sip, chew, lick, and swallow while staying totally mindful in the process. Living the sizzly tickle of a bubbly drop sliding down your throat, or feeling a chocolate truffle collapse on your tongue as the masala of earthy flavors melts into your being, the taste, the aroma, and the ritual all act as the object of your attention. In a chocolate-tasting meditation, you can delicately savor a truffle or another fine piece of chocolate as if it were the last piece of chocolate on earth, truly taking your time to feel its textures, density, aromas, complexity of flavors, and intricacy of fragrances as it slowly melts in your mouth until *you become* the chocolate . . . and it becomes you. When your attention drifts away to thoughts or sounds, ever so gently drift back to the liquefying of the chocolate on your tongue. You can perform this meditation alone or with others. I like to celebrate/meditate in this way at least once a week.

So even in mindful eating there is an *A-ha!* moment—that very first moment when the sumptuousness of the flavor explodes on your tongue or as the aroma first hits the back of your nose—and in the melting process as the flavors/aromas shift, evolve, and transform. But ultimately, the present moment experience ends as the flavors and sensations of the last morsel become a sweet memory.

Yet even if these immersions don't provide the longer-lasting benefits of a non-sensory meditation practice, they still offer value: a fun way to be present. As long as you consciously stay mindful during these types of experiences—eating and drinking mind-fully—they will nourish you and reinforce your ability to more consciously witness yourself and life. When we are able to more consistently witness our behaviors, we can see our non-nourishing behaviors in a more objective light, and rather than being defensive, we can then make more conscious, life-affirming choices.

Body Meditations

Mindfulness meditation, to a certain extent, is a "body" meditation, because you are taking in energy and information from all your senses—hearing, seeing, smelling, tasting, breathing—and feeling everything in your body that you can feel, including the largest organ, your skin. And, watching your breath as it moves in and out, has a certain sense of *activity* to it. But there are also more intimate physical forms of meditation that involve the connection between two people, such as partner yoga, massage, and lovemaking.

A gifted massage therapist can open up, step out of the way, and channel the universe in a dynamic exchange of energy between themselves and the object of their attention. Giving someone a massage can even be a meditation in itself for the giver. Surrendering to the nurturing and healing touch of massage treatment is one of the most stress-relieving things you can do as you open your physiology and your heart. Receiving a massage is a fully present-moment awareness experience. Regardless of where your mind wanders, you are continuously brought back to the object of your attention: wherever you are being touched in a given moment and whatever energetic or emotional connection the sensation of touch triggers.

There are thousands of books and videos on massage, but over the last 15 years, I have become most familiar with traditional Ayurvedic massage, which uses warm, herb-infused oil designed to balance one's mind-body personality. I am also a devotee of Thai massage, which is most often practiced clothed. It is similar to having someone do yoga *to* you. Your Thai massage therapist actually moves you into positions akin to yoga asanas and then holds you in those positions as you breathe into them. Slowly and effortlessly you stretch, millimeter by millimeter, further than you otherwise thought you could. Stretch your body . . . stretch your mind . . . stretch your heart. And it is very easy under these circumstances to fully surrender to the present moment.

Partner yoga has gained popularity over the years, inspiring such powerful offshoots as family yoga and contact yoga. *Contact Yoga*, based on the healing power of love and intimacy, was founded by American yogini and philanthropist Tara Lynda Guber, who also created Yoga Ed., the nationally recognized yoga-for-schools program. Contact Yoga acts as a powerful body meditation as you use partnering poses to explore *relationship* in your life— your deepest patterns of connecting and distancing, loving and protecting, giving and receiving—patterns that usually remain unconscious until they are brought into the light of a yoga practice.

The Yoga of Sex

For thousands of years, sex, the act of lovemaking, even the moment of orgasm have all been described as meditative experiences because of the wave of present-moment awareness that can sweep through the participants. Lovemaking can be a meditation if the shared focus is the present-moment journey and not the destination, moving from an expectation to the preciousness of each moment, where the object of your attention is each breath and every physical movement you experience. In that kind of atmosphere, the practice takes on a powerful body*mind* connection as our physical experience flows into an emotional experience. The moment of orgasm has been defined as pure, present-moment awareness, where your thoughts are not in the past or future but in the now! Unfortunately, that present moment only lasts a few moments, but the actual act of lovemaking can last for hours, keeping the present moment alive as each lover moves through wave after wave of merging two physical bodies into one. The ancient Hindu treatise on sexual behaviors known as *The Kama Sutra* is considered the most well-known guide on love, lovemaking, and the sexual act. Sexual meditation is essentially a form of body-centered restful awareness that is a fusion of static and dynamic prana, or life force, within our bodies. Although nourishing chemicals and nurturing hormones serotonin and oxytocin are released into the bloodstream during this sensory voyage, it is one of personal, physical activity—and *paying attention to the internal and eternal activity* rather than of stillness.

Tantric Meditation

The wise sage Osho once said, "Yoga is suppression with awareness; tantra is indulgence with awareness." Tantra is a body of ritualized spiritual mysticism and esoteric study that has survived for millennia. Tantra is historically not a single coherent system but rather a school of thought, almost tribal in nature, within both Hinduism and Buddhism. Tantra deals primarily with spiritual practices and ritual forms of worship that aim at liberation from ignorance and *samsara* (the cycle of rebirth). Several obscure offshoots of Hindu tantra have embraced sensory celebration and sexual meditations as ways to expand, grow, and achieve higher states of consciousness. In fact, the Sanskrit word "tantra" comes from two Sanskrit words: *tanoti*—"stretch" or "expand," and *trayati*—"liberation."

The science of tantra has two main branches or paths: *vama marga* (the "left-hand way") and *dakshina marga* (the "right-hand way"). Vama marga, the left path, combines sexual life with yoga practices in order to connect the energy of the universe with the primal energy within us. Dakshina marga, the right path, is yoga without sexual connection. In several left-path Tantric sects, various sexual practices and rituals are described in detail as devotional offerings to the goddess Shakti. One ritual is participating in the sexual rites of vamamarga, a fusion of masculine and feminine energies leading to an ecstatic spiritual experience. The seamless fusion of opposing sacred energies (creating one-ness) is considered a path to enlightenment, and the *non*physical, spiritual orgasm that occurs is a glimpse of this higher state of consciousness . . . one of pure bliss.

The sexual union practices of early Hindu tantra known in Sanskrit as *maithuna* (pronounced *my-t'huna*) were designed for practitioners to evolve their personal sexual energy into sacred energy and to then achieve higher states of physical and spiritual awareness as they exchanged this sacred energy. As the two prac- titioners move deeper into maithuna, they reach ecstatic sexual states and lock into what is referred to as a static embrace. The orgasm in this ritual takes place when the transfer of *spiritual* energy between the two practitioners culminates in the union of their subtle bodies. There is no physical ejaculation but a merging into one-ness of the Shiva (masculine) and Shakti (feminine) ener- gies between the two of them.

Long ago, many of these Tantric rituals shifted from sexual practices in the physical realm to a more metaphorical and metaphysical practice without actual sexual penetration. It should also be noted that historically only a minority of Tantric sects practiced sexual rites. Yet, our culture has embraced the misconception that tantra is all about sex. Modern tantra expressions celebrate cosmic consciousness through sensory pleasure. A powerful form of tantric sexual meditation is about awakening the god or goddess within—your most divine sensual aspect—giving yourself to another person in a devotional way and taking the time . . . until time stands still . . . to use your senses to exchange energy with one another, merging two beings into one while you are both totally present. Regardless of what you choose to share, Tantric meditations are all about giving to one another and making sure that your bodies, minds, and spirits are on the same path.

As two people begin the practice of a lovemaking meditation, they set the intention for the experience to be a sacred journey in which they witness their own feelings and emotions, those of their partner, and the union of the two. This intention of sacredness and an ongoing awareness of each other's breaths, the rise and fall of each other's bellies, moisture awakening on the skin, the sound and sensation of the rapid beating of each other's hearts, words spoken and unspoken, the most subtle of aromas, tastes, and healing touch will move the couple to a higher plane of individual, empathetic, and collective consciousness. The sense of spiritual one-ness experienced when two people merge intimately into each other is akin to any *A-ha!* moment one can have. Just touching this level of unity once will help a couple move their relationship to a higher plane of existence. If nothing else, as you explore your emotions, your senses, and your sense of Self with your partner through Tantric meditation, you will understand yourself better, and that is the perfect starting point for cultivating a relationship with another being. This is a wonderful meditation to use to strengthen and enhance your relationship with yourself as well as with your partner.

How Does Yoga Relate to Meditation?

Yoga means union. Therefore, yoga is meditation. And meditation is yoga. Any practice that brings about a state of present-moment awareness or a stilling of the mind is a form of meditation: that moment during running or cycling or swimming or dancing or riding a roller coaster, or practicing the eight limbs of yoga. That moment when you are totally present . . . in which there is no past or future, in which time has no meaning, where there is no thought, when you are totally in the zone . . . that moment when you are in total sync with your body, your mind, the moment, the universe. There is only a state of pure present-moment awareness. It is this one-ness that is the true definition of yoga—pure being, pure unity.

Most people think of yoga in terms of a physical practice that occurs on a mat in which you move your body into postures or poses known in Sanskrit as "asanas" (pronounced *AH-sah-nah*). Then, depending on your school of practice and your philosophical orientation, you "live" the pose and then flow to the next. Each school of yoga spends varying amounts of time in the pose and also focuses on a select few of the hundreds of asanas. In this context, yoga has the ability to harness that dynamic interplay between stillness and activity. You breathe into the pose . . . you become the pose . . . you let yourself *be*. Asana is a beautiful expression of *consciousness in motion*.

But then you get back into the physical world and change poses. And then you change poses again. Over time, virtually every student of yoga develops an evolved homeostasis in the body's internal rhythms leading to better flexibility, focus, and balance; increased physical and mental confidence; often greater patience; increased strength; and powerful easing of the symptoms of PMS and of pre-, peri-, menopause, and post-menopause.

Science Now Confirms . . .

Research performed in 2010–2012 by the *National Institute of Health* demonstrated that hatha yoga can be an effective practice for healing lower back pain. And a 2016 study published in the *Journal of the American Medical Association*, compared 340 test subjects with back pain after eight weeks of three different therapies: (1) ibuprofen and pain medications (2) cognitive therapy, and (3) yoga and meditation. At the end of the eight weeks, it was the groups who had cognitive therapy and yoga/meditation practice that reported 50 percent less pain versus the group taking pills. According to Memorial Sloan Kettering Cancer Center, "yoga improves the quality of life in both newly diagnosed and long-term cancer survivors by reducing stress and fatigue, and improving sleep and mood."

The *Meditation Room* section of davidji.com is continuously updated with the most cutting edge scientific studies and clinical trials on yoga and meditation—especially for pain treatment. I invite you to visit and check out the various studies we post and search the web for "yoga pain study" or "yoga cancer study" and *thousands* of links will appear in the search results.

There are so many types of yoga classes, though stillness and silence during the practice is usually *not* where most teachers take you during yoga class. But there are great teachers who give you permission to explore your being. And there are talented and intuitive teachers who can guide you to powerful experiences that open you, center you, relax you, invigorate you, awaken you, soften you, and expand you; this is why yoga is referred to as a practice of body-centered restful awareness.

Infinite Flexibility

Any practice that adds value to your life is worth exploring. For more than 20 years, I have been a practitioner, and student, of myriad yogic practices from the four main paths of yoga: *raja, bhakti, karma,* and *gyan*. During my first Teacher Training when I was certified as a 200-hour yoga teacher, most of the students in my class had no intention to ever teach. They simply wanted to deepen their yoga practice. Over the past 15 years I've noticed a similar trajectory in meditation. Most meditation teachers-in-training take that route—not to teach others but to better understand and ingrain their own meditation practice. I honor any student of any age or philosophy who ventures into a yoga studio. Whether it's Kundalini, Anusara, Ashtanga, Bikram, Jivamukti, Iyengar, Vini-Flow, Swaroopa, hot yoga, Joe's yoga, or your own lying on the floor in your living room watching a video! The key is engaging in the practice.

Many schools of yoga emphasize a physical workout or achieving perfect poses, which build strength, flexibility, and balance yet keep us more focused in the physical realm. Other schools place greater emphasis on going deep into one's soul while in a particular pose rather than achieving perfection in the asana, shifting your awareness back and forth between silent stillness and dynamic physical activity.

Many styles of yoga incorporate a series of flowing asanas known as sun salutations, or *surya namaskar* in Sanskrit. But even during sun salutations, our moments of restful awareness are consistently brought back into the physical realm; if we are surrendering to the practice in a way that honors the original teachings, it's distinctly the present moment.

Throughout any yoga practice, the fact that the practice is *body centered* keeps the practice in the physical realm. When we think of yoga we envision someone practicing an asana. But the practice of asana is only one aspect of yoga, which is a broad philosophy that encompasses all aspects of life. In the raja (royal) yoga tradition that developed in ancient India, the great yogic teacher, sage, and wisdom translator Patanjali defined yoga as yoga citta vritti nirodha, *the progressive quieting of the fluctuations of the mind.*

Yoga's Eight Limbs

It was more than 2,000 years ago that the sage Patanjali wrote down the foundations of yoga philosophy in *The Yoga Sutras*. This sacred text describes an eight-limbed path that forms the structural framework for a program of right living. None of the eight branches of the tree is more important than any another, each being a part of a holistic regimen that brings a person into total wholeness of body, mind, and soul.

According to Patanjali, the *asanas* are just one of eight limbs of yoga, but there are seven others that are as important. The eight limbs (known in Sanskrit as *ashtanga; ash = eight; tanga = limbs*) are:

1. *Yama:* ENLIGHTENED CONDUCT (Behavior)

The yamas are a universal code of commandments or moral imperatives (essentially the DO-NOTs) that describe evolutionary behavior or how enlightened beings should live. In Sanskrit yama means death. The yamas are essentially the way we bring about compassionate death to our ego. In the ancient Indian texts, The Upanishads, they have been referred to as the "restraints." There are five yamas:

    i.   *ahimsa:* nonviolence

    ii. *satya:* truth in word and thought

    iii. *asteya:* nonstealing

    iv. *brahmacharya:* conscious choice-making regarding intimate behavior (traditionally Brahmacharya is associated with celibacy or *"thou shalt not have sex,"* but I prefer to see it as *"let us pay attention to the choices we make in our relationships"*)

    v. *aparigraha:* non-coveting or absence of greed—essentially, gratitude for what we *do* have

2. *Niyama:* PERSONAL OBSERVANCES (Choices)

The niyamas are the prescribed actions and personal observances that reflect the internal dialogue of conscious people. If the yamas are the *Universal* DO NOTs, the niyamas are the *Personal* DOs. These observances include practices and teachings for making the most evolutionary personal choices in life. Historically, the niyamas are:

i.   *shaucha:* cleanliness of body and mind

ii. *santosha:* contentment with what one has

iii. *tapas:* austerity

iv. *svādhyāya:* study of the Vedic scriptures to better know the Self; (essentially *Self-study*)

v.   *ishvarapranidhana:* surrender to God or connecting more deeply with your higher power

Tradition dictates that the yamas and niyamas are foundational observances to master along this path of awakening to our true Self.

3. *Asana:* BODY POSTURES OR POSES

The intimate relationship between our personal and extended bodies. Feel free to pick the asana philosophy that resonates most with you from challenging poses to chair yoga and everything in between!

4. *Pranayama:* BREATHING EXERCISES AND CONTROL OF PRANA (vital energy)

Awareness and integration of the rhythms, seasons, and cycles of our life.

5. *Pratyahara:* CONTROL OF THE SENSES

By withdrawing our five senses, we can tune into our subtle sensory experiences—seeing beyond our eyes, hearing without our ears, smelling without our nose, tasting without our mouth, and feeling without our body.

6. *Dharana:* CONCENTRATION

Attention is the very first step in the process of meditating: fixing your consciousness on one point or region and cultivating our ability to hold that attention steady without being distracted from it. Dharana is the evolutionary expression of attention and is the active practice of refining one's ability to maintain a single point of focus.

7. *Dhyana:* CULTIVATING INNER PERCEPTUAL AWARENESS

The second step in the process of meditating—*once attention has been mastered*—is the non-judgmental observation of that object. It's one thing to place your attention on a fixed object, it's another thing to then observe it continuously with no judgment. Patanjali referred to this as meditation, essentially when the act of concentrating becomes perfected and *there is no longer the need to try or do* in order to connect one to a non-dualistic state of consciousness, to the junction between the personal and the universal aspects of our being.

8. *Samadhi:* UNION WITH THE DIVINE

Samadhi is the third piece of the meditative practice once *Dharana* and *Dhyana* have been mastered. Once you have cultivated attention and meditation skills, samadhi is one-ness—*the progressive expansion of the Self.*

These last three branches of yoga are historically referred to as *samyama* (which is translated as binding up or tying together). Essentially, three of the eight limbs of yoga are about meditation. So there is actually historical linkage that shows yoga is meditation and meditation is yoga!

Yoga is a rich, broad, beautiful fabric that weaves through every aspect of existence . . . our physical bodies, our environment, our mind, intellect, ego, emotional being, our daily interactions, and our spiritual Self—our soul. Yoga connects them all through the practice of the eight limbs. The next time the word *yoga* flows into your awareness, expand your perception beyond the concept of asana to include the other seven limbs. Then you'll truly be practicing yoga on and off the mat.

Although the physical and emotional benefits of a daily yoga practice are well documented and are a magnificent foundation for personal healing, stress-release, and creating a mindful state of living, we must remember that the practice of *asana* always keeps us in activity. Even when practicing the most spiritual or meditative type of asana, *the body-centric nature of the practice still keeps us in activity.* Yoga is essentially consciousness in motion! So unless, your savasana (the final pose of the practice—also referred to as corpse pose), contains an extended period of stillness and silence (no talking, no music), you will not receive the scientifically recognized long-term benefits of a meditation practice. It is only during meditation that we truly transcend activity to experience stillness and silence. Meditation creates that *passive state of awareness*—the pure experience in which we are neither in the past nor in the future but are solidly immersed in the present moment.

SECRETS OF BUDDHIST MEDITATION

*"There is no need for temples, no need for
complicated philosophies. My brain and my heart
are my temples; my philosophy is kindness."*

— HIS HOLINESS, THE 14TH DALAI LAMA

Prince Siddhartha (which means "he who achieves his aim")
Gautama, commonly referred to as the Buddha or "one who is
awake," is said to have lived approximately 2,500 years ago. His
father, Śuddhodana, was the ruler of the Shakyas, a large clan or
group of tribes during the 5th century B.C. Tradition tells us that
Siddhartha was born in the town of Lumbini, located in what we
now refer to as Nepal. During the first few days of Siddhartha's
birth, an oracle visited Suddhodana and told him that his son
would either be a great king or spiritual sage. The story continues
that the father, desiring his son to be a great king, shielded him
from anything that would derail that path. So Siddhartha was kept
away from all religious and spiritual teachings and any suffering
that could be experienced in the outside world. At the age of 29,
after being protected from the darker aspects of the outside world
for almost three decades, the young Siddhartha ventured out
beyond the palace walls for the very first time and witnessed a
whole new reality—one of suffering, aging, illness, and death. This
totally blew his mind! So he left the protective walls of his father's
palace and set off on his own journey of discovery initially intent
on transcending the pain of these realities of life. This led him
to choose a path of poverty, withdrawal from all worldly desires,
self-denial of earthly pleasures, and self-starvation. He dedicated

himself to a life of austerity, asceticism, and meditation. Of course this created a very thin and austere meditator.

One day when he was close to the point of death through self-starvation, a young girl offered him a bowl of rice, and he accepted it. At that moment, he realized that severe austerity would not lead to enlightenment. From then on, Siddhartha encouraged people to follow a path he called "the middle way"—devotion to moderation between the extremes of self-indulgence and self-denial. His followers became disengaged, believing he had lost his focus and lost his mind. So they left him.

That night he sat under a pipal tree, meditating in the north Indian town of Bodhgaya, vowing not to stop until he had attained Truth. He practiced *anapanasati*, a meditation practice in which you focus your awareness on following your breath in and out. (Sounds like mindfulness to me!) After meditating for 49 days, he experienced enlightenment at the age of 35. From that point on, he was known as the Buddha—*the awakened one*. Stories are told that because Buddha had no witnesses to the enlightenment that came to him during that meditation, he moved his right hand down from his lap and touched the ground beneath his folded knee so the earth could be his witness. This is why you often see statues and paintings of the Buddha meditating with his right hand reaching down from his knee.

After achieving enlightenment, the Buddha spent four months each year with his monks, discussing and practicing his teachings. After his death, his followers shared these teachings, at first by continuing the oral tradition and then by writing them down. Buddhism has flourished in many areas of the world, and its philosophy and practices have become increasingly popular in the Western world as people recognize their value, wisdom, and practicality.

What's It All About?

You don't have to be a Buddhist to practice Buddhist meditations. At no point during a Buddhist meditation is it required or requested that you pray to the Buddha or believe in the teachings of the Buddha. In fact, all Buddhist meditations are about attention and mindful awareness, not about worshipping a person or a deity. Buddhist meditations can even help you get closer to Jesus Christ or whomever your higher power is, through the doorway of compassion.

The core of Buddhist teachings is what is known as the Four Noble Truths (*ariya sacca*), and they are simply:

1. ***The nature of Suffering***, or *dukkha*, is the suffering that is a predominant experience in life. More specifically, dukkha is the unsatisfying nature of our ever-changing life and the short-lived, transient nature of all things.

2. ***The root of Suffering***, or *dukkha samudaya*, is our clinging to desires, *resisting* the reality of an ever-changing existence.

3. ***The cessation of Suffering***, or *dukkha nirodha*, comes about through ceasing to cling—the powerful act of letting go of our attachments to outcomes and no longer trying to keep things the same.

4. ***The path leading to the cessation of Suffering***, or *dukkha nirodha gamini patipada magga*, can be attained by practicing the ***Noble Eightfold Path*** *(ariyo aṭṭhaṅgiko maggo)*, which describes eight core characteristics to embrace to end our suffering.

The Noble Eightfold Path is a practical guideline for an individual's spiritual, moral, and mental development. Buddha instructed if you live each day with these eight characteristics as your guiding principles, you transcend the conditioned attachments, illusions, and delusions that create suffering in your life.

Following these guidelines leads to a deeper understanding of all things, which includes the expansion of:

wisdom through:
1) right view, and,
2) right intention

moral conduct through:
3) right speech,
4) right action, and,
5) right livelihood

mental development through:
6) right effort,
7) right mindfulness, and,
8) right concentration.

According to Buddhism, practicing the guidelines of the Eightfold Path in daily life while having a deep understanding of the *Four Noble Truths* is how one attains a higher level of existence and ultimately reaches Nirvana, a state of union with all things—Buddhism's version of one-ness.

Practicing a Buddhist meditation is simply resonating with the vibrations of the universe through the guidance of one of the most amazing teachers to have ever lived and connecting to his traits of peaceful coexistence and unconditional love, as well as expressing compassion and loving-kindness to others. This would seem to support the tenets of Christianity, Islam, Judaism, Hinduism, Jainism, Sikhism, Taoism, Confucianism, Sufism, even atheism . . . and even the most fundamental or detached expressions of devotion to a higher power.

The Bhavanas

The primary purpose of Buddhist meditation is to train the mind to slow down and ultimately, be still. The Buddhist term for meditation is *bhavana*, or "mental cultivation," and the three most well-known bhavanas are:

(1) *metta*—loving-kindness, (2) *samatha*—tranquility, and (3) *vipassana*—insight. Let's explore each of these.

1. METTA—LOVING-KINDNESS

In *metta bhavana*, you concentrate on sending out *metta*, translated as unconditional loving-kindness, to all living beings. In metta meditative exercises, my personal technique is to start with directing thoughts of benevolence, love, and compassion *inward*. Although self-directed loving-kindness was never specifically instructed by the Buddha, I have found that starting the meditation this way quickly engages and empowers me by providing a very clear object of attention. I have asked Master metta practitioners, Buddhist monks, and even His Holiness, The Dalai Lama, if self-directing metta is acceptable in starting a metta meditation, and they have all assured me that other Buddhist writings imply that it may be an appropriate start to the practice.

The 13th-century, Sufi poet Hafiz wrote, "I am a hole in the flute through which the Christ breath flows." And if you can see yourself as conduit of *metta*—not the flute and not the breath—but simply as a hole, a channel, a conduit, an empty pathway, then you can flow unconditional loving-kindness in and flow it back out without becoming attached to it. We use our breath as the vehicle to transport metta *first* into our heart *and then* back out to others, using your heart as a point of reference for gradually radiating loving-kindness outward.

The Practice

First, you take a long, slow deep breath in of metta and feel it fill your heart. Then you flow it back out to those you deeply respect, such as your most revered teachers or life guides. Next, take a long, slow deep breath in of metta and feel it fill your heart, then radiate loving-kindness to your loved ones—those living and those who've left this earthly realm. Then take a long, slow deep breath in of metta and feel it fill your heart, and then radiate it out to your friends. Then take a long, slow deep breath in of metta and feel it fill your heart, and shower it onto someone you know who may be suffering. Next, take a long, slow deep breath in of metta and feel it fill your heart, and then send it to someone with whom you have a grievance. (I often do that one twice to expand my capacity for forgiveness, acceptance, and compassion.) Then take a long, slow deep breath in of metta and feel it fill your heart, and radiate it out to all sentient beings on the planet. Notice that as you continue to expand your circle of loving-kindness, you direct metta to your most intimate relationships, to your enemies, and finally toward all beings on the planet. At a certain point in the practice, you realize you are simply a conduit of love, that your heart is just bursting with metta, and you've got enough love inside for the whole world!

It's at this point that I take a long, slow deep breath in of metta, feel it fill my heart and then radiate that love out into the universe, sending it to every corner of the galaxy. I stay in that space, breathing it in from every nook and cranny of the cosmos and then radiating it back out so it has no limits. I can sit in a space like this for 30 minutes, opening my heart, feeling gratitude in every cell of my body, flowing forgiveness, and feeling self-love . . . self-compassion . . . self-forgiveness . . . ripple through me.

I have found metta meditation to be a very nourishing practice. Both first-time meditators and seasoned meditators alike appreciate its simple sweetness and its powerful softening ability. If you are holding a grudge, carrying around anger, overwhelmed with sadness, or find yourself pointing fingers, the metta bhavana will transform you to a healing state very quickly.

The ancient Buddhist teachings suggest that one should master metta bhavana before moving on to any other type of meditation. Interesting, right?

Always start with your heart. I recommend that you take your time cultivating this practice. Start with just five minutes, get comfortable there, and simply slow each phase of the process down until the conduit of your heart flows in and out in slow motion. Over time, see if you can stretch it to 10, then 15 minutes—the perfect amount of time to receive the optimal benefits of a heart-opening practice.

After a few weeks of practicing this teaching, the metta meditation will become the gentle way you start your day. You'll quickly notice that your heart is more open, you are more tolerant of irritations around you, and you have a ripple of a smile flowing through every word, thought, and action. You'll also realize that it is a pure present-moment experience to help you connect to your essence.

2. SAMATHA—TRANQUILITY

Samatha bhavana is the practice of bringing about calm to the mind through single-mindedness of concentration. *Samatha* can be translated as calm, peace, or tranquility. The meditator focuses on one object or action, such as witnessing your breathing or soft-gazing at a drishti point. Samatha bhavana practitioners believe that by concentrating on just one thing for an extended period of time, the mind will become stilled to the point of calmness and *tranquility*, hence the name samatha. *Samatha bhavana is specifically designed to cultivate your abilities of concentration* and thought to prepare the mind for the third type of Buddhist bhavana, *vipassana*, or insight meditation. Master Buddhist meditators advise spending years cultivating the mind through samatha bhavana before moving on to vipassana, the more advanced bhavana. The key to any physical practice, fitness exercise, or sport—whether you are lifting weights, running, climbing, swimming, dancing, or cycling—is to strengthen the bodymind. And for Buddhist meditations that exercise is samatha. Yet, as American Buddhism has flourished over the past 40 years, attention on samatha bhavana has withered and vipassana has thrived because the high achiever in us wants to skip ahead to the end result without taking the time to practice and really cultivate our ability of concentration. But this method is revered because this type of meditation technique was first used by the Buddha to cultivate *his own* concentration.

One of the more common forms of samatha bhavana is using a basic visual object of attention known as a *kasina*. There are 10 *kasina* mentioned in the ancient Buddhist scripture known as the *Pali Tipitaka*:

1. earth *(paṭhavī kasiṇa)*

2. water *(āpo kasiṇa)*

3. fire *(tejo kasiṇa)*

4. air, wind *(vāyo kasiṇa)*

5. blue, green *(nīla kasiṇa)*

6. yellow *(pīta kasiṇa)*

7. red *(lohita kasiṇa)*

8. white *(odāta kasiṇa)*

9. enclosed space, hole, opening *(ākāsa kasiṇa)*

10. consciousness *(viññāṇa kasiṇa)* or a bright light *(āloka kasiṇa)*

The *kasiṇa* is typically described as a colored disk, with the particular color, properties, and dimensions based on which kasina is being used as the object of attention. In the beginning stages of kasina meditation, an actual physical object is used as the object of concentration. For example, to meditate using the earth *kasiṇa,* you'd paint or draw a red-brown circle on a canvas or piece of paper, or find a chunk of earth or clay to gaze at—even the top of a hill or mountain in the distance will work as long as there are no moving objects between you and the kasina. Then you softly gaze at it, similar to a Drishti meditation, which we discussed in Chapter 6.

In time, as you become more advanced in your concentration abilities, after gazing at the image for 10 minutes, you would take the training wheels off and close your eyes allowing the mental image snapshot to reproduce itself in your mind's eye. Once you have cultivated samatha kasina meditation, you simply close your eyes as you begin your meditation and recall the image into your awareness—similar to the practice of Sri Yantra. Try it right now. Select one of the 10 kasina and simply close your eyes and gaze at your version of the image in your mind. When you drift into thought, gently drift your attention back to the kasina. Do it for a minute and I'll wait right here.

Pretty easy, right?

3. Vipassana—Insight

Now that you have opened your heart through metta bhavana and calmed your mind and cultivated your ability of concentration through samatha bhavana, it is ready to be trained further through the practice of *vipassana bhavana* (known as insight meditation), in which you are mindful of all your thoughts and feelings and witness them with detachment until you have the experience of insight into the truth of your life. When you experience thoughts, sounds, or physical sensations, you don't react to them. Rather, you stay present with them as they occur and witness them with no judgment, without defining each moment as good or bad, right or wrong, pleasant or unpleasant. You simply let them *be* and allow yourself to also *JUST BE*. In time, as this silent witness who simply watches everything that unfolds within you and around you, you begin to notice that your thoughts actually create sensations in your body and then the sensations create thoughts. You become aware of the vicious cycle that can hijack our consciousness—but you do nothing with it. It is your awareness of the process that brings insight.

WHAT'S ALL THE BUZZ ABOUT MINDFULNESS?

Vipassana is the root of what our current culture refers to as *mindfulness* and increasingly more and more Buddhist teachers have shed their robes, edited out the Buddhist connection, changed the languaging, made it more about stress reduction—and in so doing, have made vipassana much more understandable and accessible to the mainstream. After attending many lectures and teachings on mindfulness, I've noticed that what also has been edited out is the tenderness of truly being mindful. In its place is a more stress-relief based conversation. I understand that teachers of this teaching are attempting to reach the masses and not scare them away by keeping the languaging more scientific, non-denominational, and distinctly non-"spiritual," but in the process, the true *heart* of mindfulness has been lost. It's turned into a buzzword and marketing tool, and has even become trendy, taking on a coolness or a cache of *hipsterism*. I feel that whatever can get people meditating is great. And I would encourage you that if your orientation to mindfulness was from one of these types of classes or books, that you go deeper and take some time to explore the ancient Buddhist foundations of this magnificent practice.

Probably, the most prolific teacher of vipassana in the mainstream is Dr. Jon Kabat-Zinn who developed the *Mindfulness Based Stress Reduction (MBSR)* program at the University of Massachusetts Medical Center in 1979. He tactfully kept it science-based, secular, and simple, positioning the ancient practice as a tool for physical and emotional healing and stress reduction—things we all grapple with every day. Over the past 30 years, he evolved MBSR into a common form of complementary medicine addressing a variety of health problems where it is now offered in over 200 medical centers, hospitals, and clinics around the world, including some of the leading integrative medical centers such as the Scripps Center for Integrative Medicine, the Duke Center for Integrative Medicine, and the Jefferson-Myrna Brind Center for Integrative Medicine.

Dr. Kabat-Zinn has authored many research studies using MBSR. And, in addition to the obvious scientific benefits we attribute to meditation such as lower blood pressure, more restful sleep, less emotional reactivity, and heightened immune function, MBSR is now widely used to lessen chronic pain, increase workplace well-being, decrease drug dependency, increase self-esteem, and ease anxiety. MBSR is a fusion of mindfulness meditation and yoga and is usually taught as an eight-week intensive. And, because it is languaged as a healing lifestyle program and explained more scientifically, it is probably more palatable to corporate decision-makers and hospital administrative committees that approve these types of programs. The brilliance of Jon Kabat-Zinn is that he is so tender and real-world in his content and teaching style. When you learn directly from him, the compassion of the Buddha effortlessly flows through his words and guidance, even though he is sharing a very modern translation of the ancient teachings.

Most people first experience vipassana at 10-day (or more) vipassana retreats usually led by a Buddhist teacher or a vipassana devotee. The common thread in all vipassana retreats is that they take place in total silence—you don't speak; you don't read; you don't make eye contact; you don't drink alcohol or indulge in recreational substances; you rise before the sun; you meditate for several hours; you eat one big meal around 11 A.M.; you meditate for several hours; and you are in bed by 9 P.M. Other than receiving guidance on how to sit, how to witness, and instruction on some basic Buddhist elements such as the *Four Noble Truths* and the *Noble Eight-fold Path*, there are no lectures or entertainment. The process is very specific and everything is simple. After you have gotten over the shock of giving up your cell phone and the discomfort of being silent, you begin to see life as so simple and your needs and desires in a less complex way. Being in silence for 10 days, you realize how much you judge everything, project yourself into other people's minds, and fantasize about what they are thinking or believing. You slowly realize most of what you say doesn't need to be spoken. It's very intense, and it can feel a bit rigid. Each day as you descend more deeply into silence, it is filled chock-full of *A-ha!* moments. But it's not for everyone.

If It's Good Enough for the Buddha . . .

As I mentioned before, *Vipassana* is known as the meditation practice that the Buddha used to attain enlightenment. I find vipassana to be very simple and inclusive. I practiced it for several years just because of its ease and found the practice to be a nurturing and gentle form of meditation. I recommend you experience vipassana at some point in your life, but unless you desire to explore the first two Bhavanas in advance, you may find this beautiful practice quite jarring.

There is something sacred and holy about Buddhist meditations. Not in a religious sense, but in the purity and simplicity of the practice which is so heart-based and *self*-compassionate. We beat ourselves up so regularly—judging, ruminating, relentlessly second-guessing our choices, woulda-coulda-shoulding ourselves, regretting our words or actions, grieving over past decisions. Yet the practices of metta, samatha, and vipassana have a special power to soften us and to give us permission to be okay with ourselves no matter what is happening in our lives in a given moment.

When I first became familiar with Buddhist meditations, I dove deep into metta meditation. After a year, I began incorporating it into my every morning (and more than 15 years later, I still start my day with it). When I felt I was ready for samatha, I dipped my toe in but very quickly discovered mantra meditation. Instead, I began a daily mantra practice to cultivate my ability to concentrate (the New York control freak in me would not wait for samatha to take hold). I then began exploring vipassana at several silent retreats. I found them enlightening, restorative, soothing, and very tenderizing, but then I would return home to my mantra as my core practice. I don't know whether my impatience helped or hurt me in my practice, because it has now been many years that I have been practicing *Nakshatra Mantra Meditation*, and I have found profound richness and expansive one-ness as I move through my life. Several times a week I practice mindful meditation usually in the middle of the day between my bookends of mantra meditation. And quite often, when I am teaching larger groups of people for a day or two, I will teach them metta and mindfulness meditation. Once a year, I create my own pattern interruption by retreating from the hustle and bustle of my world for 10 days and going into silent contemplation. When I come back to "reality," I see the world with new eyes. I feel invigorated, rejuvenated, energized, and peaceful. This overarching sense of calm literally lasts for months.

Each month as I connect with thousands of people around the world exploring meditation, I am always touched by the sweet energy emitted by those who walk in the path of the Buddha. Not necessarily those who claim they are Buddhists, but those who practice mindfulness on a daily basis regardless of their "official" philosophy or religion. They practice loving-kindness without expectation of acknowledgment or recognition; they are gentle beings and, therefore, create gentleness in their world. They are less caught up in drama because they judge less, worry less about the past and future, and stay in the moment. I learn so much about myself and about the world from them. Most often, these people tell me that they are not necessarily Buddhists but that they have a daily heart opening or meditation practice such as metta bhavana.

CHAPTER 12

SECRETS OF MANTRA MEDITATION

"A human being is a part of the whole, called by us 'Universe', a part limited in time and space. He experiences himself, his thoughts and feelings, as something separated from the rest, a kind of optical delusion of his consciousness. This delusion is a kind of prison for us, restricting us to our personal desires and to affection for a few persons nearest to us. Our task must be to free ourselves from this prison by widening our circle of compassion to embrace all living creatures and the whole of nature in its beauty."

— ALBERT EINSTEIN

My current mantra meditation practice is one borne of my life-long spiritual voyage, which began in my mother's womb. She believed in the concept of the unbounded universal Self, and she and I explored it in many ways throughout my youth before her body died. I still feel a very deep spiritual connection to her even though she left this earthly plane decades ago. She was always open to new teachings and guided me to expand my reference point beyond the traditional religious, philosophical, and spiritual tutelage I received.

My comfort with a poly-philosophical approach to our existence has allowed me to embrace the Torah as well as the Vedas, Christ consciousness, Islam's mystical Sufism, Osho's Taoism, Guru Nanak's heart-based Sikhism, the loving-kindness of Buddha's compassionate teachings, and the universality of religious science. I see them all as different paths to the same outcome, alternate narratives of the same archetypal story, all resonating the same frequency and common theme: a life of purpose, peace, compassion, love, and fulfillment.

Studying and practicing a blend of these diverse teachings has helped me transcend the many traumas, struggles, and challenges that I have experienced in my life. It has helped me to move into the present and help others find deeper fulfillment in their lives. It has taught me that I can't undo the past—I can't unring the bell—I can't unhurt those I have wounded. But I can make different choices in *this moment* to right my past wrongs, to *say now* what I couldn't or didn't say then, to *listen now* to what I couldn't hear then, to add sweetness to the lives of new people in my life in the same way I brought pain into the lives of those in my past. We can all bring closure to the past in our heart and in our mind, and take responsibility for all our past actions, as well as our current feelings, interpretations, and dreams.

What Is in a Mantra?

The traditional image of a meditator is someone sitting cross-legged with eyes closed and their hands resting on their knees, with thumbs and index fingers touching to form a circle as they chant the sound *Om*. That chanting of *Om* is what's called the chanting of a mantra, and if you remember all the way back to Chapter 1, the word *mantra* comes from two Sanskrit words: *man*, which means "mind," and *tra*, which means "vehicle" or "instrument." So your mantra is your mind vehicle and your mind instrument. It is simply another tool to transport your mind from a state of activity to one of stillness and silence. We get the words "**tra**in," "**tra**vel," and "**tra**nsportation" from the Sanskrit root *tra*. Most traditional mantras are created from the 50 letters of the Sanskrit alphabet, but there are Chinese, Sikh, Tao, and Vietnamese Buddhist mantras that have their own origins. There are even mantras meant to be carved into stones as a form of meditation. The Thai KATHA MANTRA is meant to be chanted while gently holding an amulet energetically charged by a saint.

Mantras can consist of a single letter, a syllable or string of syllables, a word, a phrase, a sentence, or several sentences strung together. Typically, most mantras are sounds, syllables, or vibrations that don't necessarily have a meaning. Their value lies in their *vibrational quality*, not in any meaning that humans, society, culture, or civilization has placed on them over the last few thousand years. In fact, the oldest mantras are said to have been chanted before language was created! For this reason, they go beyond the realm of sound. And they take you deeper, because they are vibrations that have existed since the dawn of creation.

The Hymn of the Universe

Om, often referred to as the hymn of the universe, is the oldest mantra sacred to Hindus, Buddhists, and Jains. *Om* is considered the ultimate vibration because it contains every vibration that has ever existed and every vibration that will ever exist. Just as white light contains all the colors of the spectrum, *Om* contains every sound in the vibrational spectrum, even those we can't hear with our ears. One of the clearest visual representations of this is on the cover of Pink Floyd's album *Dark Side of the Moon*. It shows a beam of white light coming into one side of a prism and all the colors of the spectrum coming out the other side. The same could be said for *Om*; it's the white light of sound.

Historically, *Om* is first mentioned in the twelve verses of the ancient Vedic text the *Mandukya Upanishads*, which explains the three basic states of consciousness: waking, sleeping, and dreaming. In its original spelling and pronunciation, *Aum* (pronounced *ahh-uhh-mmm*) is a blending of those three states of consciousness into the one-ness of three distinct syllables: A, U, and M. These three vibrations also represent the three stages of our known existence: birth, life, and death.

The vibration "A" (pronounced *ahh*, like the sound you make opening your mouth for the doctor) represents the waking state and the beginning of all things. Just as the letter *A* is the first letter of most every alphabet—the first letter of the Rig Veda, the Koran, Homer's *Odyssey*, even the first word of the New Testament—the vibration *A* heralds creation . . . the beginning. Vedic sages refer to it as the *A-kara*, and it represents the realm of *form* and shape—the physical realm.

The vibration *U* (pronounced *uh*) is referred to as the *U-kara* (pronounced uk-kara), and represents the dream state, the realm that is devoid of form or shape—the ethereal realms of air, water, fire, dreams—ever-changing aspects of the *formless* world around us.

The vibration *M* is known as the *Ma-kara*, which represents the state of deep sleep—neither form (like the akara) nor formless (like the Ukara), actually *beyond* shape or shapelessness—the realm of consciousness in hibernation, waiting to unfold.

In Sanskrit grammar, when the letters *A* and *U* are combined in writing, they are translated as the letter *O*. That is why we so often see *Om* written instead of *Aum*. Over thousands of years, the writing of *Aum* has taken a backseat to *Om*, and that has led to *Om* being the sound that is most often chanted by both Western students and teachers of yoga, meditation, and Vedanta. In India, where people have a greater familiarity with Sanskrit from daily prayer, the sound is still pronounced Aum.

When the three individual vibrations are combined, a fourth vibration is created, like a chord in music made up of individual notes. *Aum* (pronounced *aaahhh—uhhh—mmmmmm*) represents the fourth state of consciousness—transcendent consciousness, or *turiya*, and what we call enlightenment or one-ness. In Hinduism, it's the unity of the Divine made up of its three components: *Brahma*—creation, *Vishnu*—preservation, and *Shiva*—destruction and rebirth. The chanting of the mantra *Om* heralds our individual and collective universality, which is why we usually chant *Om* before and/or after meditation and yoga practice, and when we read sacred, ancient texts.

By repeating a vibration or sound over and over, it will become part of your physiology; it will become your mind; it will become *you*. There will be no separation between you and the vibration that is resonating right now.

Om—The Hymn of the Universe

This is the Sanskrit symbol for the vibration *Om*. The large curve on the lower left represents the material world of the waking state—the Akara. The smaller curve on the upper-left represents deep sleep—the Makara. The curve on the right that extends to the right from the intersection of the two left curves represents the dream state—that tender line between waking and sleeping—the Ukara. The dot at the very top is akin to the dot (or bindu) in the center of the Sri Yantra discussed at length in Chapter 6, "Secrets of Visual Meditation," and represents the universe in all its abundance. This state is often referred to as *turiya* (pronounced *toor-yah*), a Sanskrit word for "absolute consciousness," "the universe," or "one-ness." And the curved line under the bindu represents maya, the illusion of existence that separates our bodymind from one-ness and must be transcended for us to return to the whole. Ommmmm!

Mantras can be uttered aloud or silently. When a mantra is chanted out loud, it is intended to concentrate, intensify, and expand consciousness. Ancient Vedic texts maintain that a whispered mantra is a thousand times more beneficial than a spoken one, and a silent mantra is a thousand times more powerful than a whispered one.

Meditating on Om

We can meditate right now using the mantra *Om*. Say it out loud and feel the vibration a-u-m as it is birthed, then sustains, and then dies out as you purse your lips. And notice the silence before and after it is uttered. Now let's whisper it. *Om*. And now begin slowly repeating it silently to yourself. *Om* . . . *Om* . . . *Om* . . . *Om* . . . over and over again. Allow it to linger and allow the silence to settle in before the next *Om*. To practice any type of mantra meditation, close your eyes and silently repeat the mantra over and over. When you notice that you have drifted away from the mantra to thoughts in your mind, sounds in the environment, or sensations in your physical body, gently drift back to the mantra. It will get louder and fainter, faster and slower; it will even become jumbled, distorted, and inaudible. However the mantra changes, simply keep repeating it, and when you notice you've drifted away just gently drift back. Back and forth and back and forth again. Gently surrender to the back and forth. Let's try it for a few moments right now. Just for a few moments. But first take a deep breath in through your nostrils and hold it for a moment and then slowly let it out. Do that again. And then close your eyes and begin silently repeating *Om*.

Now, let's meditate on *Om* for a few moments.

How did that feel? What did you feel?

Mantras with Meaning

Early in Vedic history, teachers began categorizing mantras as either meaningful or meaningless. Meaningless mantras are simply sounds used for their vibrational quality—similar to the vibrations of the seven chakras. Meaningful mantras, on the other hand, inherently contain some intention or meaning that is determined by the culture and language in which they arise, as well as a personal meaning. These mantras both connect the reciter with a particular intention and serve as a meditation vehicle, helping to awaken a specific state of consciousness. Examples of meaningful mantras include the famous four sutras known in Sanskrit as the *Mahavakyas*, or "master sayings" (maha—great or master; vakya—saying):

- **Prajñānam brahma**—*The universal Spirit is pure wisdom* from the *Rig Veda*

- **Ayam ātmā brahma**—*My Soul is the universal Spirit* from the *Atharva Veda*

- **Tat tvam asi**—*You are that* from the *Sama Veda*, and

- **Aham brahmāsmi**—*I am the Universe*, or *I am Divine*, from the *Yajur Veda*.

As I've indicated above, the Mahavakyas are drawn from the four main ancient Vedic texts. But there are many timeless mantras beyond the mahavakyas such as:

- **So hum**—*I Am That*—(popularized by the late great modern sage Wayne Dyer)

- **Sat chit ananda**—*Truth, Consciousness (or knowingness), Bliss*

- **Moksha**—*I am emotionally free* (popularized by David Simon), and

- **Sarvam khalvidam brahma**—*Everything is Spirit* (which MJ Vermette whispers in the closing moments of *You Are the Gap* on our album *Journey to Infinity*).

If you're looking to meditate with a mantra, I encourage you to select one that feels comfortable and has a meaning with which you connect. Aham brahmasmi is one of my favorites, and

I encourage you to try it as well. I've been using it consistently for about 10 years and often say, "Aham brahmasmi, baby!" to sign off from my radio show. It resonates with me and it's empowering. On a vibrational level, it quickly soothes me into stillness and silence.

Mantras Used for Their Vibrational Quality

In mantra meditation, we use the repetition of a word or phrase to disconnect us from the activity around us—the thoughts, sounds, and physical sensations that are a part of every moment we are alive. In contrast with mindfulness or vipassana meditation, where practitioners place their attention on the breath, mantra meditation uses the *silent repetition of a meaningless syllable, syllables, or vibrations* to disconnect us from activity. We keep our present-moment awareness solely on the mantra's vibration, not the many other possible activities of the moment such as breathing or thinking. After consistent silent repetition, the mantra becomes the sole object of our attention. We have between 60,000 and 80,000 thoughts each day. That's about a thought every second, which brings a simultaneous awareness of meaning that leads to mental activity. By repeating a meaningless syllable or syllables, such as a chakra vibration or *Om*, over and over and over again, the meditator can disconnect from meaning and slip into a space between thoughts, where there is no activity. By repeating something that is meaningless over and over and over again, an open, undefined space washes over every aspect of you—beyond your labels, beyond your definitions, beyond your meanings and understandings—and into the space of one-ness.

Your mantra is your hyperlink to the nonlocal domain.

The Power of Mantra

Once this space of stillness and silence becomes you, you truly detach from thoughts in your mind, sounds in the environment, and physical sensations in the body. Your heart rate slows . . . your breathing slows . . . the past drifts away . . . the ongoing speculation about the future ceases. There is a subtle awareness of moving from activity to stillness; thoughts and sounds pass through you instead of being received and processed by you. A lightness of being flows into you. The concept of YOU expands from a breathing human being to a silent observer and then to a unified being, seeing the sacred in every face, flower, and object around you. Ultimately, you merge into everything without distinction. You become one.

This is "it"—what is commonly referred to as "being in the gap." And the beauty is that you can't know you're there; it's beyond space and time. You stay in this higher state of consciousness until your body pulls you out of it by drifting back into activity as your awareness drifts to a thought, a sound, or a physical sensation—and you flow out of one-ness and back to duality.

At the moment you begin to drift out of the stillness and silence, you start to apply meaning to the moment. That is when you realize you were "in the gap"; it's always after the fact. It is at that moment you recognize the difference . . . the separation between *that* and *this*, or the duality of our individual local existence and the universal nonlocal one. Meaning comes back into your awareness. You can't recognize the gap while you are in it, because you are not separate from it. It's like a fish swimming through the ocean, unaware that it's fully immersed and integrated into the water until it chooses to leap out into the air—then it truly realizes separation.

It is at this moment—as you become aware of your thoughts again—that you drift back into the realm of meaning and activity. As you drift out of the stillness, you become aware of the mantra or perhaps a new thought, a sound, or a physical sensation. This is normal, common, expected; this is part of the meditation. But regardless of where you find yourself, *just gently drift back to the effortless repetition of the mantra. The mastery of meditation is when you can comfortably drift back and forth.*

This is meditation, plain and simple, drifting ever so gently back and forth between the object of attention—in this case, the mantra—to the realm of activity and thoughts, sounds, and physical sensations . . . and then back again to the mantra. Don't torture yourself; don't try to control anything. As soon as you become aware you are no longer repeating the mantra (which is the most common experience), just gently drift back to it. The repetition of the mantra is effortless, *like mist rising off a lake at dawn*. Any more effort and you're working way too hard.

There are literally millions of mantras because they are sounds or myriad combinations of the infinite sounds of nature. And they are used for many different purposes (devotional, destressifying, spiritual, healing, manifesting, mystical, material)—and in many different ways (silently repeated, chanted, whispered, sung in chorus, and read by a leader and responded to). I believe in the power of the mantra, and almost any mantra used with the right intention in a daily practice can take one from a very personal constricted state of existence to higher states of consciousness, including more expanded and universal states.

USING A BIJA

The Sanskrit word *Bija* (pronounced *bee-jah*) means "seed" and, as such, is a metaphor for the cause or origin of something. Thousands of years ago, the *rishis*, or seers, in what is now the Indian subcontinent identified what they believed to be the original sounds of nature. They called them Bija sounds or seed syllables. The oldest of these Bija sounds—*Om*—is first referenced in the ancient Vedic text known as the Upanishads. In Tibetan Buddhism, the three sacred seed syllables are: a white *Om* (representing the *enlightened body* and the one-ness of the Universe), a red *Ah* (representing *enlightened speech and prana*—our energetic voice in the world), and a blue *Hūṃ* (representing the *enlightened mind* that rests in the heart). Since then, powerful Bija sounds have been used as mantras because they are organic, pure, universal vibrations.

In the late '60s and early '70s, meditation was reintroduced to the masses, creating one of the most powerful shifts in human consciousness on the planet. With legendary Beatle George Harrison setting the tone, millions around the world, especially in the United States, Australia, and Western Europe, tapped into mantra meditation as a way of life. George traveled to India and was taught to meditate, using a Bija mantra, by his guru, the esteemed Maharishi Mahesh Yogi who created and popularized Transcendental Meditation in the 1970s. Since then, thousands of people have learned to meditate using this technique to help them disconnect them from activity, while connecting to the stillness and silence that rests within.

When used as a mantra in meditation, seed sounds can connect you directly to source. The value of using a Bija is that it's not a word that has meaning; it's simply a vibration—a vibration that has existed forever. Because it was never intended to have meaning, its vibrational quality is what holds our attention, which is then drifted away from things that have meaning.

Using Your BirthStar Mantra—Nakshatra Mantra Meditation

The mantra practice that has worked most powerfully for me, the one that I teach attendees at my workshops, and the one that I have trained my Certified Meditation Teachers to share with the world, is the ancient technique known as *Nakshatra BirthStar Mantra Meditation. Nakshatra* (pronounced NAK-SHATRA) is the

Sanskrit word for *Birth Star*. According to the ancient Jyotish calculation of heavenly bodies, *this is the star in direct alignment with you at the moment you were born—the first star the moon saw as you passed into this earthly realm.*

The Moon orbits completely around the earth every 27.3 days. This is known in modern astronomy as a sidereal month containing 27 days of 24-hour periods. And yet, thousands of years ago, the ancient scientists of the sky not only calculated this information, but also gave each 24-hour period in the month a Sanskrit vibration based on the star or star clusters visible during that time. Ancient Chinese, Babylonian and Egyptian astronomers also used the concept of *Nakshatra BirthStars*, to track the seasons, mark the passage of time, and celebrate auspicious occasions.

We now know it takes thousands and—in some cases, millions—of light-years for the light of a star to be visible on planet Earth. When you learn the Sanskrit name of the light from the star that heralded the 24-hour period when you passed from the unmanifest into the manifest—from stardust into birth—it is one of the most magnificent sounds you will ever learn. The vibration of this mantra will resonate on the deepest level and guide you to that stillpoint that rests at the core of your being.

Taking You Back to the Source of Everything

At the moment of your birth you were pure, and whole, and perfect. But it's been a few years since that moment and a lot has happened since then. Since a Nakshatra is a 24-hour period, your vibration includes several hours when you were in the womb, the moment of your birth and the hours when you first stepped foot (or peeked your head) into this world—the whole cycle of your individuation. When you practice *Nakshatra Mantra Meditation*, every meditation brings you back to that divine moment of your pure perfection, and reconnects you to the purity and perfection of your unconditioned essence.

I believe practicing *Nakshatra Mantra Meditation* has altered my DNA, taken me deeper than other techniques, and provided amazing experiences along the way. It has sharpened my clarity, provided tranquility, taken me deep into stillness and silence, released anxiety and stress, strengthened my understanding of existence, offered insights, expanded my capacity for compassion and forgiveness, profoundly connected me to source, opened my heart, and given me immeasurable gifts. Most importantly, it has peeled away layers of my conditioned existence and reconnected me to the sacred moment of my birth when I took my first breath, heard sound through air, and the umbilical cord that tethered me to my mother was severed.

I have experienced amazingly powerful results from this technique over the past 10 years by simply practicing 30 minutes in the morning and again in the evening, typically once in the very early morning and once in the late afternoon or evening.

> *Your Nakshatra BirthStar Mantra is the vibration the universe was making at the moment you passed from the unmanifest into the manifest and came into this world of form and phenomena.*

How Your BirthStar Mantra Is Calculated

There are hundreds of thousands of meditators around the world who practice *Nakshatra Mantra Meditation*, and millions who have practiced it dating back to the most ancient times. There are 27 Nakshatra Bijas (or seed sounds) in this school of meditation, and they are raw, pure, and universal. In *Nakshatra Mantra Meditation*, each meditator uses their unique BirthStar sound as a mantra that reflects the vibration or the atmospheric quality of the universe at the moment of his or her birth. Every moment in life contains a certain energy inherent in the atmosphere in a particular place at a specific time. You can feel it right now wherever you are. There are certain qualities to this very moment based on where you are and what's going on. So imagine going back thousands of years and drinking in the bigger picture—the relationship of the earth, the moon, and the stars that were present in a particular 24-hour period.

To determine someone's *Nakshatra Mantra*, the place, date, and time of a person's birth is correlated to the specific vibrations of the universe that were written down in Sanskrit thousands of years ago. Based on your birth information, a Vedic mathematics program then calculates the vibration from the 27 possibilities. Once identified, that vibration is merged with several other vibrations, including other Bija sounds, to create an individual's personal *Nakshatra Mantra*. Once you learn your personal mantra, you repeat it silently during your meditation to move more easily into stillness and silence.

It's pretty powerful to meditate using the sound that the universe was making at the moment you passed from the unmanifest into the manifest. It's also very powerful to know the exact alignment between the earth, the moon, and the stars that existed at the moment you were born is the exact same relationship that existed among the earth, the moon, and the stars 5,000 years ago, when this vibration was first discovered and written down. We humans come and go every hundred years, but the sun, the moon, the earth, and the planets have been signposts of the galaxy for more than 15 billion years!

Mantras in Religion

All the world's major religions include some form of mantra meditation in their practices. Chanting the Catholic rosary, practicing Kabalistic hitbodedut meditation, praying one of the Buddhist Lam Rims, repeating Allah's name in Islamic dhikr, or the responsive reading of the Yoga Vasistha—all are repetitive devotional practices giving glory to the Divine.

Although meditation in itself is not a religious practice, I find the daily practice of drifting into stillness using a mantra brings me closer to my most universal Self. Thousands of my students who are deeply religious—Catholics, Hindus, Orthodox Jews, fundamentalist Christians, and devout Muslims alike—have found that meditating with a mantra has helped them quiet their minds so they can feel even closer to their God.

Regardless of your religious orientation, when it comes to living a meditation practice, go with what resonates with you. Feel free to choose a mantra that you will be comfortable with and one that supports whatever spiritual or religious philosophies you have. Mantra meditation is a beautiful practice that will complement any other religious rituals or spiritual practices you employ.

Whether or not you are religious, you know that there is something bigger—something higher, grander than you—even if it's no more than a belief in a godlike intelligence or a creative, universal energy. If you were brought up practicing a religion, even if you've moved away from those teachings, you probably still have some devotional aspect to your life. Wherever your belief is directed, I believe that a meditation practice can enhance and uplift your personal devotion to your god, power your prayer, and reaffirm your belief in the divine aspects of life outside of you and within you.

Meditation is simply a tool to help you connect more fully with your most expansive Self—the better to feel God, Jesus, or the Universe's love, open yourself to it, and then pour it back into the world. Life is circulation. When the circulation ceases, life ends. When the circulation is total and expansive, you can experience a blissful existence in whatever area of your life that is open to that expansion.

What's the difference between prayer and meditation? *Prayer is talking to God; meditation is listening.* Meditation does not take the place of prayer. If you have a prayer or devotional practice, your meditation will expand it and make it more powerful. Meditation slows the swirl around you, so you hear the most subtle whispers of God. Meditation heightens your spiritual connection to your higher power, your god, the universe, and your most universal Self.

The Universal Mantra

When David Simon was first diagnosed with a malignant brain tumor in June of 2010, he began incorporating the repetition of what he referred to as "the universal mantra" into his daily practice. In Judaism, it is not appropriate to utter the name of the Lord out loud, so other words are substituted to reference the almighty. The most common of these "no-names" is spelled using four Hebrew letters:

Yud   Hey   Vov   Hey

Read left to right, these four consonants YHVH would appear to spell out *Yahweh*, or *Yehovah*. The original Hebrew used no vowels and is read right to left, so it would be spelled from right to left like this:

The English translation of Yahweh and Yehovah—this personal no-name of the supreme being—is "I am," or "I am that I am." When it is spelled from top to bottom, it appears:

As you can see, it looks like a person with a head, shoulders, arms, and torso, with hips and legs that extend down to the earth. So, using this mantra is essentially the heralding of God at the same time you are acknowledging your human-ness.

When you repeat a word or phrase over and over again, it becomes part of your physiology—one with your essence—an integrated aspect of who you are.

To practice what I now refer to as the Universal Mantra meditation, close your eyes and silently repeat *Yud* (rhymes with should), *Hey, Vov* (rhymes with love), *Hey* over and over. When you notice that you have drifted away from the mantra to thoughts in your mind, sounds in the environment, or sensations in your physical body, gently drift back to *Yud, Hey, Vov, Hey*. As you repeat it silently, it will get louder and fainter, faster and slower; it will even become jumbled, distorted, and inaudible. However, the mantra changes, simply keep repeating it, and when you notice you've drifted away, just gently drift back. Back and forth. Let's try it for a few moments right now. First take a deep breath in through your nostrils, hold it for a moment, and then slowly let it out. Do it again. Then close your eyes, and begin silently repeating the mantra. Let's meditate together now.

How did that feel? What did you feel?

This type of meditation inspired me to write the following Sanskrit sutra:

> *Yogastha kareem karuna.*
> *Yogastha kuru karmani.*
> *Yogastha karuna brahma.*

Which means: *Established in BEing, it is a blessing to perform compassionate action. Established in BEing, perform action. Established in BEing, performing compassionate action is the Ultimate truth.*

The phrase "yogastha kuru karmani" is from the ancient text, the *Bhagavad Gita*, in which Lord Krishna counsels the great warrior Arjuna on the purpose of life. Arjuna is deep in the midst of a profound spiritual dilemma, as he knows his purpose in life is to be a fierce warrior, but he is agonized by fear, grief, uncertainty, sadness, and regret as he readies his troops for a calamitous battle in a huge family feud, pitting friend against friend, cousin against cousin, teacher against student, and patriarch against son.

As he stands with Krishna as his charioteer in the middle of the vast plains of Kurukshetra in northern India, Arjuna gazes intently at the two opposing armies of his relatives that now face each other poised for battle. He is paralyzed by the gravity of the task before him—leading the charge of one army against the other and, in the process, causing the death of hundreds of his friends, esteemed teachers, and relatives. He asks his divine guide how he can possibly live with his decision, and Krishna replies with a spiritual dialogue spanning 18 chapters on yoga, self-realization, dharma (or purpose), devotion to God, the meaning of life, and ultimately, the nature of reality. When Arjuna asks his higher power, "Oh dear Lord, how shall I move forward in life?" Krishna replies in Chapter 2, Verse 48, "Yogastha kuru karmani—establish yourself in the present moment, and then perform action."

To meditate on the teachings, select a phrase, such as "yogastha kuru karmani" (pronounced *yoga-stah koo-roo kar-mani*), close your eyes, and silently repeat the phrase over and over as the object of your attention. When you notice that you've drifted away to thoughts, sounds, or physical sensations, gently drift back to "yogastha kuru karmani."

Let's try it right now for a few minutes. Start by saying it out loud three times: yogastha kuru karmani, yogastha kuru karmani, yogastha kuru karmani. Then whisper it three times. Now repeat it silently to yourself three times. Then take a deep breath in and slowly exhale. Now take a few minutes . . . and when it feels comfortable, close your eyes and continue silently repeating the mantra. I'll wait right here.

Did you notice that your attention flowed to and from the mantra, disconnecting for a moment here and there from your awareness of thoughts, sounds, and physical sensations. Did you notice yourself drift back and forth? What did you feel? How did it feel?

Mantra Myths

Many spiritual teachers assert that there is a specific protocol to rigidly observe regarding mantras—that they need to be taught in a certain way, used in a certain way, used only at certain times. This makes sense to a point so you can understand the basic structure and process of a mantra meditation and get grounded in it. But I have observed that when the practice starts to take on a rigid atmosphere of "musts" and "rules," personal commitment and passion seem to ebb. There are no rules in *Nakshatra Mantra Meditation*, which separates it from the other mantra meditation schools I have been a student or a teacher of. Structure is a healthy component of a practice and it acts as a helpful set of guardrails to keep you on track. Rigidity in any philosophy can start to feel constricting. For example, one of my teachers of a mantra meditation technique I once practiced used to stress the importance of not meditating with your baby or your pet because they would steal your energy. David Simon and I used to meditate a lot with our dogs and they would lovingly curl up next to us and even add value to the experience. Pets and babies have the sweetest, most divine energy and to merge with that innocence in a meditation is a special gift. Sometimes you simply have to listen to your heart and remind yourself that "the guru rests inside."

Meditation is simply a tool. It is not a religion and should have no dogma attached to it. So if you find that you've stopped resonating with a particular technique, mantra, or school of meditation, feel free to keep exploring!

Meditation and the desire to do it must flow naturally from who we are as people and should feel like something we *want* to do, not something we feel we *must* do. Infinite flexibility is the key to happiness and fulfillment. This applies to use of the mantra as well.

There is so much conversation about mantras in the meditation community that I wanted to share my thoughts on the most popular assumptions and misconceptions regarding mantra practice and demystify some of it.

1. THE MANTRA MUST BE PRONOUNCED PERFECTLY.

Everything in our world is about attention and intention. If your intention is to connect to the subtle essence of the vibration, don't be critical of yourself regarding the pronunciation or the esoteric meaning of the mantra you're using. While some claim that a mispronounced mantra will be ineffective, if your intention is pure, the mantra will resonate and have purpose, even if you are pronouncing it differently from how it was originally uttered. Repeating a mantra is meant to be an effortless practice, a practice of surrender. Remember, it's just a faint idea. It's a vibration, so allow it to unfold gently and gracefully. There are many Sanskrit dictionaries and pronunciation websites online, so feel free to explore the many expressions of Sanskrit—and have fun in the process.

2. MANTRAS ARE TO BE TAKEN SERIOUSLY.

Many of the mantras we use so casually today had their beginnings in devotional or religious contexts. And while many of them often use the name of various gods as metaphors—such as awakening your Christ consciousness, opening your heart to your true Buddha nature, or enlisting the Hindu elephant-headed god Ganesha to help you solve problems—when invoking mantras with deities, one should have sensitivity to their depth of sacredness. All mantras (meaningful and meaningless) should be treated with reverence, essentially *handled with care* in a lighthearted, innocent, and gentle way. They should be treated not with the seriousness of someone about to perform a science experiment or a medical operation but as someone appreciating the effectiveness of the tool. That being said, too much seriousness or importance on the mantra brings you into the realm of meaning, of thought, of activity. That's why the silent repetition of the mantra will always take you deeper than the out loud repetition. Silence is passive. Vocalizing out loud has many moving parts, such as breath, voice, tone, timbre, volume, and the sound itself as it leaves your lips, travels through air into your ears, and vibrates your chest, creating another entire loop of activity. Also, saying a mantra aloud will turn it into a word in your mind—and then you'll move back into meaning. The lighter the practice, the easier the practice. The easier the practice, the more likely that you will continue the practice. The more consistent you can be, the more quickly you will see and feel changes. So lighten up!

3. To be effective, a mantra should be received directly from a self-realized teacher so that it's infused with the teacher's spiritual energy.

All forms of interaction carry an energetic exchange—smiling at someone, having a conversation, shaking hands, honking your car horn, even reading this book, and, of course, receiving your mantra from a teacher. But it must be kept in perspective; a mantra is just a tool. A great teacher can help you to use that tool by egolessly channeling the knowledge of the universe and open you to wisdom that already rests within you. It's important to remember that once information has been transmitted to you, the true teacher holds no further claim on the information or what you do with it.

Receiving your mantra directly from a teacher is ideal because you can continue working with the teacher as your practice evolves. But the teacher is simply a conduit for you to open to the practice, receive your mantra, refine your technique, and evolve in its ongoing use. Every teacher is a little different. Some teachers carry a higher vibration. Some have greater depth. Some are better facilitators of your learning process. Some are better communicators. Some have a teaching style that may resonate more with you. It's important to consider all these factors when choosing a teacher, but regardless of your teacher's energy or state of consciousness, *you* are the only one who can give value to your mantra. That happens only through daily practice. So right now, with the support of this book, you will be able to comfortably meditate. Don't stress about the power of the teacher; believe in the power of your practice . . . the power of *you*. Use the tools, and see where your life goes.

4. TO KEEP THE POWER OF THE MANTRA AT A HIGH LEVEL, IT SHOULD BE KEPT IN STRICTEST SECRECY AND NOT REVEALED TO ANYONE ELSE.

The mantra is your mind vehicle that takes you from activity to stillness and silence. You wouldn't use sound to take you into silence, so what keeps the mantra powerful is keeping it in a sacred place and not using it casually or out loud, even when you're by yourself. If I gave you a seed for a magnificent flower, you planted it. And then months later, if I bumped into you and asked how your seed was growing, you wouldn't dig into the earth and show me your seed. You'd say, "I planted it; it's growing; and it's blossoming." It's the same with our mantras. We keep them planted in the stillness and the silence to be used as our *mind vehicle* in the sacred fertile soil of our practice.

By speaking your mantra out loud, you bring it from the silent ether into this physical world. Sharing it with others will also lead to you applying some kind of meaning to it, defeating the purpose of a *meaningless* vibration.

Of course, sharing your mantra with someone won't trigger some cosmic retribution upon your karma. Yet you can't unring the bell. You can't take it back. So if you'd like your mantra to have its optimal effectiveness, it starts with not sharing it and keeping it in the realm of meaninglessness. If someone is asking, do they really care? Or are they simply being polite? I recommend keeping it private until you are comfortable with it being planted firmly within. I prefer to keep mine private so that it most effectively disconnects me from meaning and activity.

To keep your mantra in an optimized state, when you find yourself repeating it or using it when doing some activity other than meditation, just let your awareness drift back to your thoughts in the same way that you drift from thought to the mantra during meditation. Deep attachment to the mantra as a word or incantation will move you deeper into meaning and into activity. Remember that we use the mantra to disconnect us from activity and connect us to stillness and silence, so don't spend time on its meaning or definition. Use it for its timeless, meaningless, effortless, vibrational power.

5. Your mantra can help you fall back to sleep.

If you're having trouble sleeping, don't use a mantra you use in meditation to help you fall back asleep. You don't want to reinforce a Pavlovian connection between saying your mantra and falling asleep. Instead, use the sleep mantra, *Om Agasthi Shaheena* (pronounced *om ah*gah-*stee sha*-hee-*na*). Although it works whether you repeat it silently or out loud, my recommendation is to start by saying it out loud three times, soften to a whisper, and then move into silence.

Mantra or Mindfulness? Which is better?

Mantra meditation is also a tool that heightens your awareness, but it is designed with a different intention. The purpose of using a mantra is to drift your attention away from thought and back to the mantra as the object of your attention. This means when we have a thought, rather than watching it or observing it as we do in mindfulness, we instead pay it no mind and drift our attention back to the mantra—and begin repeating it again. In mantra meditation, we are not watching our thoughts with detachment when they arrive. Instead, we take that as the cue to drift back to the mantra. When we practice mantra meditation, we are cultivating our ability to drift back to the mantra

. . . back to the mantra . . . back to the mantra. Essentially, training ourselves to effortlessly drift back and forth. Thoughts are coming into our awareness and they all carry some type of meaning. Yet we are repeating a vibration, which has no meaning, and at a certain point they cancel each other out! *And there is NO thing—nothing. It is in that moment that you are neither in thought nor mantra. Instead you are in a place of nothingness, which can last for a millisecond, a second, or a few seconds. In time, through repeated visits to this space of nothingness, we spend more and more time there. This is the space between our thoughts—this is the gap, a realm of unconditioned perfection. And as you get really proficient in this practice, those moments become more frequent and their duration increases. Over time, they begin to weave themselves into your day-to-day interactions with the world and then you begin experiencing a relaxed state of restful awareness.*

One day, a student of five years visited me to discuss her meditation practice. On returning home from a Buddhist meditation retreat, she had continued her daily mindfulness practice and let go of her mantra practice. Two weeks had passed, and although she felt peacefulness, she sensed that something had shifted. She had practiced mantra meditation for almost five years and experienced higher states of consciousness, but for the past month, as she practiced mindfulness, she had drifted away from those higher states of consciousness and wanted to reconnect to them. I celebrate meditation in all its forms so it didn't matter to me what type of meditation she did, as long as she was finding it added value to her life.

She insisted that this questioning wasn't about which meditation technique was more effective but instead her understanding of what was actually happening within her by shifting from a mantra practice to a mindfulness practice. At the time, I had journeyed in the other direction—from a vipassana practice to a mantra meditation practice—and my experiences had gotten deeper and more powerful over time.

There is no right or wrong meditation technique; neither is better than the other. It depends on what you are looking for at a given time.

My student was now at a meditation crossroads, and my concern was that she would stop meditating all together. I needed a way to articulate the difference in the two styles while giving her permission to choose either. After discussing my concern with a friend and meditating, I had this profound sense of clarity.

Later that afternoon, I met with my student and encouraged her to practice her newfound method for at least 40 days and then choose her preference from an unconditioned space. I reminded her that the higher states of consciousness she experienced from her mantra practice would always be there waiting for her if and when she desired to return to a mantra practice. She smiled and breathed a sigh of relief that all options were open to her. All options are always open to us, though our constricted, ego-based view of the world sometimes doesn't reveal them to us. But with fear released and a bit of encouragement to expand her comfort zone, my student dove more deeply into her meditation practice, ultimately becoming a certified Masters of Wisdom and Meditation teacher, where we celebrate both practices.

CHAPTER 13

SECRETS OF CHANTING MEDITATION

*"Some scenes you juggle two balls,
some scenes you juggle three balls, some scenes you
can juggle five balls. The key is always to speak in
your own voice. Speak the truth."*

— VINCENT D'ONOFRIO

The sun was just beginning to crest above the horizon, as I glided down the Mekong River in northern Cambodia. The thick balmy air was penetrated by the occasional voices of monks performing their first prayers of the day. As we silently drifted downstream, passing one Buddhist temple after another, the chanting became louder and more frequent. As we winded our way down the river, one voice ahead would fill the air as we approached and passed by, then trail off as we glided downstream to the next new voice ahead of us, which would fill the air, and fade into the distance as we continued on.

This gauntlet of Theravada Buddhist prayer created an ongoing vibrational blanketing of my senses as one monk's voice faded out and an approaching one faded in. The chanting continued for miles as we silently followed the current downstream. Eyes closed, I sat quietly at the bow of the boat, drinking in the singsong of prayer. The repetition of Buddha's teachings in the ancient Pali language surrounded me for over an hour. As we passed the last temple, the final monk's prayer vanished like the subtle waning vibrations of a gong slowing into stillness. Surrendering to the rising and falling waves of sweet devotion in a language I did not even understand connected me deeply to some sweet core of my being and disconnected me effortlessly from any mental activity, such as the past or the future. In surrendering to the chanting, I had ultimately become the vibration and had absorbed its devotional intentions even though I could not decipher the words. It was a profound meditation.

To this day, in addition to my daily practice, I enjoy chanting mantras out loud to bring me to higher states of consciousness. One of my favorites to chant out loud is the death-defying mantra known in Sanskrit as the *Mahamrityunjaya* (pronounced maha-mritt-yoon-jaya) *Mantra*, and also referred to as the *Tryambakam* (pronounced try-am-bakam) *Mantra*, I created a hip-hop version of this mantra back in 2003 after David Simon taught it to me and recorded it on *Journey to Infinity*. It is the perfect mantra to help someone in a weakened state rejuvenate, heal, and gain strength. It goes like this:

Aum tryambakam yajāmahe
Sugandhim pusti-vardhanam
Urvārukam iva bandhanān
Mrtyor muksīya māmrtāt

It is translated as:
We invoke the sweet smelling three-eyed God who nourishes
all the creatures of the Universe and releases us from death
for the sake of immortality. Just as the cucumber detaches
from its vine, we implore the Lord to liberate us from death.

Chanting performs many of the same functions as a silent meditation but instead of stillness, the chanter achieves a state of physical/emotional trance through continuously repeating a sound, word, mantra, or the name of God.

Devotional chanting dates back thousands of years and has been celebrated as a way to achieve deeper contact with the Divine by focusing on the present moment. The premise is that during this process, your attention can only be on the sounds you utter or hear—not on any other thought, sound, or sensation. This is exactly what I experienced that morning cruising down the

Mekong River in Cambodia. The continuous repetition of words, mantras, vibrations, or sutras—whether in the form of prayer, song, or responsive reading—creates a state of higher consciousness, but the delivery system is one of the physical and mental realms.

When you utter sounds, you are using the tools of your voice (your mouth, tongue, vocal chords, uvula, throat, lungs, and breath). The effect is for the outer ear to capture sound waves and direct them down into your external ear canal. The vibration sends signals toward the brain, creating a neural message that we understand as sound. It is then that the intellect, and then the soul, resonate with the sounds.

While drifting down the river that morning, I was in a passive state, one of innocence and receptivity. I wasn't chanting, moving my lips, or pushing air through my mouth with any force. I was simply absorbing and vibrating. It was more like experiencing a glorious Gandharva Sound Meditation. In the Buddhist traditions, chanting the Buddhavacana (considered the direct guidance of the Buddha) is a powerful way of effortlessly etching the teachings of Buddhism into one's being. They were etched into my being that morning on the river as wave after wave of the ancient devotional wisdom rippled through my body.

Buddhist chanting is not practiced by Westerners so much as a religious ritual but rather as a way to develop mindfulness. The Buddhist meditation practitioner does not actually worship the Buddha or ask for forgiveness or blessings. Instead, the practitioner honors the divine teachings and if there is any devotional aspect for the uninitiated, it is simply in the form of respecting the Buddha for his supreme achievement.

As most early Buddhist texts were written in the language of Pali, much Buddhist chanting stays true to that lineage. Hindu chanting, which often *is* devotional and does ask various Gods for forgiveness or blessings, is in Sanskrit. The teachings of these two belief systems have been interwoven for thousands of years, and transmitting these texts orally has been the most organic method of keeping the teachings alive and growing throughout generations.

Whether uttered in Pali or Sanskrit, this measured, monoto-nous song or prayer is repeated over and over to create a trance-like, vibrational state that moves the chanter and the listener from meaning to meaninglessness, and from a state of egoistic individu-ality to one of expanded awareness or universality. At the same time, through ritualized repetition, the teachings get woven into every fiber of the chanter's and the listener's being.

Japa

When the chanter brings the chanting down to a whisper and repeats the same prayer or phrasing over and over, this whispered repetition is known as *Japa*, which in Sanskrit means "muttering," or "whispering." Most Japa is accompanied by a ritual in which the chanter counts the number of repetitions of the mantra on a *mala*, a prayer bracelet or necklace made of 108 beads. Usually held in the right hand during Japa practice, the mala is often draped over the middle finger so that you can flick one bead and then the next with your thumb as you repeat the mantra over and over. In Eastern traditions, the index finger is said to represent the ego, which is seen as the biggest obstacle to experiencing self-realization. Therefore, in Japa practice, we don't touch the mala to the index finger. After you have rolled 108 beads over with your thumb, you arrive at a larger bead known as the *meru* or "guru bead" or "head of Shiva," which signals you to stop and flick the beads in the opposite direction. This way you can track how many repetitions you've done without opening your eyes or keeping track in your mind by counting. It's an effortless meditation timer! The practice of Japa is thousands of years old, beginning as the personal expressions of the thousands of verses in the sacred Rig Veda, Hinduism's oldest and holiest scripture, which was shared solely in oral form for 2,000 years before being written down around 3,500 years ago. Over time, the mantras used in Japa evolved from non-Vedic sources as well, such as the Hindu Tantric texts or those cognized by meditating rishis.

Bhajan, Kirtan, and Namavali

Any Indian devotional song is referred to as *bhajan* (which comes from the Sanskrit term *bhakti*, meaning "devotion"). While Japa is always meant to be whispered or chanted to one's Self, when the words or mantras are sung rather than whispered, it is considered bhajan.

When the group becomes larger and there is a leader, this group chanting is known as *kirtan*, meaning "to repeat" in Sanskrit. The person conducting the kirtan—the *kirtanker*—leads the group in call-and-response Sanskrit chanting. Kirtan practice involves chanting hymns or mantras to the accompaniment of instruments such as the harmonium (a hybrid instrument that is a cross between a mini lap piano and an accordion), two-headed Mridanga or a Pakawaj drum, and Karatal hand cymbals. Kirtan was first popularized as a part of Vaishnava worship (a form of worship of the Hindu god Lord Vishnu, the maintainer of the Universe), Sikhism, and specific Buddhist traditions. In recent years, however, Kirtan has also become a frequent feature of the yoga and meditation communities perched at the door of the mainstream market.

Paramahansa Yogananda (philosopher, guru, author of *Autobiography of a Yogi*, and creator of the Self-Realization Fellowship) was one of the first Eastern spiritual teachers to bring Kirtan to the West. In 1923, he led a Kirtan with 3,000 people at New York City's Carnegie Hall, chanting Guru Nanak's "Hey Hari Sundara" ("Oh God Beautiful").

Kirtan is currently becoming more widely known in the West, with the increased popularity and celebrity of skilled Kirtankers and practitioners of *Namavali* (songs that worship Hindu deities such as Lord Rama or Lord Krishna with devotional anecdotes or by recounting episodes from scriptures or verses that chronicle the multiple names of God). Modern masters of these meditative practices have expanded on the groundbreaking, multi-decade careers of master Kirtankers Krishna Das, Jai Uttal, and Bhagavan Das to include the edgy styling of MC Yogi, who blends Kirtan with rap; Larisa Stow, who mixes devotional music with motivational interludes; and Dub Sutra, who uses an eclectic mix of electronic down-tempo beats with live instrumentation and devotional chants.

An easy way to learn about chanting is by listening to chants or playing them as background music to your day. The chanting recordings of those I've just mentioned are amazing ways to experience the timeless chanting of mantras in very different styles and a great foundation to exploring the realm of Kirtan and Namavali.

Part III

FURTHER ALONG THE PATH

By now, you understand the history, art, and science of meditation; its powerful, clinically proven benefits; and the most popular ancient and modern practices and techniques. We've meditated together and perhaps we've even spent some time in the gap together. But the real secret of meditation is showing up every day and keeping your personal practice alive no matter what else is going on so you can better manage all life's twists, turns, and surprises. This is where most people stop and yet the key to better health, abundance, expansiveness, and personal transformation rests in your commitment to keeping it going so your life can continue to blossom and bloom. I've crafted this section as your daily resource guide to help you get comfortable with the practice that resonates most and stay on the path. In the following pages are tips, tools, and answers to some questions you may have as your practice evolves. Let's begin by discussing what's supposed to happen when you meditate so we can demystify this somewhat secretive stigma surrounding the experience.

CHAPTER 14

EXPERIENCES IN MEDITATION

*"Do you have patience to wait until your mud
settles and the water is clear? Can you remain
unmoving until the right action arises by itself?"*

— LAO-TZU

Only a few things can happen when you meditate. And they are
all valid experiences. No matter what method you are using as the
object of your attention (mantra, visual, breath, chanting, chakra),
there are only three things that can actually happen when you
meditate *in addition* to the object of your attention:

You can *have thoughts.* You can *fall asleep.* You can *experience
stillness.*

This stillness is referred to as "the gap," an expression often
attributed to Maharishi Mahesh Yogi, the great sage and founder
of the Transcendental Meditation movement, yet used by millions
worldwide to describe the experience of pure consciousness
during meditation. My mentor, friend, and teacher Dr. Wayne
Dyer referred to the gap as the place where we "join forces with
our sacred energy and regain the power of our Source (God)."
Building on Wayne's most eloquent explanation, I define the
gap as a place of no space and no time. No space means you can't
know you're there; no time means you can't know for how long.
Yet everyone is trying to get there!
Just a few months following the 9/11 attack on the Twin
Towers of the World Trade Center, I was meditating in the historic
town of Oxford, England. It was the day of the week that they

mow all the lawns within the grounds of the university, which stretches for miles throughout the city. We were in the middle of a heat wave. Giant green mowing machines 25-feet wide buzzed the thousands of acres surrounding the thick stone walls of our medieval-era room, vibrating the narrow Rapunzel windows at each end of the castle. The sound was deafening. Even though the room temperature was a sweltering 90 degrees, I got up to close the two sliver windows to block out the noise. As I got up, Deepak asked me where I was going.

When I responded that I was trying to block out the noise so it wouldn't distract me during meditation, he smiled and said, "There's no difference between the sound of those mowers, a beautiful love song, a baby crying, the sound of your mantra, or even me whispering in your ear. They are all simply thoughts, and when you notice that you have left the mantra and drifted into any thought, any sound, or any sensation, just gently drift back to the mantra." I sat back down.

For more than 15 years, those words have stuck with me. Often in my meditation, as I become aware that I have been making mental lists or thinking about a conversation or a challenge that is before me, and upon realizing that I have drifted away from the mantra to thoughts, sounds, or physical sensations, I simply return my attention to the mantra. It's important to underscore that the three activities of the mind and the physical realm—*thoughts*, *sounds*, and *physical sensations*—are actually all versions of having thoughts. But to understand the process of going beyond them, let's first explore them.

Thoughts During Meditation

With our 60,000 to 80,000 thoughts a day, we have a thought about every one to 1.5 seconds. But you are *not* your thoughts. You are the space between each thought. And in this space of infinite possibilities lies the pure potentiality of the next thought. Most people think they are their thoughts, but we simply receive our thoughts.

Thoughts have two characteristics: they are silent, and they have meaning. So throughout our lives, as thoughts drift into our awareness, we build a foundation of meaning and then we continue to build more and more meaning around that thought and build that even larger or move to another thought. That next thought is birthed from all your experiences, coupled with infinite possibilities of potentiality. That's why the next thought can be anything. No matter what that next thought is, *it still is not you*. It is simply another thought—regardless of how profound it may seem.

So it is normal to have thoughts . . . thoughts of saying to yourself, "It's not working," or "I'm not doing it right," or, "I'm thinking about my love life," ". . . my job," ". . . money," etc. It's common to suddenly find yourself in deep list-making mode, holiday-planning internal dialogue, or working out the pros and cons of a solution to a problem. All these thoughts are normal, and when you first become aware of the waterfall of thoughts during meditation, it's simply your conditioned bodymind letting you know it's not used to stillness. Be gentle and stay the course. With each meditation, you will become more comfortable with the gentle drifting back and forth between thought activity and stillness.

So our thoughts are constructions and constrictions that keep us in activity as we try to make sense of every moment in some way. But we are not our thoughts. Which means, in any moment, we can simply give ourselves gentle permission to drift away from the thought that has just arrived and back to the object of our attention, such as our breath or the mantra.

Sounds During Meditation

Sound is a powerful creator of thought and a subcategory of thought. As long as we are gifted with functional eardrums, we will hear sound. We can close our eyelids to stop seeing, but we don't have a biological mechanism to stop sound. And because none of us lives in a soundproof booth or a recording studio, we will hear sound in our daily life and as part of our daily meditation.

Dogs bark, airplanes fly overhead, car alarms go off, and phones ring. Meditation takes you beyond sound, so don't feel the need to do anything with it. Let it in. Witness it. Observe its flow into your awareness. Hang with it a bit if you care to and then observe it flow away as your attention drifts back to the mantra, your breath, or the object of your attention. Remember: Do nothing with it. You are the one who gives the sound relevance, so at first you will want to listen and have an internal dialogue about it, which will most likely create thought and more dialogue. When you notice you are having an internal conversation about a sound, ever so gently drift back to the mantra, or your breath, or whatever the object of your attention is during the meditation.

Try to listen to two conversations simultaneously. You can't really do it. Try it with your TV or radio. Ask someone to engage you in conversation while you are deeply engrossed in a show that contains dialogue. You can really only follow one series of vibrations. You may drift back and forth, quickly grabbing a word here or there from both conversations, and your eardrum is vibrating to accommodate all frequencies being transmitted to it. But at the intellectual level, you are in overload and can't actually process them both simultaneously. Now envision that the ongoing conversation in your head is the ongoing repetition of a mantra. As long as you are always willing to drift back to it, the mantra will disconnect you from thoughts and especially sounds.

Just like your thoughts, sounds are not interruptions in your meditation; they are part of the fabric of your meditation. They *are* your meditation. Simply let the sound vibrate, and then gently drift back to the mantra, your breath, or the object of your attention. Ultimately, *the mantra or the inhale and exhale of your breathing can be the loudest sound in your awareness.* It's the intention we bring to the sound that determines its relevance in the moment. The longer you stay on a particular sound, the closer it leads you to some kind of meaning. Then a parade of thoughts will begin as you play out a dialogue. It is our desire for—and our connection to—*meaning* that sparks all thought. So do nothing with sound. Let it come; let it go; be unconcerned.

Another example of attention and intention regarding sound is happening right now as you read this book. There may be many sounds in the background, but as long as your attention is on the words on these pages and your intention is to keep reading, the outside sounds drift in and out and don't take you away from the flow of information. But if you weren't resonating with a particular sentence or paragraph, you are more susceptible to being interrupted by a sound. Remember, watching yourself breath or repeating the mantra can always be the loudest, most primary vibration in your awareness.

THE POWER OF INTENTION

It's the intention we have about objects and experiences that defines them in our life. That's why some of us love dogs and some of us are afraid of them. Some of us love Metallica, while others resonate with Taylor Swift. Some of us love pasta and others crave gluten-free offerings. But that's simply the intention *we* bring to a given situation. It's not those things that are inherently good or bad or right or wrong; it is the intention each of us brings to a particular object or experience. See how so many beliefs and affinities in your life would shift if just a few of the things you rejected, detested, feared, and repressed suddenly were on your like list. Everything would be different. Each day, unravel one thing you reject and embrace it just for the day. Show compassion for someone you are mad at; smile at something that usually makes you grimace or groan; instead of rolling your eyes, offer help.

The Sanskrit word *san kalpa* (pronounced *san kalp*) means "subtle intention." Try meditating using the mantra *san kalpa* for a week. Simply repeat it over and over, and when you realize you've drifted back to a thought, drift back to *san kalpa*. Throughout the day, every time you experience one of the things that make you constrict, ask yourself, "What if I didn't feel this way?" and silently whisper to yourself, "san kalpa." Effortlessly, in just a few days, you'll start to open to new ways of thinking. You may not change your opinion or belief system; but you'll become more aware of the constricted, mindless, or knee-jerk ways with which you respond to the world and shut out others' viewpoints. Your expanded awareness will lead to greater empathy, deeper understanding, and less implicit bias in your decision-making. This subtle meditation exercise will open your heart and your mind a bit more to all the things you reject in a conditioned way. And within a week, you will feel a powerful shift in your willingness to receive greater diversity in your thinking. Ahhhh . . . the power of intention!

Sensations During Meditation

Another generator of thought is our physical body. Physical sensations are a fact of life. We have a flesh casing, which in Sanskrit is called the *annamaya kosha*, the "illusionary sheath covering made up of food." We are indeed DNA wrapped in food. As long as we have the blessing of a physical body, we will experience sensation. We will wring our hands, furrow our brow, feel gurgles in our stomach, rise and fall with each breath, and scratch the proverbial itch. Don't let the fact that you have a physical existence frustrate or upset you during meditation. Celebrate that your flesh vehicle has moved you through your entire life right up to this moment.

When it comes to your body, always move toward comfort. *In meditation, comfort is queen!* If you have anxiety about how long you've been meditating, open your eyes and look at the clock or your watch. If your legs have gotten numb from sitting, uncross them. If your head has slouched down, gently lift it back to a more comfortable position. If that doesn't work, find a blanket or pillow to support your neck. Find a chair where you can be comfortable. Yes, it's okay if it reclines a bit. You don't want to lie down or recreate a sleeping position, but pretty much any chair you feel comfortable in will work.

When I'm meditating while sitting in a chair, I don't cross one leg over or rest my ankle on my other knee because I know that my ankle gets pins and needles in about 14 minutes. My attention flows to my numb ankle, and *boom*, I'm back here in the local domain in the realm of activity as I uncross and stretch my legs. Get yourself as comfortable as possible so your physical body is not a factor during the meditation.

When I sit in a chair to meditate, I like to have my feet touch the ground. If there is no chair, or if I am at home, I can sit comfortably on a fat (six inches high) zafu pillow with my legs crossed for about an hour before I need to readjust. Since you are only meditating for 30 minutes at a time, your goal should be to find some seating arrangement that will feel comfortable for at least that period.

If your back hurts, stop and rub it a bit, or stand up and stretch it. Finish meditating for the remaining minutes of your practice. Honor your body with any need that you have. Then gently re-immerse yourself into your practice by taking a few deep breaths and then floating back into your mantra or following your breath.

If you have engaged in strenuous physical activity, yoga, or exercise, allow yourself a cool-down before leaping into meditation. You don't want to enter the practice hyperventilating.

You also don't want to bring any alternative medicines, such as caffeine, cannabis, or alcohol, into your meditation. Wait until after you've meditated before you choose whether to ingest a recreational additive, as they will get in the way of authentic experiences. They will make it more challenging for you to genuinely "feel" the beauty of the actual meditation and, most likely, the post-meditation follow-through of your unconditioned Self. There's plenty of time throughout the rest of your day to bring in one or more of these "healing" supplements. I enjoy wine and the occasional margarita. Yet, when I am meditating a lot, I have no desire to drink. I just want to hang in that higher state of consciousness forever, and I have noticed that any "additive" dulls the clarity and the benefits of my meditation practice.

As long as we are alive, we will feel. We are pure, unbounded consciousness wrapped in this flesh casing of tender molecules for the span of a lifetime, and as many have observed, "No one gets out of here alive." Sensations are a part of life and, therefore, a part of meditation.

How Do I Know If It's Working?

Most of the time, thinking, hearing, and feeling are the primary activities we actively engage in during meditation. In addition to the object of your attention (repeating a mantra, following your breath, or chanting some no-name of the Divine), there are only the three experiences you could genuinely have during the meditation of falling asleep, having thoughts, and drifting into the stillness and silence known as being in the gap. *All are signs of a verified meditation.* If any, all, or a combination occur during your practice, that is the sign of a verified meditation.

Every other experience (worry, regret, expectation, hearing, visuals, sensations) is a version of a thought. So let's explore some of these more subtle, yet very common, experiences that we can have.

Common Beginner Experiences

New meditators often comment they feel a sensation in their head. Some cite an overall peace of mind or a calming feeling that, over time, continues to weave through all aspects of their life. Other new meditators cite boredom and restlessness. This is very common and expected. We spend every single moment of our life in activity. To suddenly stop that activity addiction or do nothing

. . . *really* do nothing . . . is an interruption to the person who has been trying to fill those empty spaces with mindless social media, obsessive texting, relentless TV watching, or self-medication. Most new meditators quickly experience a new peace of mind. Yet, a small group of beginners report either a slight dizziness, tightness in their scalp, throbbing temples, or an outright headache. If this happens to you, it usually means you are working too hard. Take a few more deep breaths before and during meditation. This will allow you to release a bit of stress before you drift into stillness. And don't work so hard on perfecting your practice. Stop trying; don't do anything. Let go, and the tightness in your head will fade away.

Still others report a gentle tingling around the location of the third eye. Throughout time, this energy center has been linked to one's connection to source, to a spiritual practice, to intuition, to spirit itself. This is a common place to have feeling during meditation. If you feel sensation in your third eye, simply see it as an energetic connection between you and your soul. It's still just a thought, so try not to place too much meaning on it.

Releasing Stress

One of the first things new meditators experience is the release of stress. Throughout your life, you have built up tension in your body, impacting and influencing your emotional and physical health. Meditation helps release stress, which we can define as *all the wishes, dreams, expectations, and desires in which a need you had was not met.* (For some of us, that's a lot of tension!) These disturbances weave their vibrations into every aspect of our being, and unless we interpret it differently or get closure, it will continue to fester at the most subtle level. Since this has built up within you over the course of your entire life, it won't get released in one or two meditations. But over time, the stress will begin to drip off of you. If you'd like to explore stress in your life and how to truly move beyond it, I suggest you read *destressifying*, which I wrote as the transformational life tool for transcending stress. *destressifying* will take you on a powerful journey of transcending stress by teaching you how to master your needs, your emotions, your communication, and your purpose in life. But, before you leave *Secrets of Meditation*, let's first master your awareness!

It is very common for a new meditator to express the release of stress in different ways: some smile more, some cry, some feel the release in their bodies, some feel more grounded, some have flashes of clarity, some have *A-ha!* moments, some become more sensitive or more emotional, some have flashes of compassion or empathy where they did not previously, while others have visual experiences. This is you becoming more aware of your unconditioned Self.

As you begin to witness these experiences, try not to shut down. A lot of these feelings and sensations signal the "waking up" of your true Self, which has been dormant under layers of emotionally toxic plaque that has built up over years from every unmet need throughout the course of your life. This process of emotional release and the weight slowly lifting off you is the beginning of your journey to emotional freedom and the catalyst for bridging your heart to a realm of unconditional love, happiness, and peace of mind. Be gentle with yourself as the "new" lighter you begins to emerge, and some of your less nourishing patterns start to drift away. Stress can also release itself through the physical body in the form of lightness or heaviness in the upper body, tingling sensations, cold or hot feelings in the hands or feet, pins and needles, and soft waves of energy flowing through certain parts of your body. In the first two weeks of a new meditation practice, you will have myriad experiences through which you will express the release of stress. Write about these experiences in your journal—not simply what you experience *during* the meditation but what happens in the other 23 hours of your day . . . your experiences *outside* of meditation. Write these down in the MY MEDITATION EXPERIENCES worksheet on page 253 and after just a few days, you will see a very clear correlation between your meditation practice and the behaviors you exhibit in your waking state.

Visual Images

Some of us are more visual than others. We see the world through images. During meditation, it would be natural to see geometric shapes, saturations of color, the mantra or other words, symbols, drawings, photographs, or even videos. Many people see the faces of people they have never met as well as the faces of loved ones, or those who have passed on from this earthly realm. When you see colors, it means there is an energetic movement in the chakra of that color.

If you see red, it means there is some energetic movement in your root chakra—some expansion going on in your grounded-ness—your connection to another person. If you see orange, it means there is some energetic movement in your second chakra—some expansion going on in your creativity center—your birth-ing of new projects, directions, relationships, or mind-sets. If you see yellow, it means there is some energetic movement in your solar plexus chakra—some expansion going on in your follow-ing through, moving through a blockage, your sense of personal transformation. If you see green, pink, or black, it means there is some energetic movement in your heart chakra—some expansion going on in your compassion, forgiveness, acceptance, your abil-ity to receive love. If you see blue, it means there is some energetic movement in your throat chakra—some expansion going on in your self-expression, your voice, your capacity to let yourself be heard. If you see purple, it means there is some energetic move-ment in your third-eye chakra—some expansion going on in your intuition, your ability to discern, your decision-making. And if you see white, it means there is some energetic movement in your crown chakra—some expansion going on in your spiritual awak-ening—your connection to Source. For more details on the mean-ing of each chakra, refer back to Chapter 8, "Secrets of Energy Meditation," and explore your experience in greater depth.

The encouragement here is to let it happen, let it flow—the images, the thoughts, the sounds, the stress release, the stillness—and within two weeks, you will be operating on a higher plane than you were only a few weeks earlier. This will not weaken you; it will not make you a slacker, lazy, or uncaring. It will give you a broader perspective on life.

That's where you will see signs of how meditation is benefiting your life. You will be amazed by what you find after only a month, and that will be the best confirmation of your personal transformation. You will see more; you will understand more. You will love more deeply. You will live more deeply.

CHAPTER 15

THE FIVE MYTHS OF MEDITATION

"What's the message in Metallica? There is no message, but if there was a message, it really should be look within yourself, don't listen to me, don't listen to James, don't listen to anybody, look within yourself for the answers."

— LARS ULRICH

Meditation has held a niche position within our popular culture for almost 100 years. In the 1940s, Somerset Maugham's tale of experiencing one-ness in *The Razor's Edge* captivated the literary world. Two years later, it became the very first major motion picture produced by Hollywood that featured meditation. In the 1960s, meditation had a huge surge as the Beatles popularized Transcendental Meditation as taught to them by the Maharishi Mahesh Yogi. But meditation's big mainstream breakthrough came in 2008 when media mogul Oprah Winfrey (also a practitioner of Transcendental Meditation) discovered a book called *A New Earth* by Eckhart Tolle and decided to partner with him in the first-ever online meditation series. Her promotion of the event on network TV for 10 solid weeks rallied more than 500,000 people around the globe to log on to the web series, bringing meditation into the mainstream and turning *A New Earth* into a *New York Times* #1 bestseller.

Every few years, a TV show, mainstream movie, or best-selling album reinvigorates awareness of meditation and that is sure to continue as the practices embeds itself more deeply into our culture. Many new meditators get their first experience while lying in savasana at the end of a yoga class; while others sample an online guided meditation and are hooked forever! Wherever you got your original understanding of meditation (and maybe it's this book), there are five basic myths that we all come across at some point in our journey of developing a practice. And if this is not your first go-round, then probably embracing one of these myths helped us rationalize that our lives would be better off *without* meditation. Ultimately, this rests at the core of why we may have stopped or let it slip away. But if you can embrace these myths as just that—myths—then release them, you will more easily give yourself permission to begin or reengage your practice.

Myth #1: The first thing you need to do is to clear the thoughts from your mind or at least still them.

As if!

You have approximately one thought every 1.2 seconds. You will not stop them so don't even try. They are not interruptions in your meditation; they *are part of* your meditation, so let them come and let them go. Simply drift back to the mantra, or your breath, or whatever object of attention you were using to disconnect you from activity. So many meditators stop meditating because they have thoughts, but having thoughts flowing in, out, and through your meditation is so perfect. This is your chance to process each day's activities that otherwise would go buried, unaddressed, and unprocessed.

That doesn't mean to pay attention to them, and that includes not resisting them either. To resist is to pay attention, and where attention goes, energy flows. Let them drift in, and let them drift away. Don't engage them. Simply drift back to the object of your attention—the mantra, your breath, the drishti, and so on. Here's how much effort to use when you meditate: Like mist rising off a lake at dawn. Stop now, and envision morning mist ever so gently lifting off a field or a lake. There is virtually no movement. Over time, you will find that during meditation you spend more time in mantra land or "follow-your-breath land" than in thought land. And as you meditate each day, the fluctuations of your mind will slow.

Myth #2: Something special or transcendent is supposed to happen during meditation.

Nothing special is supposed to happen during meditation. Blissful, calming, and entertaining experiences *can* occur during meditation, but that is not a requirement and not our goal. Special moments don't have to happen for the experience to have its emotional, physical, or spiritual benefits. But if cool things happen during meditation, hang out and enjoy them. As you immerse more deeply in the experience and drift from the mantra, you will see yourself move from witnessing the experience to thinking about it. As you begin to apply greater meaning to your experience, you will move back into activity from your stillness. At that point, you are essentially back where you started: in activity. That's okay. It's all part of the process. When you realize you have moved back into thought, just gently drift back to the mantra or the object of your attention.

Your meditation session is part of your daily practice. Have you ever been to the gym? Most likely the reason that you go there is to work out. You don't go to the gym to get magically fit in an hour or necessarily to be entertained. Your hour-long sessions at the gym bring you strength, flexibility, and balance throughout the day and night. That's where the benefits of the practice come through. And eventually from those regular one-hour workouts, there comes a subtle shift in your body and your emotional state.

The reason you work out is so you are more physically fulfilled in the rest of your life. You're not that concerned with achieving your peak health *in the gym*. The gym is your practice. It's the same thing for yoga classes.

And it's the same for your meditation practice. These 30-minute sessions are the practice for the rest of your day, week, and life. You aren't serving the world when you're sitting and meditating in the dark. It's when the session is over and you open your eyes and go back with the rest of us that you can be more creative, more intuitive, more compassionate, more fulfilled, and more open to infinite possibilities.

This, of course, is in addition to all the other physical benefits that ripple through your physiology. Cool visions and intense sensations can occur during your meditation. You can experience deep energetic and spiritual connections, and you can witness your astral body and even the gap. But those aren't the signs of a successful meditation. A successful meditation is one you *do*. The magic happens when you open your eyes. So, just show up and don't judge the experience.

Myth #3: I don't think I'm doing it right.

So many of us perfectionists out there want to know that we are "doing it right."

How many times have we asked ourselves right before, during, and after meditation, "Am I doing it right?" Or because you didn't experience the Buddha or nirvana, because you didn't see colors, or because you had thousands of thoughts, you resigned yourself to the fact that you weren't doing it right?

Whenever you ask, "Am I doing it right?" the answer is, "Yes, you are doing it right!" Now and forever, know that the pressure here is off. In meditation, as long as you are doing it, you're doing it right. The only bad meditation is the one you don't show up for! Who's your biggest critic? It's you. And judging your meditation practice is no different. There's no need to be so hard on yourself. Surrender to the unknown. Surrender to the fact that you have only one purpose in meditation, and that is to innocently repeat the mantra or follow your breath, depending on which meditation practice you choose. As long as you do that, you are doing it right. So congratulate yourself for just *doing* it. After several consecutive days of meditating, you will hear, "Hey, you look more relaxed."

Or, "Wow, great idea! I didn't expect that from you." Or, "Hey did you have some work done?" Or, "I want some of what you've got!"

Myth #4: If I meditate long enough, I will achieve enlightenment.

In your very essence—at your very core—you were born enlightened, and enlightened you shall die. But from the time you were born into this world, you have been layered with interpretations, perspectives, and conditioning. From each moment since your birth, these layers have covered that wholeness, purity, perfection, and pure consciousness from which you were formed.

Will you become enlightened? That is the wrong question. You already are. You simply may not be awake to it. But each time you meditate, you get an opportunity to peel away more layers of that conditioning. Will you awaken yourself to your wholeness? Yes. Meditation by meditation, moment by moment, you will wake up to more of your already enlightened Self.

Myth #5: If I meditate, I am a superior human being, because I am spiritual.

Meditation is a gift, a gift you give yourself each time you practice. It's also a gift that you give to the world around you. There is no spiritual hierarchy of humans based on whether they meditate or for how long. This is a spurious claim used by insecure individuals under the guise of spiritual expertise. This is the same claim that fundamentalists of all religions and belief systems have used for millennia to elevate themselves and distance nonfollowers. I do not believe meditation embraces a spiritual hierarchy. I believe it embraces the Golden Rule.

Having a daily meditation practice doesn't make someone better than anyone else. Meditation allows you to connect more deeply and more frequently to the stillness and silence that rests within each of us. The more you can tap into your unconditioned Self, the easier it is to experience empathy and see your universality, which is essentially seeing yourself in others and seeing others in yourself. In that state of one-ness awareness, there is no comparison between you and anyone else.

NAMASTÉ
I HONOR THE DIVINE IN YOU

Namasté (pronounced *nahmah-stay*, with the emphasis on the last syllable) is a Sanskrit word meaning *I bow to you*. Most people translate the salutation as, "I honor the divine place in you that is also in me. And I know that when you are in that space and I am in that space that we are one." *Namasté* is used as a traditional salutation when greeting someone (similar to *shalom, aloha,* and *assalamu alaikum*) and saying good-bye. It's used as a way to herald the universal essence—the one-ness—that connects two people.

The last time I checked, there were close to eight billion people on the planet. At the end of our lives, when we leave this earthly existence and reach the pearly gates, top of the mountain, or wherever we are going, we will see that there are eight billion paths to get there. Ours was only one path of the billions that exist.

If it works for you, do it. But a meditation practice, yoga practice, or religious practice will not make you superior to anyone else. In fact, these teachings state that you are neither above nor below anyone else. Each relationship is simply a mirror of yourself. In Sanskrit, the sutra *tat tvam asi* means "You are that." Whatever you judge in another person is a reflection of you, what you recoil from is what you'd like less of in yourself, and what you praise in others is an aspect within you that you praise and often desire more of. I believe our words, thoughts, and actions in our daily life—the threads of our relationships—are the criteria to which we should pay attention, not how much time we spend sitting in darkness and repeating a mantra. To determine what kind of person you are, listen to the answers to these questions:

Are you aware of your impact on others? On yourself? Are you forgiving? To others? To yourself? Are you kind to yourself? Have you learned from your pain? How many times a day do you sense a feeling of gratitude? Do you realize the power of your ripple? Can you learn from unanticipated uncertainties in your life? Can you grow from struggle? Can you embrace your ego? Can you embrace your own unconditional love? Do you leave ojas (sweet nectar) instead of ama (toxic residue) when you send an e-mail or text, exit a room, leave a job, end a relationship? And what do you do once you realize that you have left ama?

Whether you meditate, practice yoga, or are deeply devoted to some divine being, you will still be human and subject to all the vagaries, challenges, and opportunities that humans face each day in their bodies, their minds, and their souls. A regular meditation practice can help you enjoy and appreciate the life you currently live and take it to an even deeper level of fulfillment.

CHAPTER 16

CULTIVATING A DAILY MEDITATION PRACTICE

> *"The practice of mindfulness begins
> in the small, remote cave of your unconscious
> mind and blossoms with the sunlight of your
> conscious life, reaching far beyond the people
> and places you can see."*
>
> — EARON DAVIS

In order to bring this peace and stillness into your life on a daily basis, you must have a practice that supports the process. So many of us have meditated either through a guided meditation, lying on our backs in savasana at the end of a yoga class, or simply sitting in silence for a few minutes. Each of these experiences brings a sense of calm to our lives, but they don't necessarily shift our consciousness over the long term. Changing the way we view the world, our life, others' words and actions, and our own behavior requires a shift in our pattern of behavior.

To achieve this shift, you must dip into that stillness and silence on a regular basis. The optimal duration is 30 minutes (but you can start with a mere 16 seconds), and the ideal frequency is twice each day—once in the morning and once in the afternoon or evening (but I suggest you begin slowly and lock down a morning meditation practice of any duration first, and then lock down your afternoon or evening practice).

Feel free to use any of the mantras mentioned throughout this book. Find one that resonates with you, and use it consistently for a week and see how it feels. Use one mantra and stay with it. If you change the mantra too often, it will end up creating thought and activity. We use the mantra to disconnect us from activity, so don't feel the need to synchronize your breathing to the vibrations of the mantra. If you determine that you'd like to use a mantra, there are some classic universal sounds, including the traditional mantra *Om*, the so hum mantra, the many sutras I've discussed, and the mantra we just used in the *I Am Meditation*, or any of the other mantras you've enjoyed.

If you can commit to meditating 20 to 30 minutes every day for 40 days straight, your life will change forever, and you will want to meditate every day for the rest of your life. Following the guidance contained in this book can help you start your practice if you've never meditated or to reengage if you have drifted away from your practice. But in the end, *you* have to see the value, so you will want to continue on a daily basis. Make a commitment today to show up every day for 40 days to allow the practice to settle in comfortably. Most likely you will miss a meditation here or there. Just pick up the next day, and you'll still feel the cumulative results. Try not to miss consecutive days. Are you ready to take your life to the next level? You can start right now by meditating with me for five minutes with a free guided meditation in *The Meditation Room* on my website.

Most people who slip away from a meditation practice become *crisis* meditators. They know the value of the practice, but they have stopped meditating for some reason. Then when they begin interpreting their lives as filled with challenges, they turn to meditation for a few days, weeks, or months.

There's a big difference between meditating once in a while and having a meditation practice. Having a practice is when you can successfully string together consecutive days of meditation until it is ritualized. Ideally, this will become part of your daily routine, no different than brushing your teeth. So why is it so hard?

It's really not. Yet former meditators cite two main reasons for why they stop a perfectly fulfilling practice after only a few days or weeks: *lack of time* and *subtlety of results*.

Excuse #1: I Don't Have Enough Time

The number one excuse people give for not meditating is that they don't have enough time. They have time for watching TV, streaming videos, texting, talking, partying, checking e-mails, Facebooking, commuting, flying, seeing the doctor, etc. which means they've got at least five minutes where they are waiting around. We determine what activities we fit into each moment of the 24 hours of our day. Of course, realistically you have the time to meditate for 20 to 30 minutes every day, even if you just shaved one minute from each of your morning activities. Time is not some independent being that imposes itself on our schedule. We develop our schedule based on our values and beliefs. We decide what we think is the best use of our life energy and how much time we are willing to allot to various activities.

What I have found is when you incorporate a meditation practice into your life, suddenly there is time for everything. You approach everything from a point of greater clarity and ease. Deadlines evaporate as you finish projects ahead of schedule. You experience more restful sleep, which gives you greater vitality and the ability to focus. You become more efficient in all your work, so there is finally some free time and some breathing room. You realize the non-nourishing behaviors you were expending energy on, and you are able to replace them with more nourishing, more efficient behaviors—ways of living that support you more. But you have to take the first step, so I suggest you commit to this week of a daily meditation practice and see how the time in your life expands to fit everything you want and more.

Excuse #2: I Don't Feel the Results

The second most common reason people cite for not meditating is they think the results are too subtle so they can't see any value in continuing. Again, this goes back to our misconceptions about what meditation is supposed to be. If your expectations are to levitate and see colors but you are only aware of drifting back and forth between the mantra and thoughts, you will assume it's not working and give up. You may even think you're doing it wrong because you don't have any *A-ha!* moments during your practice.

The benefits happen in the 23 hours a day we are not meditating. So be patient and stop looking for the higher state of consciousness to arrive. It will flow into you when it is time, so don't worry or be concerned. Just keep meditating, and after a few days, you will recognize distinct changes in the way you interact with life, stress, disappointments, unmet needs, and your own thoughts.

Having a meditation practice is no different than doing some form of physical exercise every day. Exercise subtly tightens your body; meditating every day gently eases your mind into a sense of well-being. Why wouldn't you want to do the same thing for your emotional state, your physical body, and your spiritual possibilities?

The Exception to the Rule

Many schools of meditation perform certain rituals before the actual meditation occurs, such as chanting *Om*, saying a prayer, setting intentions, or asking questions. The purpose is not to then bring these questions actively into your meditation. In fact, it's to get certain intentions and dialogues out into the ether. I like the question-and-answer format prior to meditation because it allows me the opportunity to settle into the key things going on in my life and to bring some intentions—not just my attention—to them.

New meditators who are high achievers often apply that same level of effort, focus, and concentration they have applied to every other aspect of their life. It usually brings results in our world, and their track record might be brilliant. In fact, most of us were taught the following equation at a very young age:

focus + effort = success

We were also taught that if we increase the effort, the level of success will expand as well. The lesson we absorbed was work hard enough, and we can have everything we want. But as you may have noticed, this supposed law of life doesn't always apply to every aspect of life. In fact, in time it becomes more of a personal style—a way we live our life—rather than a law that we consciously follow. But this "natural" law of our society doesn't always translate life's challenges into expansive solutions. By coming from a different perspective or withdrawing so fully and then reimmersing, we sometimes see something once familiar with a new set of "eyes," infinitely increasing the possibilities for expansion and growth.

In meditation, it's the exception to the rule that brings us success. The best results occur when we let go of all effort. We let go of focus, replacing it with innocence, and the innocent repetition of the mantra. The formula for an effective meditation is:

surrender + innocence = success

It goes against everything we've been taught. Surrendering is counterintuitive for successful, accomplished, or powerful individuals who have *worked* hard to achieve all their positions and possessions. All that you've accomplished in this life is based on DOing. Meditation is about BEing. So you require a different set of tools to connect with your divine inner Self that rests beneath all these positions and possessions—to just BE.

When Should I Meditate?

In the era when these teachings were first made popular, almost 5,000 years ago, most people were farmers. They rose before sunrise, they washed, they prayed and meditated, and then they went into the fields at the first hint of sunrise. They worked in the fields with their animals and they retired for the day before sunset. They meditated before dinner, and they slept as the sun slept. For more than 5,000 years, Ayurveda has taught that the ideal times to meditate are between the hours of 5 and 7 A.M. and between 5 and 7 P.M. According to Ayurveda, these times of the day are at the lightest part of the morning and evening (the end of vata time: 2 to 6). This, of course, corresponds to the rising and setting of the sun, which is how these ancient civilizations guided their lives. Ayurveda was developed long before night shifts, nightclubs, and round-the-clock emergency rooms, and long before planes, trains, and buses moved through the night. So this ancient guidance had little knowledge that we would be living in an age where people went out to dinner when it was already dark, and many of us rose long after the sun had come up.

The Power of Ritual

So when is the right time? I used to say to myself, *I'll meditate at 10 o'clock every morning.* But 10 never comes. You know what it's like. The phone rings. The dog needs attention. You spend more time than you thought you would on sending an e-mail, going to a store, or dealing with a challenge. Then it's noon, and you have a lunch meeting. You plan for 3 o'clock but then you get pulled away, so you promise yourself you will meditate as soon as you get home. But a friend calls and asks you out to dinner. And then you go to a movie and then to a club for dancing, and before you know it, it's midnight and you haven't meditated.

If you lock your meditation in like a seamless ritual, it will flow without thought. The easiest way to lock in your daily meditation practice—and most important, your morning meditation—is to ritualize it. Make it part of a series of activities you do based on each activity flowing from one into the other, rather than what time it is while you're performing them.

For example, when you wake up each morning you look at the clock—then you pee. You don't say to yourself, "It's 6:30; time to pee." Then you do the next thing on your invisible list of morning activities and then the next. You don't know what time you brush your teeth every morning, because you don't do it based on time; you do it based on following some order of rituals you've created over the years. We have between 8 and 15 that we deploy in a certain sequence on waking.

The Effortless Ritual: RPM

To solve the difficulty that most meditators have ensuring that they lock in that first meditation of the day, I developed a ritual known as RPM, which stands for Rise, Pee, Meditate. It's based on the fact that you wake up each day. So what time do you wake up?

It's not too big a leap to think that within a few minutes of waking, you're going to pee. Well, you're two-thirds of the way there! If the very next thing you do is sit down to meditate, then within 35 minutes of opening your eyes in the morning, you'll have a half-hour of stillness and silence inside you to greet every moment as you move throughout the rest of your day.

If the first thing you do when you wake up is meditate, then logically, there will be fewer distractions to begin the practice. How much time is spent checking your e-mails, reading your Facebook or Twitter feed, standing in the shower, watching TV, or going online? Couldn't you take a few minutes from each of your morning ablution rituals and wake up 15 minutes earlier? Then you'd have that sweet unhurried 30 minutes to start your day. If the answer is no, then revisit what time you go to bed and try going to sleep 15 minutes earlier for a few weeks in a row. It will suddenly be a part of who you are. So, yes, Ayurveda says to meditate between the hours of five and seven, but you have to do what works best for you. Whatever works!

Over many years, I had popularized the concept of sunrise meditation—sitting down in the total blackness of the morning, setting an intention for the next 24 hours, and then meditating as the very first rays of light peek above the horizon and the sun kisses the day and blesses those intentions. There is something special about manifesting the day—being the silent witness to the birds waking up; the wind beginning to stir; and the warmth of the sunrise bathing your face, as the earth begins one more light-filled rotation through space. It reminds you of how inter-connected and interdependent every flicker of life is. This works especially well if your house is filled with our beings. But even if you live alone, I suggest you experiment with my pre-dawn ritual.

Evening Ritual: RAW

The evening is more difficult because you have time issues on both sides of your meditation practice, and your mind is very active. For the afternoon or evening meditation, I suggest the acronym RAW (Right After Work). Make it the very, very, very last thing you do before you leave work or the very, very, very first thing you do when you get home. This way it's ritualized, and there aren't any time pressures.

If you meditate using the RAW ritual, you will ever so gently coast into your evening before it explodes with activity: dinner, kids, stories of the day, TV, Internet, pets, workouts, and anything else you cram into those last remaining hours you are awake. You will be bringing a bit of stillness and silence into the activity of your evening. And you will be in alignment with the timeless wisdom of Ayurveda as well as the circadian rhythms of nature. If you can have your evening meditation under your belt, you handle it all with grace and aplomb. If it feels better for you to meditate closer to your bedtime, do that. Just remember meditating too close to bedtime will "steal" your sleep, rejuvenating you so much that you may have trouble getting to bed. Maintain this philosophy: When it comes to your afternoon or evening meditation, do whatever works!

How Long Should I Meditate?

Time is on your side. And I recommend you start gently and small. Start with 16 seconds . . . move up to a minute. Add a minute every week. And then suddenly, YOU HAVE A PRACTICE! Then see if you can truly own a 10-minute practice twice a day—

one in the morning and once in the afternoon or evening. Slowly work yourself up to it so it gets ingrained and reinforced. That would be spectacular! Once you really feel comfortable with those two bookends of your day, begin the process of adding an extra minute to your RPM every week. When you realize that you've hit 20 minutes every day, celebrate and gift yourself something special. Don't add any more time to your afternoon practice until you feel totally comfortable you have showed up every day for 40 days. Then add a minute each week. This gentle, slow, incremental methodology will allow you to truly master your practice.

As for timing your meditation, feel free to face the direction of a clock, watch, or timer. I place a clock right in front of my gaze so that if I should open my eyes a crack, I'll see the time in less than a second, and I can seamlessly drift back into my meditation. I prefer that to waiting for an alarm, but it's a matter of preference. And if you'd prefer to be signaled at the 10-, 20-, or 30-minute point or a specific interval, every cell phone on the planet has an alarm, and most phones have ringtones and apps that mimic chiming Tibetan bowls or similar soothing sounds to gently take you out of the meditation. Ideally, choose a soft sound that gets progressively louder.

Where Should I Meditate?

I meditate each morning with *Peaches, the Buddha Princess*, curled up on another zafu right next to me. I sit in front of a coffee table that I place a digital clock on. I don't use a timer or alarm. I meditate and open my eyes when I am aware I'm thinking about time. I glance at the clock, take in the time, close my eyes, and go back into meditation. What should you do? First, leave your bed. Find a spot you don't connect with other ritualized behaviors. Pick any relatively quiet place where you can be relaxed and comfortable. In extreme circumstances, meditators have meditated in their bathrooms, their cars, and even their closets. But that shouldn't be necessary. Find a quiet spot that feels somewhat sacred or special, a place you can imagine sitting in every day, and find a cushion, pillow, or chair that you can hang in for at least 30 minutes. Move toward the most comfortable seat and the most comfortable position. Always keep moving toward comfort, wherever that is.

If you have trouble getting out of bed or you repeatedly tap the snooze button on your clock, then I suggest you use the meditation technique taught to me by Vedic Master Tiffany Murray. I call it the *Snooze Button Meditation*! As soon as your alarm goes off and you touch the snooze, use that as your meditation timer. With your eyes closed, slide your tush up to your headboard, pull your blanket up around you to keep your comfort level high, and begin your sitting up meditation practice. When the alarm sounds again, you will have a solid 10 minutes of meditation embedded in you.

Feel free to meditate while commuting (as long as you are not driving), at the doctor's office, in the airport, at a sporting event, at a rock concert, or during any long trip you are taking. The next time you have five free minutes, see what it feels like to use those precious minutes tapping into the stillness and silence that rests within. It doesn't matter what direction you face: God is everywhere. I like to face east to feel the first light of morning come into my meditation. Usually this is followed by hearing birds, but every day is different . . . all so special. If you need to peek, peek. If you need to move, move. If you need to stretch, stretch. Do whatever you need to do: sneeze, cough, scratch, yawn. Always move toward comfort. If you are pulled out of meditation by some disturbance, tend to your urgent situation and then return and meditate for the remaining minutes.

If for any reason you find that you have skipped a day or a meditation, give yourself a hug for noticing. Cut yourself some slack and dive right back in. The practice is cumulative, so don't worry if you slip away as long as you are willing to slip back in.

THE 9.5 MOST VALUABLE KEYS
TO A SUCCESSFUL DAILY PRACTICE

Whether you meditate using your breath or using a mantra as the object of your attention, there are several keys to an effortless and comfortable daily practice:

1. **Comfort is queen.** Make sure you are comfortable in every moment. If you're comfortable, you'll continue to meditate; if you're not comfortable, most likely you'll stop. So no matter what the disturbance, don't resist. Stop and deal with it (stretch your legs, look at your watch, rub your neck, turn off your phone, scratch your cheek), and drift back to mantra.

2. **Create a ritual.** Don't pin your meditation to a time on the clock. Use a ritual such as RPM (Rise, Pee, Meditate) or any other ritual that works for you. The afternoon ritual can be RAW (Right After Work) or any other ritual that feels comfortable. Allow your meditation time to be sacred.

3. **Remember to let go.** Ask your questions, say your affirmations, set your intentions innocently before you meditate and then let them all go. Don't bring anything into the meditation (no intentions, agendas, or targets) other than the mantra, following your breathing, or the object of your attention.

4. **Stay innocent.** See if you can master the Buddhist concept of beginner's mind—seeing every meditation as the very first. Show up like a curious child. Don't force your practice. Let it innocently unfold.

5. **Witness.** Let go of any expectations you may have about the practice. Nothing is *supposed* to happen. Observe whatever flows into you and drift back to the object of your attention.

6. **Keep drifting.** Treat any interruption, sound, old mantra, idea, mood, feeling, or emotion as you would any other thought, and gently drift back to the object of your attention: the mantra or your breath.

7. **There is no meaning.** Don't get distracted with the meaning of any sutra, affirmation, mantra, or intention that you've planted. If you are repeating a mantra, remember that it's only a vibration—the meaning will take care of itself.

8. **Surrender.** How hard should you try? Like mist rising off a lake at dawn. Any harder than that, *and you are trying way too hard!* If you are using a mantra, don't say it; *listen* to it. Let it bubble up.

9. **You are perfect.** Whatever happens is perfect! Do not judge the experience. Every meditation is like a snowflake, unique and never to be repeated.

9½. **Enjoy!** Do not get too serious. This is a lighthearted practice, so enjoy!

CHAPTER 17

FREQUENTLY ASKED QUESTIONS

"There is no God other than life itself."

— OSHO

There are thousands of frequently asked questions regarding what one experiences during meditation, and I have addressed the most frequent of the frequent. The simple fact remains the answer to every questions rests within you. Simply meditate, follow the guidance in this book, and when you have a question, the answer will most likely come from inside. If it doesn't, e-mail me at secrets@davidji.com, and we can figure it out together. So before you ask any questions, just show up and meditate every day for 40 days!

After you have accomplished this magnificent process, your life will be different, and you will then be able to ask yourself, *Do I like my life more when I'm meditating or more when I'm not meditating?*

If you like it more, keep going, and your life will continue to blossom and bloom. If you aren't sure, keep meditating for another month. After you hit your second month of daily meditation, send me an e-mail and tell me how it feels and what's gone on in your life. Tell me your challenges and your triumphs. Ask any questions you'd like, and I'll personally reply to you

If you don't feel that 40 days of meditation has provided any value in your life, pass this book on to someone else. Send me an e-mail, and let's chat about it before you decide to move on.

What's the difference between prayer and meditation?

Prayer is talking to God; meditation is listening. Quiet your mind through meditation, and you will connect more deeply to whatever God you pray to. You've been asking questions in the form of prayer for many years. In the quietude of your heart, you will finally hear the whispers of God's reply.

How can I tell if I'm ready to embark on a spiritual journey or attend a meditation workshop?

We've all heard the saying, "When the student is ready, the teacher appears." When people begin asking themselves whether they'd benefit from a more intense inner journey, they are usually ready. At a meditation retreat, most attendees are like-minded in terms of being open to the concepts of expanded states of consciousness and deeper states of peace. The energy of the collective is tangible and can be an empowering experience to help you take bolder steps in your life. If that sounds overwhelming, start more slowly and learn to meditate with a teacher in a more intimate environment. If you'd like to start or deepen your practice, reach out to me and we can chat about your next steps.

What should my goal be during meditation?

It's paradoxical but your goal is to simply BE . . . not DO. So depending upon the type of meditation you choose, just do that. For example: In mantra meditation, just repeat the mantra. In breath awareness, just breathe. In drishti meditation, just gaze. It's a rookie mistake to try to intellectualize or add ANYTHING to the process. Simpler is better. Less is more.

Where do I find a teacher?

The ideal way to deepen your meditation practice is directly from a practicing teacher. They don't have to wear monks' robes or Indian saris to teach you. My criteria is that they meditate daily, understand the teachings, and have an open heart. If so, they can share the practice with you and support you. Feel free to visit **davidji.com**'s meditation resource page to find a certified teacher near you.

What mantra should I use to start?

Select a mantra that you will feel comfortable with—not for its supposed meaning but from its vibration alone. Feel free to use any of the mantras listed below, or learn your personal mantra through a certified meditation teacher. The following mantras can work very effectively until you receive your mantra:

> *I Am*
> *So Hum*
> *Om*
> *Om Ah Hum*
> *Yud Hey Vov Hey*
> *Aham Brahmasmi* or any of *the mahavakyas*
> *Om Ganapati Namah*
> *Yogastha Kuru Karmani*
> *The Chakra Vibrations: Laam, Vaam, Raam, Yaam,*
> *   Haam, Shaam, Om*
> *Moksha*
> *Om Mane Padme Om*
> *Gratitude, Trust, Love, Peace*
> *Om Namah Shivaya*
> *So Hum Namah*

Should I try to synchronize the mantra with my breath?

This is another trap for those who have practiced a form of breathing meditation and then try to use a mantra. When you breathe as the object of your attention, your breath rises and falls, speeds and slows. The same thing happens to the mantra. They will diverge at some point, similar to rubbing your belly and patting your head at the same time. There is no way to really synchronize or coordinate the two. If you have a breath awareness practice and you want to move to a mantra-based practice, try synching the breath and the mantra for a few minutes and then let go of the breath and solely drift your attention to the mantra.

Can I listen to soothing meditation or yoga music during the meditation?

You can do anything you like, but if you use music during your meditation practice, you are staying in activity. So, I don't recommend it. The reason you like music is because it soothes and relaxes you. But it also reminds you of something relaxing and therefore you are introducing meaning to the meditation, which will drift you into thought. My strong suggestion is the only way to experience pure unbounded consciousness is through stillness. *Yogastha kuru karmani! Established in presence, perform action.* If you can create stillness as the bookends of your day, then feel free to add any other kind of meditation or practice in between. That practice will soar as long as you bracket it with experiences of non-activity.

I fell off the wagon and stopped meditating! Help!

First of all, take a deep breath right now. Life can get busy and sometimes feel overwhelming. This can create a domino effect in which certain "noncritical" daily rituals get dropped. This simply means that you have chosen to allocate 30 minutes to another activity in your day over the perceived value of meditation in your life. You have certain expectations, and you're not feeling the results, so you don't see the value. That's a common response from those who stop practicing meditation. But if you want to, you can easily reconnect with your most centered Self, starting now. You can gently drift back to your practice today by selecting a few moments to celebrate that you are even having this conversation. Now pick a time today when you can dedicate 10 minutes and work your way up to 30 minutes by increasing one minute per day. Don't feel constrained or pressured, but make sure you truly dedicate your attention and intention to this gift that you are giving yourself.

Meditation Training Wheels to Get You Back on Track

We've already spoken about the power of 40 days and the ease of which we can surrender to daily guided meditations. If you've lost your meditation mojo and you don't know how to get it back, *do not despair!*

When I launched *40 days of Transformation* as a free online program, thousands of "crisis" meditators reached out to me and said the 40-day process saved their lives. As, I mentioned earlier, the "40 days of Transformation" is based on the Sufi poet Jelaluddin Rumi's quote, "What nine months does for the embryo, forty early mornings will do for your growing awareness."

Most religions reference a 40-day transformational experience as well. There are many biblical and historical references to 40 days. Moses prayed for 40 days on Mt. Sinai; David and Goliath fought twice a day for 40 days; the ancient Egyptians packed the bodies of the dead for 40 days before mummifying them; the prophet Muhammad fasted and practiced abstinence for 40 days; Buddha meditated for 40-plus days under the Bodhi tree before experiencing enlightenment; and Jesus fasted in the wilderness battling the devil for 40 days (which is why Lent is 40 days).

Simply doing an online search for "40 days" turns up hundreds of references to this 40-day connection.

40 days of Transformation heralded that connection. Each day, meditators from all over the world—at every level of experience and practice—logged on, turned up their speakers, and journeyed with one of the many types of meditation offered for 40 days in a row. Each meditation is followed by a metta moment, an act of loving-kindness that each of us can flow into the world that day. The beauty of the *40 days of Transformation* is that it's an immersion into mantra meditation, mindfulness, sound healing, and metta bhavana in one seamless experience, allowing you to experience the union as well. Every meditation starts with a lesson, then contains a period of silence from 5 minutes to 30 minutes where I ring a crystal bowl or chime every few minutes, so you can stick around and meditate for as long as you like. At the end, the metta moment gives us an intention for the day—and that is actually how we transform the world—by transforming ourselves!

Can you imagine the ripple effect of this sweet silence spanning the globe as meditators in every time zone log on together for 40 days? The power of the collective is profound and for 40 days tens of thousands of us share a universal journey of one-ness. It's gone viral so right now, in this very moment, thousands of people are meditating to the *40 days of Transformation*. Cultivating mindfulness and sharing acts of metta is a beautiful daily practice, and I recommend it to you—no matter what your style of meditation is.

MY INTENTIONS

This is your opportunity to transform your good intentions into life-affirming choices. Below are seven sacred questions that I encourage you to ask yourself right now to place a stake in the ground as you truly commit to a powerful daily practice. The answers that flow from your heart will deliver you to where you need to be in your life. But before you answer, close your eyes, place your hand on your heart, and allow yourself to get still.

1. WHY DO I WANT TO MEDITATE?

    _____

    _____

    _____

    _____

2. WHAT DO I HOPE TO ACCOMPLISH THROUGH HAVING A
    DAILY PRACTICE?

    _____

    _____

    _____

    _____

3. WHAT IS MY DEEPEST DESIRE?

_____

_____

_____

_____

_____

4. WHAT AM I GRATEFUL FOR IN THIS MOMENT? AND WHY?

_____

_____

_____

_____

_____

5. WHAT TRAITS AND CHARACTERISTICS DO I HOPE TO CULTIVATE AND NOURISH THROUGH MY PRACTICE?

_____

_____

_____

_____

_____

6. WHAT NON-NOURISHING BEHAVIOR, HABIT, OBSESSION, OR COMPULSION DO I WISH TO RELEASE FROM MY LIFE?

_____

_____

_____

_____

_____

7. WHAT NEW BEHAVIORS AM I COMMITTED TO IN ORDER TO MANIFEST MY DREAM LIFE?

_____

_____

_____

_____

_____

MY MEDITATION EXPERIENCES

Each day after your meditation, write down the length of your morning practice and what happened during your meditation. There are no right or wrong answers. A few minutes after your meditation ends, write down how long the practice lasted. Then jot down a few impressions of the experience. So if you fell asleep, saw colors, had thoughts, felt restless or agitated, experienced calm or peace, etc., write that down. At the end of your day, write a few words that express your defining moments of the day, such as, "I was irritable." "I got in an argument." "I forgave someone." "I executed brilliantly." "I felt in the zone." Feel free to comment about your sleep patterns, level of vitality, or overall demeanor. At the end of each month, look back and review. You'll see in black and white—that the way you see and respond to the world around you is directly linked to your daily practice. And that will inspire you to keep it going. Send me an e-mail after 40 days letting me know how your life is unfolding with a constant daily meditation routine.

Day	Length	Experiences in Meditation	Experiences Out of Meditation
1			
2			
3			
4			

Day	Length	Experiences in Meditation	Experiences Out of Meditation
5			
6			
7			
8			
9			
10			
11			
12			
13			
14			
15			
16			
17			
18			
19			
20			
21			
22			

Day	Length	Experiences in Meditation	Experiences Out of Meditation
23			
24			
25			
26			
27			
28			
29			
30			
31			
32			
33			
34			
35			
36			
37			
38			
39			
40			

AFTERWORD

Meditating every day has opened my world to lean more deeply in the direction of my dreams and away from what no longer serves me. It's a process and a lifelong journey. I am now aware when words leave my lips that don't create peace and harmony. I'm now aware when I have thoughts that really don't serve me. Meditation has awakened the silent witness within me, and that has made all the difference. I feel truly blessed to walk on this sweet earth.

I believe this comes from seeing the daily benefits and results of this practice. I look forward to connecting to the stillness and silence that rests within because I now know it is the source of all existence.

You are not alone on this journey. We are all together, stumbling through each day to put some food in our bellies and receive love. In the process, we can share that love, light, acceptance, forgiveness, encouragement, and peace with everyone we touch.

If we can do this—even just a bit more than we did yesterday—then this life of ours, as transient and uncertain as it is, will be the most amazing journey one could ever fathom.

Each of us shares a sacred obligation to nurture and protect all the sentient beings on the planet. This includes animals in shelters and on factory farms, wild game, our beautiful oceans and the life that teems within, cops who serve and protect us, and the brave military veterans and their families who have served and sacrificed so we could have one more day of freedom. But we need to take it deeper every day by opening our heart just a little bit more. As Leonard Cohen said, "Ring the bells that still can ring. Forget your perfect offering. There is a crack in everything. That's how the light gets in." Remember to love yourself . . . love thy neighbor . . . and adopt your next pet.

READING

Chödrön, Pema. *When Things Fall Apart: Heart Advice for Difficult Times.* Boston: Shambhala Library, 1997.

Chopra, Deepak. *The Way of the Wizard.* New York: Harmony Books, 1995.

Dyer, Wayne. *Wishes Fulfilled.* New York: Hay House Publishing, 2012.

Hafiz. *The Gift: Poems by Hafiz, the Great Sufi Master.* Translated by Daniel Ladinsky. New York: Penguin Books, 1999.

Houston, Jean. *A Mythic Life: Learning to Live Our Greater Story.* San Francisco: Harper San Francisco, 1996.

Rosenberg, Marshall B. *Nonviolent Communication: A Language of Life.* Encinitas, CA: PuddleDancer Press, 2003.

Satchidananda, Sri Swami. *The Yoga Sutras of Patanjali.* Translated by Alistair Shearer. New York: Random House, 1982.

Shankara, Adi. *Adi Shankara's Crest Jewel of Discrimination: Timeless Teachings on Nonduality.* Translated by Swami Prabhavananda and Christopher Isherwood. Hollywood, CA: Vedanta Press, 1975.

Simon, David. *Free to Love, Free to Heal: Healing Your Body by Healing Your Emotions.* Carlsbad, CA: Chopra Center Press, 2009.

Simon, David. *The Ten Commitments: Translating Good Intentions into Great Choices.* Deerfield Beach, FL: Heath Communications, 2006.

Yogananda, Paramahansa. *Autobiography of a Yogi.* Los Angeles: Self-Realization Fellowship, 1997.

IN GRATITUDE

Ollie, Eddie, Annie, Francis, Monroe, and sweet Mazy. Meditating in the nonlocal. You are my daily spirit guides. Shanti, shalom, and peace.

Deepak Chopra was the first teacher who taught me to access the answer to the questions *Who am I? What do I want?* and *What is my dharma?* I am forever grateful for his willingness to share with me his brilliance, his passion, his creativity, his articulation, and his compassion.

David Simon saw something inside me and invited me into his heart. There I have stayed since the day we met. And there I will stay until I leave this earth. He has guided me through darkness into light and from pain and constriction to moksha—emotional freedom. And it has been my privilege to serve his vision of global healing through higher consciousness and love.

My dear teachers Osho, Paramahansa Yogananda, His Holiness the 14th Dali Lama, Yogi Bhajan, and Dr. Wayne Dyer—you move me each day to live a life of greater service, peace, creativity, acceptance, expansion, humor, compassion, love, and abundance.

Rosanne Drucker, my loving wife, brilliant musician/singer/ songwriter, and true believer. You've known me a very long time, and through it all, you have always encouraged my next step, no matter how difficult or random it seemed. You believed in me when I could not see my own light, and that has made all the difference. Your generosity of spirit has been the dharma beacon I have chased all these years. Your creativity, verve, and ability to flow the emotions of the universe into music and lyrics are unpar-alleled. Your unwavering open heart and your unconditional love have given me the freedom to explore the universe, and in that journey, I have found my soul. There could be no greater gift than your expanded being. Thank you . . . again and forever.

Peaches, the Buddha Princess, you are a living meditation and my unconditional companion who teaches me surrender in each moment and reminds me every day to open my heart just a little bit more.

Somyr Perry, words cannot express my deep gratitude for you taking my life to the next level. Your perseverance, desire to grow in all aspects of your mind, heart, and soul, and your generous essence have transformed the members of the *davidji SweetSpot Community* forever. Thank you for always pushing me to challenge myself. You are the Universe!

Nancy MacLeod, I'm in awe of you. You shatter the definition of comfort zone and show us all the meaning of courage, determination, and heart. You inspire me every day.

Tiffany Murray, you are the embodiment of grace under fire. Your devotion to—and seamless integration of—the teachings of timeless wisdom make you the role model for all Vedic masters to follow. I am proud to call you my dear friend and one of my certified Masters of Wisdom and Meditation Teachers.

Michael Bloom, my dear friend, brother, and guide who understands the true meaning of enlightenment and the power of the present moment, you rock!

My human family that has made it all possible to evolve each day into the best version of myself: my amazing dad and best friend, Jay Ji, and his devoted wife, Charna. Stanley Drucker, the greatest clarinetist who ever breathed life into a licorice stick; my unconditional loving mother, Naomi Drucker; my beloved sister, Susie, who has stuck by my side since I ventured out of the womb; my truly authentic brother, Jeffrey; and my soul nephew, Eddie Gilbert. You all have held space for me in my darkest abysses, championed my climbs, and celebrated with me on the peaks. I always feel your love and support regardless of where I am on my journey. I love you dearly.

Karla Refoxo, my dear friend, spoiler of Peaches, and teacher of life. You are the embodiment of tender loving-kindness merged with powerful creativity—a sweet, sensitive, divine soul, and a loving meditation teacher. You started it all with your amazing giant Buddha fresco at the Chopra Center in New York. Your vision of the covers of *Secrets of Meditation and Guided Meditations* brought deep clarity and excitement to the projects, as did your artistic sensibility. Thank you for bringing your sweet Gallega energy into my world and teaching me to keep dying to the past. You are a blessed Sufi Nagual, a gifted artist, and a trusted heart friend. Tulku rules! Tulkujewels.com

The thousand beams of light that make up the global network of the *Certified Masters of Wisdom and Meditation Teachers.* You inspire me each day as you move in the direction of your dharma, helping, healing, and serving others with your light and love. Profound thanks to the bold explorers of my *Deeper Still advanced certification.* Your commitment and deep devotion to the ancient wisdom traditions has set you apart and you have responded to the calling with power, freedom, and grace.

The thousands of meditation students around the world who have attended my workshops, joined me at one of my retreats, traveled with me to far-off places, and sat in my classes. Thank you for trusting me to share the ancient wisdom.

My reindeer sister Marianne Pagmar—The Love Shower—you have shared your heart so selflessly with the world and your life has been an inspiration for thousands who have been blessed by your timeless energy; my dream sister Rosalinda Weel, you have raised my vibration throughout the Netherlands—it has become my second home and you have taught me the meaning of pure love; and my Kundalini sister Julia Anastasiou—Yog Sundari— your bold light elevates all who come in contact with you. I am so grateful for our timeless connection.

My dear friends and loving mentors Dr. Wayne Dyer, Don Miguel Ruiz, Tavis Smiley, Barbara DeAngelis, Jean Houston, T. Harv Eker, Mike Dooley, Cheryl Richardson, and James Van Praagh.

The millions around the world who have streamed or down-loaded a meditation with me online, listened to one of my albums, or sat with me in person. We have danced in the gap together, and we have shared the magic of one-ness. You are the driving force behind my consciousness, and I am profoundly grateful.

My friends and supporters in the cosmic realm Laurent Potdevin, John Thiel, Ariana Grande, Caroline Brown, Steve Samuels, Janet Ashley, Frank Elaridi, Anna Callori, Megan

Monahan, Suze Yalof Schwartz, and Unplug Meditation—the first drop-in meditation studio on the planet.

Michael Nila, Pam Cammarata, Mia Deufel, Captain Jack Hart, Dan Schmer, Howard Powers, the Department of Justice, and the Blue Courage Team dedicated to restoring the nobility of policing.

Richard Kwakernaak and my active and veteran friends in the Dutch Navy and Special Forces—the brave BEings who have all dedicated their lives to cause of freedom.

My undying best buddy and kids' yoga expert Jodi Komitor, founder of Next Generation Yoga.

My Hay House family: the divine goddess of affirmations—the amazing Louise Hay, and the Captain of the ship—Reid Tracy; my brilliant editor Patty Gift; Carlsbad goddesses Margarete Nielsen, Heather Tate, Lindsay DiGianvittorio, & Jessica Polson; Hay House Radio, who has supported me in the studio every week on *LIVE! from the SweetSpot* for almost a decade—the incomparable Diane Ray and her brilliant engineering team: Mike, Mitch, Steve, Rocky, and Rachel; the *Secrets of Meditation* editorial and design team of Lisa Mitchell, Lisa Cheng, Nick Welch, and Christy Salinas; my sweet meditating rockstars Diane, Bryn, Stacey Smith, and Donna Abate—you guys keep it real!; and my meditation and Ayurveda students at Hay House who keep raising the roof. Hay House Radio rules!

The brilliant team of the *Hay House World Summit* and the *I Can Do It* conferences. Shay Lawry, Mollie Langer, Christa Gabler, and Chelsey Larson. Thank you for always supporting me and generously providing me with opportunities to share light with the world.

Lubosh Cech, my loving brother. Words can barely express my admiration and respect for you and your creative vision. You are a divine representation of bhakti and a generous and gifted artist. You ensure that every davidji visual expression to the world carries the perfection, elegance, and sweet intention of the source from which it was originally derived. I am in your gratitude. LuboshCech.com

Tara Lynda Guber, the generous yogi who encouraged me to own my impact. Love you, taraji!

Thank you to those along my path who have gifted me with your friendship and helped me better understand life: my oldest friend, partner, and mentor, Mark Clemente; my dear heart, mind, and confidante for so many years, my spiritual sister Anna Chosak; fearless Terri Cole; Max Simon, Rick Dore, Stanley Komitor; Pam, Sara, and Izzy Simon; Benji Moseman; Dr. Valencia Booth Porter; sweet Fran Lambert; Rookie Komitor; Robin Muto; Freddie Leonardo; Alisha Olivier Park; Judy Perl; Naadi Mohan; the spa genius Alexis Ufland; Grace Porter; Neal Tricarico; Patrick Flanagan; Tal Wilkenfeld; Trista Thorp; Ravi Meher; Dr. Suhas Kshirsagar; Deva Premal; Kimberly Willock Pardiwala; General Al Haig; Vamadeva Shastri; Gerard Butler; Sadie Drucker; Christina Warner Hill; Tipper Gore; Guru Ganesha; Maya Jeffkins; my program consultant, Vedic Master, and yogini extraordinaire Gabrielle Forleo who has stood by me all the way; Corey Booker; Abby "The Heart" Murphy; LightBridge Hospice; Sid Ganis; Sant Chatwal; Denise Reynier; Justin Drucker; Peter Guber; the crew of the *Jayavarman*; Nancy Ganis; Laura Lawee; Eliza Dushku; the one and only Wendi Cohen; Kids for Peace; Vikram Chatwal; Samara Tricarico; my friends at the Hoffman Institute; Jagatjoti Singh Khalsa; all my FB friends and fans; my Instagram posse; my Twitter followers, Cesar Millan; Holly Hatfield-Patel and Kerry Williams Gil; Rick Fox; SacredFire; Sarito Sun; Charlie Paz, Mitch Estrin; Lee Rocker; Katia Kimiya; Dave Macek; Red Lotus Society; Valerie Skonie and the tribe of the 40-day Winter Feast for the Soul; Joshua "Ganesh" Mallitt; Dave Stewart; Suzanne Dore; Lizzie Upitis; Elaine Ehrenkrantz; Jerry Kaplan; my longtime, loving friend, force of nature, and CBGB's partner Amy Berko Iles; Snatam Kaur; Damien Rose; and my dear Bloomfield brothers—Joe, Ray, Eddie, Walter, and Ted.

And profound thanks to those who have shown me the magical multidimensionality of life: Alisha Florek, Detective Bobby Goren, Liz Lemon, Damien Lewis, Jon Stewart, Jack Bauer, Shawn Carter, Patrick Jane, Dr. Gregory House, Annie Walker, and Ned Stark, who always kept it real.

ABOUT THE AUTHOR

davidji is an internationally recognized stress-management expert; corporate mindful performance trainer; meditation, yoga, and Ayurveda teacher; and author of the critically acclaimed and award-winning Amazon #1 bestseller *destressifying: The Real-World Guide to Personal Empowerment, Lasting Fulfillment, and Peace of Mind*; and *Secrets of Meditation: A Practical Guide to Inner Peace and Personal Transformation*, winner of the Nautilus Book Award and Ecuador's *Altas Conciencias* award.

davidji is credited with creating and guiding the very first 21-day meditation challenges more than 10 years ago, leading him to be referred to as the *Father of Guided Meditation* and the *Velvet Voice of Stillness*. He can be heard on more than 700 guided meditations, available on iTunes, Amazon.com, HayHouse.com, Insight Timer, GooglePlay, Spotify, Pandora, YouTube, SoundCloud, and on davidji.com.

After a 20-year career in business, finance, and mergers and acquisitions, davidji began a new journey to wholeness, apprenticing for a decade under Drs. Deepak Chopra and David Simon, serving as the Chopra Center COO, lead educator, and then as the first dean of Chopra Center University, where he trained more than 200,000 people to meditate and certified more than 1,000 meditation teachers. In 2012, he left the Chopra Center to teach the practical integration of stress management, mindful performance, meditation, and conscious choice making into our real-world, modern-day experiences. For more than 15 years davidji has helped thousands of people around the world to find balance in their lives, perform at higher levels, become more reflective and less reflexive, make better decisions, sleep better, enhance their relationships, experience abundance, and live purpose-driven lives.

He has a passion for working with entrepreneurs, business leaders, professional athletes, and those in high-pressure, high-stress situations. With support from the Department of Justice, davidji developed the *Blue Courage Awareness Training* curriculum designed to restore the nobility of policing. His teachings on stress release, conflict resolution, and mindful performance are now practiced in many of the top Fortune 500 companies, several branches of the military, and some of the largest police precincts and academies in the country. His train-the-trainer program, weaves meditation, yoga philosophy, Ayurveda, stress management, mindful performance, and conscious choice making into our real-world, modern-day experiences.

davidji is a certified Vedic Master, and every week, he hosts empowerment workshops, corporate trainings, life-change immersions, transformational retreats, and teacher trainings.

You can listen to davidji each week on Hay House Radio where he hosts *LIVE! from the SweetSpot*—a free, global internet radio show with tens of thousands of listeners around the world. To join davidji's free SweetSpot Community and receive tools, tips, techniques, and practices to take your life to the next level, visit davidji.com.

davidji

transform the world *by transforming yourself*

visit davidji.com

For more information on meditation, conscious choice-making, stress management, heart healing, and integrating timeless wisdom into your daily life, visit www.davidji.com.

join the davidji sweetspot community

Sign up at davidji.com to be a member of the davidji sweetspot community, and receive regular tools, tips, and techniques to lessen stress, ease anxiety, and bring greater balance into your life including free meditations, stress busters, and ways to connect with the millions of meditators around the world.

follow davidji

 facebook.com/flowoflove

 twitter.com/intothegap

Hay House Titles of Related Interest

YOU CAN HEAL YOUR LIFE, the movie,
starring Louise Hay & Friends
(available as a 1-DVD program and an expanded 2-DVD set)
Watch the trailer at: **www.LouiseHayMovie.com**

THE SHIFT, the movie,
starring Dr. Wayne W. Dyer
(available as a 1-DVD program and an expanded 2-DVD set)
Watch the trailer at: **www.DyerMovie.com**

AWAKENING THE LUMINOUS MIND:
Tibetan Meditation for Inner Peace and Joy,
by Tenzin Wangyal Rinpoche

THE UNIVERSE HAS YOUR BACK:
Transform Fear to Faith,
by Gabrielle Bernstein

SOUL SHIFTS:
Transformative Wisdom for Creating a Life of Authentic Awakening,
Emotional Freedom & Practical Spirituality,
by Dr. Barbara De Angelis

All of the above are available at your local bookstore,
or may be ordered by contacting Hay House (see next page).

We hope you enjoyed this Hay House book. If you'd like to receive our online catalog featuring additional information on Hay House books and products, or if you'd like to find out more about the Hay Foundation, please contact:

Hay House, Inc., P.O. Box 5100, Carlsbad, CA 92018-5100
(760) 431-7695 or (800) 654-5126
(760) 431-6948 (fax) or (800) 650-5115 (fax)
www.hayhouse.com® • www.hayfoundation.org

Published in Australia by: Hay House Australia Pty. Ltd.,
18/36 Ralph St., Alexandria NSW 2015
Phone: 612-9669-4299 • *Fax:* 612-9669-4144
www.hayhouse.com.au

Published in the United Kingdom by: Hay House UK, Ltd.,
The Sixth Floor, Watson House, 54 Baker Street, London W1U 7BU
Phone: +44 (0)20 3927 7290 • *Fax:* +44 (0)20 3927 7291
www.hayhouse.co.uk

Published in India by: Hay House Publishers India,
Muskaan Complex, Plot No. 3, B-2, Vasant Kunj, New Delhi 110 070
Phone: 91-11-4176-1620 • *Fax:* 91-11-4176-1630
www.hayhouse.co.in

<u>Access New Knowledge.</u>
<u>Anytime. Anywhere.</u>

Learn and evolve at your own pace
with the world's leading experts.

www.hayhouseU.com

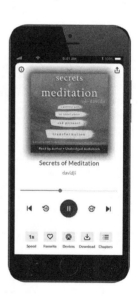